The Least You Should Know about English

ELEVENTH EDITION

form B

WRITING SKILLS

The Least You Should Know about English

ELEVENTH EDITION

form B

WRITING SKILLS

PAIGE WILSON

PASADENA CITY COLLEGE

TERESA FERSTER GLAZIER

LATE, WESTERN ILLINOIS UNIVERSITY

WADSWORTH
CENGAGE Learning

Australia • Brazil • Japan • Korea • Mexico • Singapore • Spain • United Kingdom • United States

The Least You Should Know about English, Writing Skills, Form B, Eleventh Edition
Paige Wilson and Teresa Ferster Glazier

Senior Publisher: Lyn Uhl

Director of Developmental
Studies: Annie Todd

Assistant Editor: Elizabeth Rice

Editorial Assistant: Matthew Conte

Media Editor: Amy Gibbons

Marketing Manager: Elinor Gregory

Marketing Coordinator: Brittany Blais

Marketing Communications Manager:
Linda Yip

Art Director: Cathy Richmond

Design and Production Services:
PreMediaGlobal

Manufacturing Planner: Betsy Donaghey

Rights Acquisition Specialist,
Image/Text: John Hill

Cover Designer: Hanh Luu

Cover Image: Veer Corbis

For product information and technology assistance, contact us at
Cengage Learning Customer & Sales Support, 1-800-354-9706

For permission to use material from this text or product,
submit all requests online at **www.cengage.com/permissions**
Further permissions questions can be emailed to
permissionrequest@cengage.com

Library of Congress Control Number: 2011942961

ISBN-13: 978-1-111-35025-3

ISBN-10: 1-111-35025-6

Wadsworth
20 Channel Center Street
Boston, MA 02210
USA

Cengage Learning is a leading provider of customized learning solutions with office locations around the globe, including Singapore, the United Kingdom, Australia, Mexico, Brazil and Japan. Locate your local office at **international.cengage.com/region**

Cengage Learning products are represented in Canada by Nelson Education, Ltd.

For your course and learning solutions, visit **www.cengage.com**

Purchase any of our products at your local college store or at our preferred online store **www.cengagebrain.com**

Instructors: Please visit **login.cengage.com** and log in to access instructor-specific resources.

Printed in the United States of America
3 4 5 6 7 8 9   22 21 20 19 18

CONTENTS

This book is for students who need to review basic English skills and who may profit from a simplified "least you should know" approach. Parts 1 to 3 cover the essentials of word choice and spelling, sentence structure, punctuation and capitalization. Part 4 on writing teaches students the basic structures of the paragraph and the essay, along with the writing skills necessary to produce them, and provides samples by both student and professional writers.

The "least you should know" approach attempts to avoid the use of linguistic terminology whenever possible. Students work with words they know instead of learning a vocabulary they may never use again.

Abundant exercises prompt students to identify structures, correct errors, write sentences, and proofread paragraphs. Diligent students learn to use these new skills automatically and begin to *apply them to their writing*. Most exercises consist of sets of ten thematically-linked, informative sentences on both timely and timeless subjects—anything from the death of Knut, the famous polar bear, to the book that Mark Twain made the world wait 100 years to read. Such exercises reinforce the need for coherence of details in student writing. With answers provided at the back of the book, students can correct their own work and progress at their own pace—in class and at home.

Changes to the eleventh edition continue the "Least You Should Know" tradition, with updated explanations, examples, and exercises throughout the text. Part 1 now presents "Spelling" before "Word Choice," discusses dictionary use throughout, and includes new ways to distinguish between "Words Often Confused." Part 2 on "Sentence Structure" further clarifies the use of first-person, second-person, and third-person pronouns. Part 3's coverage of "Punctuation" now cross-references Part 4's completely new section on "Choosing and Using Quotations." This comprehensive new section offers "Guidelines for Including Quotations," complete with explanations and samples of signal phrases and punctuation practices unique to quoting. Finally, Part 4 now includes discussions and examples of first-person and third-person approaches to writing, and a total of fourteen updated Writing Exercises follow key discussions throughout the Writing section.

The Least You Should Know about English functions equally well in the classroom and at home as a self-tutoring text. The clear explanations, ample exercises, and answers at the back of the book provide students with everything they need to progress on their own. Students who have previously been overwhelmed by the complexities of English should, through mastering simple skills and through writing and rewriting basic papers, gain the ability to succeed in further composition courses.

A **Test Booklet**, available only to instructors, corresponds directly to the book's content and includes both single-sentence and paragraph-length tests/exercises within each section.

ACKNOWLEDGMENTS

For their extremely helpful commentary on the book, I would like to thank the following reviewers:

Jacen Alexander, *Bakersfield College*
Michelle Christopherson, *Modesto Junior College*
Natalie S. Daley, *Linn-Benton Community College*
Lisa Moreno, *Los Angeles Trade-Technical College*
Marjory Thrash, *Pearl River Community College, Poplarville*

I would also like to extend my gratitude to the following students for their specific contributions to the eleventh edition: Tanya Alcaraz, Frances Castanar, Elizabeth Nowlin, Jessica Ovando, Maggie Wong, and Xia Zhang.

As always, I am especially indebted to my tireless publishing team for their expertise and hard work and to my family, friends, students, and colleagues for their ongoing support and encouragement.

Paige Wilson
Pasadena City College

This book is dedicated to Teresa Ferster Glazier (1907–2004). In creating *The Least You Should Know about English*, she discovered a way to teach grammar and writing that students and teachers have actually enjoyed for over thirty years. Her original explanations and approaches have been constant sources of inspiration for this and all previous coauthored editions, as they will be for all future editions of her text.

What Is the Least You Should Know?

Most English textbooks try to teach you more than you need to know. This book will teach you the least you should know—and still help you learn to write clearly and acceptably. You won't have to learn grammatical terms like *gerund, auxiliary verb,* or *demonstrative pronoun.* You can get along without knowing such technical labels if you understand a few key concepts. You *should* know about the parts of speech and how to use and spell common words; you *should* be able to recognize subjects and verbs; you *should* know the basics of sentence structure and punctuation—but rules, as such, will be kept to a minimum.

The English you'll learn in this book is sometimes called Standard Written English, and it may differ slightly or greatly from the English you use when speaking. Standard Written English is the form of writing accepted in business and the professions. So no matter how you speak, you will communicate better in writing when you use Standard Written English. For instance you might *say,* "That's a whole nother problem," but you would probably want to *write,* "That's a completely different problem." Knowing the difference between spoken English and Standard Written English is essential in college, in business, and in life.

Until you learn the least you should know, you may have difficulty communicating in writing. Look for the misused word in the following sentence, for example:

I hope that the university will except my application for admission.

The writer probably relied on the sound, not the meaning, of the word *except* to choose it. The two words *except* and *accept* sound similar but have completely different meanings. (See page 8.) The writer should have used the one that means approve the application (*accept* it):

I hope that the university will *accept* my application for admission.

Then all of the words would have communicated clearly. Here's another example, this time with missing punctuation:

The manager fired Kevin and Chloe and I received a promotion.

This sentence needs a comma to separate its two independent clauses:

> The manager fired Kevin and Chloe, and I received a promotion.

But perhaps the writer meant the following:

> The manager fired Kevin, and Chloe and I received a promotion.

Punctuation changes the meaning of the sentence, especially for Chloe. With the help of this text, we hope that your writing will become so clear that no one will misunderstand it.

As you make your way through the book, it's important to remember information after you learn it because many concepts and structures build upon others. For example, once you can identify subjects and verbs, you'll be better able to recognize fragments, understand subject-verb agreement, and use correct punctuation. Explanations and examples are brief and clear, and it shouldn't be difficult to learn from them—*if you want to*. But you have to want to!

How to Learn the Least You Should Know

1. Read each explanatory section carefully (aloud, if possible).

2. Do the first exercise. Compare your answers with those at the back of the book. If they don't match, study the explanation again to find out why.

3. Do the second exercise and correct it. If you miss a single answer, go back once more to the explanation. You must have missed something. Be tough on yourself. Don't just think, "Maybe I'll get it right next time." Reread the examples, and *then* try the next exercise. It's important to correct each group of ten sentences before moving on so that you'll discover your mistakes early.

4. You may be tempted to quit after you do one or two exercises perfectly. Instead, make yourself finish another exercise. It's not enough to *understand* a concept or structure. You have to *practice* using it.

5. If you're positive that you've learned a concept or structure after doing several exercises, move on to the proofreading and sentence composing exercises, where you can apply that knowledge to your writing.

Learning the basics of spelling and word choice, sentence structure, and punctuation does take time. Generally, college students should study a couple of hours outside of class for each hour in class. You may need to study more. Undoubtedly, the more time you spend, the more your writing will improve.

PART 1

Spelling and Word Choice

Anyone can learn to spell better and use words more effectively. You can eliminate most of your spelling and word choice errors if you want to. It's just a matter of deciding you're going to do it.

THE IMPORTANCE OF A GOOD DICTIONARY

A current, full-featured dictionary is a basic but commonly underused resource for many writers. College-level print dictionaries provide the spelling, pronunciation, definitions, usage, and sources of words, as well as foreign phrases, famous names, and geographical locations. The latest dictionaries also offer online resources, including audio and video features that bring words, people, and places to life. Of course, most computers and word-processing programs have built-in dictionaries and spell-check capabilities. However, the automatic "corrections" they suggest may at times cause more damage to your meaning than your original mistakes would. The good news is that dictionaries of all kinds will become more useful once you learn the "least you should know" about spelling and word choice.

If you really intend to improve your spelling and choice of words, study each of the following sections until you make no mistakes in the exercises.

Your Own List of Misspelled Words

Words That Can Be Broken into Parts

Guidelines for Doubling a Final Letter

Words Often Confused (Set 1)

Words Often Confused (Set 2)

The Eight Parts of Speech

Adjectives and Adverbs

Contractions

Possessives

Your Own List of Misspelled Words

You can create your own personal dictionary on the inside cover of your English notebook or in some other obvious place by making a corrected list of all the misspelled words from your graded papers. Review and practice using the correct spellings until you're sure of them, and edit your papers to find and fix repeated errors.

Words That Can Be Broken into Parts

Breaking words into their parts will often help you spell them correctly. Each of the following words is made up of two shorter words. Note that the word then contains all the letters of the two shorter words.

chalk board	. . .	chalkboard	room mate	. . .	roommate
over due	. . .	overdue	home work	. . .	homework
super market	. . .	supermarket	under line	. . .	underline

Becoming aware of prefixes such as *dis, inter, mis,* and *un* is also helpful. When you add a prefix to a word, note that no letters are dropped, either from the prefix or from the word.

dis appear	disappear	mis represent	misrepresent
dis appoint	disappoint	mis spell	misspell
dis approve	disapprove	mis understood	misunderstood
dis satisfy	dissatisfy	un aware	unaware
inter act	interact	un involved	uninvolved
inter active	interactive	un necessary	unnecessary
inter related	interrelated	un sure	unsure

Have someone dictate the preceding list for you to write and then mark any words you miss. Memorize the correct spellings by noting how each word is made up of a prefix and a word.

Guidelines for Doubling a Final Letter

Most spelling rules have so many exceptions that they aren't much help. But here's one worth learning because it has very few exceptions.

Double a final letter (consonants only) when adding an ending that begins with a vowel (such as *ing, ed, er*) if all three of the following are true:

1. The word ends in a single consonant,

2. which is preceded by a single vowel (the vowels are *a, e, i, o, u*),

3. and the accent is on the last syllable (or the word only has one syllable).

We'll try the rule on a few words to which we'll add *ing, ed,* or *er*.

begin
    1. It ends in a single consonant—*n,*
    2. preceded by a single vowel—*i,*
    3. and the accent is on the last syllable—be *gín.*
        Therefore, we double the final consonant and write *beginning, beginner.*

stop
    1. It ends in a single consonant—*p,*
    2. preceded by a single vowel—*o,*
    3. and the accent is on the last syllable (there is only one).
        Therefore, we double the final consonant and write *stopping, stopped, stopper.*

filter
    1. It ends in a single consonant—*r,*
    2. preceded by a single vowel—*e,*
    3. But the accent isn't on the last syllable. It's on the first—*fíl* ter.
        Therefore, we *don't* double the final consonant. We write *filtering, filtered.*

keep
    1. It ends in a single consonant—*p,*
    2. but the *p* isn't preceded by a single vowel. There are two *e*'s.
        Therefore, we *don't* double the final consonant. We write *keeping, keeper.*

NOTE 1—Be aware that *qu* is treated as a consonant because *q* is almost never written without *u*. Think of it as *kw*. In words like *equip* and *quit*, the *qu* acts as a consonant. Therefore, *equip* and *quit* both end in a single consonant preceded by a single vowel, and the final consonant is doubled in *equipped* and *quitting*.

> **NOTE 2**—The final consonants *w, x,* and *y* do not follow this rule and are not doubled when adding *ing, ed,* or *er* to a word (as in *bowing, fixing,* and *enjoying*).

EXERCISES

Add *ing* to these words. Correct each group of ten before continuing so you'll catch any errors early.

Exercise 1

1. tap	**6.** fill
2. clasp	**7.** smash
3. defend	**8.** play
4. clean	**9.** pad
5. refer	**10.** deploy

Exercise 2

1. sew	**6.** unhook
2. review	**7.** quiz
3. deal	**8.** push
4. clog	**9.** aim
5. click	**10.** deliver

Exercise 3

1. snip	**6.** perform
2. buzz	**7.** confer
3. mix	**8.** gleam
4. row	**9.** clip
5. tamper	**10.** permit

Exercise 4

1. pat
2. saw
3. feed
4. play
5. occur

6. brush
7. gather
8. knot
9. offer
10. box

Exercise 5

1. help
2. flex
3. assist
4. need
5. select

6. wish
7. tow
8. construct
9. polish
10. lead

Words Often Confused (Set 1)

Learning the difference between often-confused words will help you overcome many of your spelling problems. We've divided the most commonly confused words into two sets. Study the pairs of words in Set 1 carefully, with their helpful memory tips and examples, before trying the exercises. Then move on to Set 2. If you practice each set thoroughly, your spelling should improve.

a, an   Use *an* before a word that begins with a vowel sound (*a, e, i,* and *o,* plus *u* when it sounds like *uh*) or silent *h.* Note that it's not the letter but the *sound* of the letter that matters.

an apple, *an* essay, *an* inch, *an* onion

an umpire, *an* ugly design (The *u*'s sound like *uh*.)

an hour, *an* honest person (The *h*'s are silent.)

Use *a* before a word that begins with a consonant sound (all the sounds except the vowels, plus *u* or *eu* when they sound like *you*).

a chart, *a* pie, *a* history book (The *h* is not silent in *history.*)

a union, *a* uniform, *a* unit (The *u*'s sound like *you*.)

a European vacation, *a* euphemism (*Eu* sounds like *you*.)

accept, except   *Accept* means "to receive or agree to take." Think of the two *c*'s in *accept* as two arms curling up to receive something.

I *accept* this award on my mother's behalf.

Except means "excluding" or "but." Think of the *x* in *except* as two arms crossed to block something or someone.

The airline upgraded everyone *except* Stanley.

advise, advice   *Advise* is a verb. (Pronounce the *s* like a *z*.)

I *advise* you to take your time finding the right job.

Advice is a noun. (It rhymes with *rice*.)

I took my doctor's *advice* to eat more brown rice.

affect, effect   *Affect* is a *verb* that means "to alter or influence someone or something." Try substituting another *verb* that starts with *a*—like *alter* or *amaze* or *astound*—to see if one of them works. If it does, then use this verb that starts with *a*: *affect*.

> All quizzes will *affect* the final grade. (All quizzes will *alter* the final grade.)

> That story *affected* everyone who heard it. (That story *amazed* everyone who heard it.)

Effect is most commonly used as a *noun* and means "a result." Focus on the *e* sound in *effect* and *result*, and try substituting *result* for *effect* as a test.

> The strong coffee had a powerful *effect*. (The strong coffee had a powerful *result*.)

> We studied the *effects* of sleep deprivation in my psychology class. (We studied the *results*. . . .)

all ready, already   If you can leave out the *all* and the sentence still makes sense, then *all ready* is the form to use.

> We're *all ready* for our trip. (*We're ready for our trip* makes sense.)

> The banquet is *all ready*. (*The banquet is ready* also makes sense.)

But if you can't leave out the *all* and still have a sentence that makes sense, use *already*.

> They've *already* eaten dinner. (*They've ready eaten dinner* doesn't make sense.)

> We have seen that movie *already*. (*We have seen that movie ready* doesn't make sense either.)

are, our   *Are* is a present form of the verb "to be."

> We *are* going to Colorado Springs.

Our is a pronoun that shows we possess something.

> We painted *our* fence to match the house.

brake, break   *Brake* used as a verb means "to slow or stop motion." It's also the name of the device that slows or stops motion.

> I had to *brake* quickly to avoid an accident.

> Luckily I just had my *brakes* fixed.

Break used as a verb means "to shatter" or "to split." It's also the name of an interruption, as in "a coffee break."

She never thought she would *break* a world record.

Enjoy your spring *break*.

choose, chose   The difference here is one of time. Use *choose* for present and future; use *chose* for past.

I will *choose* a new major this semester.

They *chose* the wrong time of year to travel to India.

clothes, cloths   *Clothes* are garments people wear; *cloths* are pieces of material you might clean or polish something with.

I love the *clothes* that characters wear in old movies.

Workers at car washes use special *cloths* to dry the cars.

coarse, course   *Coarse* describes a rough texture.

I used *coarse* sandpaper to smooth the surface of the board.

Course is used for all other meanings.

Of *course* we visited the golf *course* at Pebble Beach.

complement, compliment   *Complement*, spelled with an *e,* means to complete something or bring it to perfection.

Use a color wheel to find a *complement* for purple.

Juliet's personality *complements* Romeo's: she is practical, and he is a dreamer.

Compliment, spelled with an *i,* has to do with praise. Remember the *i* in "*I* like compliments," and you'll remember to use the *i* spelling when you mean praise.

My recent evaluation included a nice *compliment* from my new boss.

We *complimented* them on their new home.

conscious, conscience   *Conscious* means "awake" or "aware."

They weren't *conscious* of any problems before the accident.

Conscience means that inner voice of right and wrong. The extra *n* in *conscience* should remind you of "No," which is what your conscience often says to you.

My *conscience* told me not to keep the money I found.

dessert, desert *Dessert* is the sweet one, the one people like two helpings of. So give it two helpings of *s*. Remember also that "stressed" spelled backwards is *desserts*.

When I'm stressed, I can eat two *desserts* in a row.

The other one, *desert,* is used for all other meanings and has two pronunciations.

I promise that I won't *desert* you at the party.

The snake slithered slowly across the *desert.*

do, due *Do* is a verb, an action. You *do* something.

I *do* most of my homework on the weekends.

But a payment or an assignment is *due;* it is scheduled for a certain time.

Our first essay is *due* tomorrow.

Due also comes before *to* in a phrase that means *because of.*

The outdoor concert was canceled *due to* rain.

feel, fill *Feel* describes *feel*ings.

Whenever I stay up late, I *feel* sleepy in class.

Fill is the action of pouring into or packing a container fully.

Why did he *fill* the pitcher to the top?

fourth, forth The word *fourth* has *four* in it. But note that *forty* does not. Remember the word *forty-fourth* to help you spell both of these words related to numbers.

This is our *fourth* quiz in forty-eight hours.

My grandparents celebrated their *forty-fourth* anniversary.

If you don't mean a number, use *forth.*

The ship's passengers walked back and *forth* on deck.

have, of *Have* is a verb. Sometimes, in a contraction, it sounds like *of.* When you say *could've,* the *have* may sound like *of,* but it is not written that way. Always write *could have, would have, should have, might have.*

We should *have* planned our vacation sooner.

Then we could *have* used our coupon for a free ticket.

Use *of* only in a prepositional phrase. (See p. 63.)

She sent me a box *of* chocolates for my birthday.

hear, here   The last three letters of *hear* spell "ear." You *hear* with your ear.

When I listen to a seashell, I *hear* ocean sounds.

The other spelling *here* tells "where." Note that the three words indicating a place or pointing out something all have *here* in them: *here, there, where.*

I'll be *here* for three more weeks.

it's, its   *It's* is a contraction and means "it is" or "it has."

It's hot. (*It is* hot.)

It's been hot all week. (*It has* been hot all week.)

Its is a possessive. Pronouns such as *its, yours, hers, ours, theirs,* and *whose* are already possessive forms and never need an apostrophe. (See p. 48.)

The jury had made *its* decision.

The dog pulled at *its* leash.

knew, new   *Knew* has to do with *knowledge;*both start with a silent *k.*

New means "not old."

Her friends *knew* that she wanted a *new* bike.

know, no   *Know* has to do with *knowledge;*both start with a silent *k.*

By Friday, I must *know* all the state capitals.

No means "not any" or the opposite of "yes."

My boss has *no* patience. *No,* I am not exaggerating.

EXERCISES

Circle the correct words in parentheses. Don't guess! If you aren't sure, turn back to the explanatory pages. Correct each set of ten sentences before continuing so you'll catch your mistakes early.

Exercise 1

1. We all (know, no) what modern-day rabbits look like.

2. They (are, our) small furry creatures usually (know, no) bigger than cats.

3. (A, An) recent discovery may (affect, effect) the way we picture rabbits in the future.

4. Scientists have uncovered the remains of (a, an) huge type of rabbit that grew to be six times larger than the rabbits of today.

5. These big bunnies lived several million years ago on (a, an) island in the Mediterranean.

6. Scientists have called this (knew, new) rabbit species *Nuralagus Rex*.

7. Living on (a, an) island can have (a, an) unusual (affect, effect) on a species of animals.

8. (A, An) small animal sometimes evolves into (a, an) incredibly large animal (do, due) to the island's limited environment.

9. (It's, Its) still difficult to (accept, except) the idea of a sheep-sized rabbit.

10. Luckily, there is one thing that scientists believe *Nuralagus Rex* didn't (do, due)—and that's hop.

Source: Science News, April 23, 2011

Exercise 2

1. I just finished reading (a, an) article that offers some interesting (advise, advice).

2. If (a, an) male athlete wants to win, he should (choose, chose) red as the color of his uniform.

3. Scientists have studied the (affect, effect) of wearing red on the results of competition at the 2004 Olympics in Athens, Greece.

4. Experts had (all ready, already) looked into the ways red may (affect, effect) animal behavior.

5. They (knew, new) it increased the status and success of certain animals who "wore" it.

6. Red seems unique in (it's, its) ability to help male athletes win in competition.

7. The results of the study in Athens showed that wearing red (clothes, cloths) during competition did have a positive impact.

8. The winning (affect, effect) was the same for both individuals and teams.

9. These results may be hard for some people to (accept, except).

10. (Know, No) such studies have included female athletes yet.

Source: Discover, August 2005

Exercise 3

1. Frozen dinners (are, our) part of most of (are, our) lives.

2. They come in trays with separate sections for each (coarse, course).

3. They usually include (a, an) entree, some vegetables, and (a, an) baked (dessert, desert).

4. Swanson started selling (it's, its) first frozen dinners in 1953.

5. That year, the company had ended up with too many turkeys after Thanksgiving (due, do) to (a, an) ordering mistake.

6. A Swanson salesperson, Gerry Thomas, (knew, new) that he could find a way to sell the turkeys somehow.

7. Thomas used airline meals as a model and invented a (knew, new) kind of convenience for the American family, the frozen "TV Dinner."

8. He had the idea to (feel, fill) sleek metal trays with simple, satisfying meals.

9. These quick meals were the perfect (complement, compliment) to a night in front of the television.

10. No one could (have, of) predicted how successful the TV dinner would become.

Source: Smithsonian, December 2004

Exercise 4

1. I've lived on my own for two years, and I'm (all ready, already) tired of trying to decide what to (do, due) for dinner every night.

2. When I lived at home, I used to come home from school, change my (clothes, cloths), and (choose, chose) from all of the things my mom, dad, or siblings were eating for dinner.

3. I could (have, of) taken a plate of Dad's famous macaroni and cheese back to my room and then gone downstairs later for a slice of Mom's lemon pie with (it's, its) fluffy meringue on top.

4. Now I have to come up with a main (coarse, course) and a (dessert, desert) all by myself.

5. (Do, Due) to my lack of cooking experience, dinners of my own are either burned or bought.

6. I'm beginning to (feel, fill) a little self-(conscience, conscious) about my limitations in the kitchen.

7. I could call my parents for (advise, advice), but I don't want them to worry about me.

8. Without a doubt, I should (have, of) paid more attention when both my parents were cooking, not just have (complemented, complimented) them on the results.

9. I guess I could take a cooking (coarse, course) or get a roommate to (do, due) the cooking for reduced rent.

10. I like everything about living away from home (accept, except) making my own dinner.

Exercise 5

1. There is (a, an) old, commonly held belief that if you (choose, chose) to wash your car today, it will rain tomorrow.

2. Of (coarse, course), that's just a saying; (it's, its) not true.

3. However, if you take my (advise, advice) and wash your car at home, you will at least save the cost of (a, an) expensive car wash should this happen to you.

4. To avoid the undesirable (affect, effect) of clouding or streaking of the finish, never wash your car in direct sunlight.

5. But don't park your car under a tree to take advantage of (it's, its) shade, or you may be sorry later (do, due) to the possibility of sap falling from the tree.

6. Also, be sure that the (clothes, cloths) you use to wipe the surface are clean and have (know, no) (coarse, course) stitching or texture that might scratch the finish.

7. You don't want to (brake, break) your antenna, so it should be removed if possible.

8. Once your car is (all ready, already) to be washed, use circular motions and (feel, fill) the surface with your hand every now and then to be sure (it's, its) been thoroughly cleaned.

9. Take the time to dry the whole surface of the car with a chamois if you want to get a lot of (complements, compliments) from your friends.

10. If you've done a good job, the (clothes, cloths) you're wearing will be wet, but your car will be dry and as shiny as it was the day you bought it.

PROOFREADING EXERCISE

Find and correct the ten errors contained in the following student paragraph. All of the errors involve Words Often Confused (Set 1).

Its hard to except criticism from friends. The other day, my friend Jane told me that my voice is always too loud when I talk on the phone. She said that the way I talk hurts her ears and makes her hold the phone away from her head. I no that she didn't mean to hurt my feelings, but that was the affect of what she said. I should of told her that she snores whenever we go camping in the dessert. Next time, I will record her snoring so that she can here herself. I don't really want Jane's criticism to brake up are friendship, so I'll probably just talk to her and tell her how I fill.

SENTENCE WRITING

The surest way to learn these Words Often Confused is to use them immediately in your own writing. Choose the five pairs of words that you most often confuse from Set 1. Then use them correctly in new sentences. No answers are provided, but you can see if you are using the words correctly by comparing your sentences to the examples in the explanations.

Words Often Confused (Set 2)

Study this second set of words as carefully as you did the first. Read the short explanations, helpful hints, and sample sentences before attempting the exercises. By learning all of the word groups in both sets, you can eliminate many basic spelling problems.

lead, led
Lead is the metal that rhymes with *head*.

Old paint is dangerous because it often contains *lead*.

The past form of the verb "to lead" is *led*.

What factors *led* to your decision?

I *led* our school's debating team to victory last year.

If you don't mean past time, use *lead,* which rhymes with *seed*.

I will *lead* the debating team again this year.

loose, lose
Loose means "not tight." Note how *l o o s e* that word is. It has plenty of room for two *o*'s. Remember that *loose* and *tooth* both have two *o*'s in the middle.

My sister has a *loose* tooth.

Lose is the opposite of win. Pronounce the *s* like a *z*.

If we *lose* the next game, we will be out for the season.

passed, past
Passed is a form of the verb "to pass."

Nanette easily *passed* her math test.

The runner *passed* the baton to her teammate.

I *passed* your house on my way to the store.

Use *past* when you mean "*by*" or to refer to the time that came before the present.

I drove *past* your house. (Meaning "I drove *by* your house." The verb in the sentence is *drove*.)

It's best to learn from *past* experiences.

In the *past,* he worked for a small company.

personal, personnel
Pronounce these two correctly, and you won't confuse them—*pérsonal, personnél*.

She shared her *personal* views as a parent.

Personnel means "a group of employees."

I had an appointment in the *personnel* office.

piece, peace Remember "a *piece* of *pie*." The word meaning "a *piece*" always begins with *pie*.

Some students asked for an extra *piece* of scratch paper.

The other word, *peace,* means "the opposite of war."

The two sides finally signed a *peace* treaty.

principal, principle *Principal* means "main." Both words have *a* in them: princip*a*l, m*a*in.

The *principal* concern is safety. (main concern)

We paid both *principal* and interest. (main amount of money)

Also, think of a school's "princi*pal*" as your "*pal*."

An elementary school *principal* must be kind. (main administrator)

A *principle* is a "rule." Both words end in *le*: princip*le*, ru*le*.

I am proud of my *principles*. (rules of conduct)

We value the *principle* of truth in advertising. (rule)

quiet, quite Pronounce these two correctly, and you won't confuse them. *Quiet* means "free from noise" and rhymes with *diet*.

Golfers often ask spectators to be *quiet*.

Quite means "really" or "very" and ends with the same three letters as *white*.

The bleach made my towels *quite* white.

right, write *Right* means "correct," "proper," or "the opposite of left. "

You will find your keys if you look in the *right* place, on the *right* side of the coffee table.

It also means "in the exact location, position, or moment."

Your keys are *right* where you left them.

Let's go *right* now.

Write means "to compose sentences, poems, essays. . . ."

I *write* in my journal every day.

than, then   *Than* is used to compare. Remember that both *than* and *compare* have an *a* in them.

I am taller *than* my sister.

Then tells when. *Then* and *when* rhyme, and both have an *e* in them.

I always write a rough draft of a paper first; *then* I revise it.

their, there, they're   *Their* is a possessive, meaning "belonging to them."

They read *their* essays out loud.

There points out something. Remember that the three words indicating a place or pointing out something all have *here* in them: *here, there, where*.

I know that I haven't been *there* before.

In Hawaii, *there* is always a rainbow in the sky.

They're is a contraction and means "they are."

They're living in Canada now. (*They are* living in Canada now.)

threw, through   *Threw* is the past form of "to throw."

The students *threw* snowballs at each other.

I *threw* away my application for a scholarship.

If you don't mean "to throw something," use *through*.

We could see our beautiful view *through* the new curtains.

They worked *through* their differences.

two, too, to   *Two* is a number.

We have written *two* papers so far in my English class.

Too means "very" or "also," and so it also has an extra *o*.

The movie was *too* long and *too* violent. (very)

They are enrolled in that biology class, *too*. (also)

Use *to* for all other meanings.

They like *to* ski. They're going *to* the mountains.

weather,
whether

Weather refers to conditions of the atmosphere.

Snowy *weather* is too cold for me.

Whether means "if."

I don't know *whether* it is snowing there or not.

were, wear,
where

These words are pronounced differently but are often confused in writing.

Were is a past form of the verb "to be."

We *were* interns at the time.

Wear usually means "to have on," as in wearing clothes.

I always *wear* a scarf in winter.

Where refers to a place. Remember that the three words indicating a place or pointing out something all have *here* in them: *here, there, where.*

Where are the teachers' mailboxes?

who's, whose

Who's is a contraction and means "who is" or "who has."

Who's responsible for signing the checks? (*Who is* responsible?)

Who's been reading my e-mail? (*Who has* been reading my e-mail?)

Whose is a possessive. Words such as *whose, its, yours, hers, ours, and theirs* are already possessive forms and never need an apostrophe. See p. 48.

Whose keys are these?

woman,
women

The difference here is one of number: wo*man* refers to one adult female; wo*men* refers to two or more adult females.

I know a *woman* who has bowled a perfect game.

I bowl with a group of *women* from my work.

you're, your

You're is a contraction and means "you are."

You're as smart as I am. (*You are* as smart as I am.)

Your is a possessive meaning "belonging to you."

I borrowed *your* lab book.

EXERCISES

Circle the correct words in parentheses. As you finish each exercise, check your answers so that you will catch any mistakes early.

Exercise 1

1. Knut is the name of a polar bear (who's, whose) early life made headlines in 2007.

2. Knut became (quiet, quite) a celebrity in Germany after being born in captivity and rejected by his mother at the Berlin Zoo.

3. The tiny abandoned polar bear was no bigger (than, then) a fat kitten when (personal, personnel) at the zoo had to make a difficult decision.

4. They had to decide (weather, whether) to let the little bear cub die naturally or to go against nature and raise him themselves.

5. At the time, some people voiced (their, there, they're) strong belief in the (principal, principle) that humans should not artificially raise wild animals.

6. As a small cub, Knut's fluffy white fur and adorable personality (lead, led) newspapers, magazines, and television stations (two, too, to) spread stories and photos of him around the world.

7. Children and adults (were, wear, where) equally impressed with Knut, and they wrote songs and books about him.

8. Companies even designed candy and other products (two, too, to) look like him.

9. Sadly, Knut (passed, past) away unexpectedly in March of 2011.

10. Knut lived a shorter life (than, then) most polar bears and was only four years old when he died.

Exercise 2

1. James Dean was a famous actor in the (passed, past).

2. Even though he had a (principal, principle) role in only three films of the 1950s, James Dean's work still inspires audiences.

3. Dean's acting style was (quiet, quite) and intense.

4. His most famous (piece, peace) was the movie *Rebel Without a Cause*.

5. At the time, his performances (lead, led) him (right, write) into the spotlight and made him an instant star.

6. Unfortunately, audiences would (loose, lose) (their, there, they're) opportunity to know him better.

7. At the age of 24, Dean (passed, past) away in a legendary car crash.

8. Dean and his mechanic (wear, were, where) speeding along in his silver convertible near Bakersfield, California, when another driver wandered over the center line at a fork in the road and hit them.

9. James Dean died, but his mechanic survived, and the other driver did, (two, too, to).

10. Although over 50 years have (passed, past), devoted fans still visit that bit of highway every year on September 30, the anniversary of James Dean's death.

Source: Westways, September/October 2005

Exercise 3

1. You've probably been (threw, through) this experience.

2. (You're, Your) in a theater, auditorium, or intimate restaurant, and someone's cell phone rings.

3. The person (who's, whose) phone it is becomes (two, to, too) embarrassed (two, to, too) answer it.

4. In the (passed, past), (their, there, they're) was no way to keep this unfortunate event from happening.

5. Now scientists have invented a type of magnetic wood paneling that will maintain the (piece, peace) and (quiet, quite) of public places even if people still refuse to turn off (their, there, they're) cell phones.

6. This new wood will block radio signals and therefore keep such calls from going (threw, through) the walls of a theater, auditorium, restaurant, or anywhere else (their, there, they're) not wanted.

7. Of course, (their, there, they're) are people who do not want to (loose, lose) (their, there, they're) (right, write) to make (personal, personnel) calls wherever they want.

8. One of the best uses of magnetic wood will be to protect areas (were, wear, where) signals interfere with each other.

9. (Than, Then) wooden panels will be used (two, too, to) divide wireless signals rather (than, then) block calls altogether.

10. (Weather, Whether) (you're, your) for it or against it, magnetic wood will probably be used worldwide (quiet, quite) soon.

Source: New Scientist, June 27, 2002

Exercise 4

1. The three days following September 11, 2001, (were, wear, where) unique.

2. They offered an unprecedented opportunity to study an aspect of the (whether, weather) that could not be studied under normal conditions.

3. The situation that (lead, led) to the study was the temporary ban on nearly all airline flights over America.

4. In the (passed, past), scientists had wondered (whether, weather) the clouds produced by airplane engines affected temperatures on land.

5. These man-made clouds, called contrails, are the streaks left behind after an airplane has (passed, past) across the sky.

6. Never in the recent (passed, past) had (their, there, they're) been days when the skies were clear of contrails.

7. The absence of air traffic also produced an eerie kind of (quiet, quite).

8. Not wanting to (loose, lose) the chance to discover the effects of contrails, (two, too, to) scientists went (right, write) to work.

9. David Travis and Andrew Carleton discovered, (threw, through) comparisons of temperatures from the three days without air traffic and the same days for the (passed, past) thirty years, that the contrails do cause temperatures to cool slightly.

10. This (piece, peace) of scientific data may lead to a greater understanding of our impact on the planet's (whether, weather) overall.

Source: Discover, August 2002

Exercise 5

1. I don't know (weather, whether) I should (right, write) my own resume or pay a service to do it for me.

2. I have a friend (who's, whose) just been hired by a law firm; he told me, "(You're, Your) crazy if you don't let an expert put together (you're, your) resume."

3. Maybe he's (right, write); he's been (threw, through) the process already and was (quiet, quite) satisfied with the result.

4. He has never (lead, led) me astray before, and I'm not (two, too, to) sure I know how to (right, write) all of my (personal, personnel) information in a clear format.

5. For instance, I can't decide how much of my (passed, past) experience I should include.

6. (Personal, Personnel) offices do have strict requirements about the length and styles of documents.

7. (Their, There, They're) often harder to get (passed, past) (than, then) the people on the hiring committees.

8. In fact, the one (woman, women) who helped me the last time I tried to get a job told me that the (principal, principle) problem with my file was the poor quality of my resume.

9. I think I'll ask my friend (were, wear, where) he got his resume done and how much it cost.

10. I would rather (loose, lose) a little money (than, then) (loose, lose) another job opportunity.

PROOFREADING EXERCISE

See if you can correct the ten errors in this student paragraph. All errors involve Words Often Confused (Set 2).

In the passed, if you wanted too hear a peace of music, you turned on you're stereo. Later, you could even listen too tunes on your computer. Now, with the write equipment, you can play music threw a vase of flowers. The sound doesn't come from the vase, but from the flowers themselves. Let's Corp., a company in Japan, has created a gadget called Ka-on, which means "flower sound" in Japanese. With the Ka-on device, sound is past up the stems of the flowers, into the delicate blossoms, and out into the room. If you touch the petals, you can feel there vibrations. The Ka-on sound is supposed to be softer then music played through ordinary speakers.

Source: Current Science, May 6, 2005

SENTENCE WRITING

Choose ten words from Words Often Confused (Set 2) and write a new sentence using each one correctly. No answers are provided at the back of the book, but you can compare your sentences to the examples in the explanations.

The Eight Parts of Speech

Choosing the right word is an important aspect of writing. As we've explained, some words sound alike but are spelled differently and have different meanings (*past* and *passed,* for instance), and some words are spelled the same but sound different and mean different things (*lead,* for the action of "leading," and *lead,* for the stuff inside pencils). Besides learning to spell better, it is important to understand the roles that words play in sentences.

Just as one actor can play many different parts in movies (a hero, a villain, a humorous sidekick), single words can play different parts in sentences (a noun, a verb, an adjective). These are called the *eight parts of speech,* briefly defined with examples below.

1. **Nouns** name *people, places, things,* or *ideas* and are used as subjects and objects in sentences. **Proper nouns** that name *specific people, places, things,* or *ideas*—such as *Marie Curie, New York City, Kleenex,* and *Freemasonry*— are capitalized and can include more than one word. (See pp. 57, 63 and 133 for more about nouns as subjects and objects. See p. 193 for more about capitalizing specific nouns.)

    Ms. Kim and the other **librarians** are proud of the **success** of the new **library**.

2. **Pronouns** are special words—such as *I, she, him, it, they, who, that,* and *us*—that replace nouns to avoid repeating them. (See p. 151 for more about pronouns.)

    In fact, **they** (the librarians) are very proud of **it** (the new library's success).

3. **Adjectives** add description to nouns and pronouns—telling *which one, how many, what kind, color,* or *shape* they are. (See p. 33 for more about adjectives.)

    The **head** librarian designed the **new, state-of-the-art** facilities.

    The words *a, an,* and *the* are special forms of adjectives called **articles**. They always introduce a noun or a pronoun and are used so often that there is no need to label them.

4. **Verbs** show action or state of being. (See p. 57 and p. 91 for more about verbs.)

    She **was** an architect before she **retired** and **became** a librarian.

5. **Adverbs** add information—such as *when, where, why,* or *how*—to verbs, adjectives, and other adverbs. (See p. 34 for more about adverbs.)

    Now the library can **easily** accommodate thousands of students **daily**.

6. **Prepositions** show position in *space* and *time* and are followed by noun objects to form prepositional phrases. (See p. 63 for more about prepositions.)

    The computers lounges **in** the library are full **by** the middle **of** the morning.

7. **Conjunctions** are connecting words—such as *and, but,* and *or*—and words that begin dependent clauses—such as *because, since, when, while,* and *although.* (See p. 69 and p. 83 for more about conjunctions.)

> The library **and** its landscaping impress people **when** they first see the campus.

8. **Interjections** interrupt a sentence to convey a greeting or to show surprise or other emotions and are rarely used in Standard Written English.

> When they walk up or drive by, they say, "**Oh**, what a great building!"

To find out what parts of speech an individual word can play, look it up in a good, college-level dictionary. (See p. 3.) You'll find a list of definitions beginning with an abbreviated part of speech (*n, adj, prep,* and so on) that identifies its possible uses. However, seeing how a word is used in a particular sentence is the best way to identify its part of speech. Look at these examples:

> Our **train** arrived at exactly three o'clock.
>
> (*Train* is a noun in this sentence, naming the vehicle we call a "train.")
>
> Sammy and Helen **train** new employees at Sea World.
>
> (*Train* is a verb in this example, showing the action of "training.")
>
> Doug's parents drove him to the **train** station.
>
> (*Train* is an adjective here, adding description to the noun *station.*)

All of the words in a sentence work together to create meaning, but each one serves its own purpose by playing a part of speech. Think about how each of the words in the following sentence plays the particular part of speech labeled:

> n   prep   adj   n   adv   v   adj   n   prep n conj v
> Students at community colleges often attend several classes in a day and are
>
> adv adj conj pro adv v adv
> very tired when they finally go home.

Below, you'll find an explanation for each label:

> Students   n (*names the people* who are the subject of the sentence)
>
> at   prep (*begins a prepositional phrase* showing position in space)
>
> community   adj (*adds description* to the noun *colleges,* telling what kind)
>
> colleges   n (*names the place* that is the object of the preposition *at*)
>
> often   adv (*adds to the verb,* telling when students *attend* classes)
>
> attend   v (*shows an action,* telling what the students do)

several	adj (*adds description* to the noun *classes,* telling how many)
classes	n (*names the things* that the students *attend*)
in	prep (*begins a prepositional phrase* showing position in time)
a	no label (an article that *points to the noun day*)
day	n (*names the thing* that is the object of the preposition *in*)
and	conj (*joins* the two verbs *attend* and *are*)
are	v (*shows a state of being,* linking the subject *students* with the descriptive word *tired*)
very	adv (*adds to the adjective* that follows, telling how *tired* the students are)
tired	adj (*describes the noun* subject *students*)
when	conj (*begins a dependent clause*)
they	pro (*replaces* the word *students* as a new subject to avoid repetition)
finally	adv (*adds to the verb,* telling when they *go* home)
go	v (*shows an action,* telling what they do)
home.	adv (*adds to the verb,* telling where they *go*)

Familiarizing yourself with the parts of speech will help you spell better now and understand phrases and clauses better later. Each of the eight parts of speech has characteristics that distinguish it from the other seven, but it takes practice to learn them.

E X E R C I S E S

Label the parts of speech above all of the words in the following sentences using the abbreviations **n**, **pro**, **adj**, **v**, **adv**, **prep**, **conj**, and **interj**. Remember that proper nouns can include more than one word and that you may ignore the words *a, an,* and *the.* Refer back to the definitions and examples of the parts of speech whenever necessary. When in doubt, leave a word unmarked until you check the answers after each set of ten sentences.

Exercise 1

1. The mall near my house has a new movie theater.
2. It shows American and international films.
3. The films from other countries are in foreign languages but have English subtitles.
4. Many of the foreign films come from India.
5. I have seen three Indian films there already and have liked them very much.
6. These Bollywood movies are not what I had expected.
7. I had heard about their bright colors and their songs full of dancing.
8. However, I have particularly enjoyed the stories and characters in these films.
9. The acting has also been impressive and has often moved me to tears.
10. I guess that I can call myself a fan of Bollywood now.

Exercise 2

1. When babies want something, they often cry.
2. Now some parents teach sign language to their babies.
3. One professor of psychology tried sign language with her baby in the 1980s.
4. Then she repeated the experiment with other children.
5. The results showed that at twelve months of age, most babies are ready.
6. They can control their hands fairly well.
7. If a parent repeats signs for a few months, a child can learn them.
8. Studies report benefits for babies who learn sign language.
9. Later, their verbal test scores are high.
10. Also, they score very well on IQ tests.

Source: Psychology Today, November/December 2004

Exercise 3

1. In the summer of 2005, London Zoo opened a temporary exhibit.
2. The title of the exhibit was "The Human Zoo."
3. Zoo officials selected eight human volunteers.
4. Then they put the humans on display for several days.
5. Dozens of people had applied online for the project.
6. The exhibit showcased three males and five females.
7. They dressed in fake fig leaves that covered their shorts and bikini tops.
8. With its rocky ledges and cave-like structures, the enclosure had previously housed bears.
9. The eight humans talked, played games, and received a lot of attention.
10. Outside the exhibit, the zoo posted signs about human diet, habitat, and behavior.

Source: BBC News, August 25, 2005

Exercise 4

1. Plants need water and sunlight.
2. Sometimes houseplants wither unexpectedly.
3. People often give them too much water or not enough water.
4. I saw an experiment on a television show once.
5. It involved two plants.
6. The same woman raised both plants with water and sunlight.
7. The plants grew in two different rooms.
8. She yelled at one plant but said sweet things to the other.
9. The verbally praised plant grew beautifully, but the other one died.
10. Plants have feelings, too.

Exercise 5

1. Rabies is a disease that is usually fatal.

2. Only five people with rabies symptoms have ever survived.

3. Most people who are bitten get rabies shots before any symptoms begin.

4. These patients can avoid the deadly results of the disease.

5. Jeanna Giese from Wisconsin is unique.

6. She survived a case of rabies after a bat bit her at her church.

7. She already showed symptoms of rabies when she went to the hospital.

8. Doctors did not give Giese the rabies vaccine.

9. They put the teenager into a coma instead.

10. Their treatment worked, and it promised hope for rabies patients in the future.

Source: Los Angeles Times, June 16, 2005

PARAGRAPH EXERCISE

Here is a brief excerpt from a book called *The Question and Answer Book of Everyday Science,* by Ruth A. Sonneborn. This excerpt answers the question "Why do our eyes blink?" We have modified some of the phrasing in the excerpt for this exercise. Label the parts of speech above as many of the words as you can before checking your answers.

Your eyelids blink regularly all day long. They stop only when you sleep. Blinking protects your delicate eyes from injury. When something flies toward you, usually your lids shut quickly and protect your eyes.

Blinking also does a kind of washing job. It keeps your eyelids moist. If a speck of dirt gets past your lids, your moist eyeball traps it. Then your eyes fill with water, your lids blink, and the speck washes out of your eye.

SENTENCE WRITING

Write ten sentences imitating those in Exercises 1–5. Keep your sentences short (under 10 words each), and avoid using to _____ forms of verbs. Label the parts of speech above the words in your imitation sentences.

Adjectives and Adverbs

English has only two kinds of modifiers: adjectives and adverbs. "To modify" means to change or improve something, usually by adding to it. Two of the eight parts of speech, adjectives and adverbs, are used to *add* information to other words. Try to remember that both *ad*jectives and *ad*verbs *add* information.

ADJECTIVES

- Adjectives *add to nouns and pronouns* by answering these questions: *Which one? What kind? How much or how many? What size, what color, or what shape?*

    adj   n   adj   n   adj adj adj
    She bought a *new* textbook with *multicolored* tabs. It has *one large blue*

    n adj   adj   adj n   adj adj adj pro
    tab, *two medium yellow* tabs, and *three small red* ones.

- Adjectives usually come *before the nouns they modify.*

    adj   n   adj   n adj adj adj   n
    The *new* library stands on the *north* side of *our big beautiful* campus.

- However, adjectives can also come *after the nouns they modify.*

    n   ad   adj   adj   n   adj   n
    The land, *flat* and *accessible,* was the *perfect* location for the *new* building.

- Adjectives may also come *after linking verbs* (is, am, are, was, were, feel, seem, appear, taste . . .) to add description to the subject. For further discussion of these special verbs, see page 133.

    n   lv adj   adj
    The trees are *lush* and *plentiful.*

    n   lv   adj   adj   n   lv adj   adj
    The juice tasted *fresh* and *delicious.* (or) The juice was *fresh* and *delicious.*

- Adjectives can be *forms of nouns and pronouns* that are used to add information to other nouns.

    adj   n   adj   n   adj   adj   n
    The *tree's* owner always trims *its* branches during *his summer* vacation.

    adj   n   adj   n
    I love *chocolate* cake for *my* birthday.

ADVERBS

- Adverbs *add to verbs, adjectives, and other adverbs* by answering these questions: *How? When? Where? Why? In what way?*

  adv   v   adv   v   adv adv

  I *quickly* typed my paper and *reluctantly* turned it *in late*.

  v   adv   v

  She did *not* accept my paper at first.

  adv   adj

  I was *very* nervous about it.

  adv   adj   n

  She had an *extremely* disappointed look on her face.

  adv adj   adv   adj

  The deadline was *very* clear and *quite* reasonable.

  adv   adv adv

  Students *often* work *really hard* at the end of the term.

- Unlike adjectives, some adverbs can move around in sentences without changing the meaning.

  adv

  Now I have enough money for a vacation.

  adv

  I *now* have enough money for a vacation.

  adv

  I have enough money *now* for a vacation.

  adv

  I have enough money for a vacation *now*.

Notice that many—but not all—adverbs end in *ly*. Be aware, however, that adjectives can also end in *ly*. Remember that a word's part of speech is determined by how the word is used in a particular sentence. For instance, in the old saying "The early bird catches the worm," *early* adds to the noun, telling which bird. *Early* is acting as an adjective. However, in the sentence "The teacher arrived early," *early* adds to the verb, telling when the teacher arrived. *Early* is an adverb.

Now that you've read about adjectives and adverbs, try to identify the question that each modifier (adj or adv) answers in the example below. Refer back to the questions listed under Adjectives and Adverbs.

adj   n   adj   n   adv   adv   v

My family and I went to the farmer's market yesterday. There we watched the

adj   adj   n   adv   v   adv   adj

decoration of a huge wedding cake. The baker skillfully squeezed out colorful

    n   adj   n   adv adj adj   n   adj   adj

flowers, leaf patterns, and pale pink curving letters made of smooth, creamy

   n

frosting.

> **NOTE**—Although we discuss only single-word adjectives and adverbs here, phrases and clauses can also function as adjectives and adverbs following similar patterns.

CHOOSING BETWEEN ADJECTIVES AND ADVERBS

Knowing how to choose between adjectives and adverbs is important, especially in certain kinds of sentences. See if you can make the correct choices in these three sentences:

> We did (good, well) on that test.
> I feel (bad, badly) about quitting my job.
> Your friend speaks (really clear/really clearly).

Did you choose *well, bad,* and *really clearly?* If you missed *bad,* you're not alone. You might have reasoned that *badly* adds to the verb *feel,* but *feel* is acting in a

     v

special way here—not naming the action of feeling with your fingertips (as in "I *feel*

    adv   n   adj

the fabric *carefully*"), but describing the feeling of it (as in "The *fabric* feels *smooth*"). To understand this concept, try substituting "I feel (happy, happily)" instead of "I feel (bad, badly)" and note how easy it is to choose.

    Another way that adjectives and adverbs work is to compare two or more things by describing them in relation to one another. The *er* ending is added to both adjectives and adverbs when comparing two items, and the est ending is added when comparing three or more items.

    adj   n   adj   adj   n   adj   adj   n

The *first* group was *big*. The *second* group was *bigger*. The *third* group was

    adj   pro

the *biggest* one of all.

    v   adv   v   adv   v   adv

You work *hard*; he works *harder*; I work *hardest*.

In some cases, such comparisons require the addition of a word (*more* or *most, less* or *least*) instead of a change in the ending from *er* to *est*. Longer adjectives and adverbs usually require these extra adverbs to help with comparisons.

      adj   adv   adj   adv   adj

Food is *expensive*; gas is *more expensive*; rent is *most expensive*.

     adv   adv   adv   adv   adv

He dances *gracefully*; you dance *less gracefully*; I dance *least gracefully*.

E X E R C I S E S

Remember that adjectives add to nouns and pronouns, while adverbs add to verbs, adjectives, and other adverbs. If you learn the difference between adjectives and adverbs, your word choice will improve. Check your answers frequently.

Exercise 1

Identify whether each *italicized* word is used as an adjective or an adverb in the sentence.

1. We have many *beautiful* buildings on our campus. (adjective, adverb)

2. The old library and auditorium are *especially* impressive. (adjective, adverb)

3. Their *tall* white columns give them both a classical look. (adjective, adverb)

4. Their stone steps are *very* smooth from years of wear. (adjective, adverb)

5. The two buildings face each other with an *open* quad in between. (adjective, adverb)

6. Behind the columns are *long* walkways with benches. (adjective, adverb)

7. *Many* students like to sit in these walkways at sunset. (adjective, adverb)

8. The sunshine creates shadows of the columns in *moving* patterns. (adjective, adverb)

9. In such an atmosphere, studying for a subject like philosophy or art is *easy*. (adjective, adverb)

10. That special stillness allows for deeper thoughts *somehow*. (adjective, adverb)

Exercise 2

Identify whether the word *only* is used as an adjective or an adverb in the following sentences. In each sentence, try to link the word *only* with another word to figure out if *only* is an adjective (adding to a noun or pronoun) or an adverb (adding to a verb, adjective, or other adverb). Have fun with this exercise!

1. I reached into my wallet and pulled out my *only* coupon.

2. I had *only* one coupon.

3. *Only* I had a coupon.

4. That company *only* sells the software; it doesn't create the software.

5. That company sells *only* software, not hardware.

6. Other companies deal in hardware *only*.

7. In my Spanish class, the teacher speaks in Spanish *only*.

8. *Only* the students use English to ask questions or to clarify something.

9. My best friend is an *only* child, and so am I.

10. *Only* she understands how I feel.

Exercise 3

Choose the correct adjective or adverb form required to complete each sentence.

1. We have many (close, closely) relatives who live in the area.

2. We are (close, closely) related to many of the people in this area.

3. During the holidays, we feel (close, closely) to everyone in town.

4. My sister suffered (bad, badly) after she fell and broke her leg.

5. She felt (bad, badly) about tripping on a silly little rug.

6. Her leg itched really (bad, badly) under her cast.

7. The classroom hamster runs (very happy, very happily) on his exercise wheel.

   8. The children are always (very happy, very happily) when he exercises.

   9. My group received a (good, well) grade on our project.

  10. The four of us worked (good, well) together.

Exercise 4

Choose the correct adjective or adverb form required to complete each sentence.

   1. Of all my friends' cars, Jake's is (small, smaller, the smallest).

   2. Janna has (a small, a smaller, the smallest) car, too.

   3. Her car is (small, smaller, smallest) than mine.

   4. Ken bought his car last week, so it's (a new, a newer, the newest) one.

   5. Mine has (new, newer, newest) tires than Ken's since my tires were put on yesterday.

   6. Jake's car is (new, newer, newest) than Janna's.

   7. Ken looked for a car with (good, better, best) gas mileage than his old one.

   8. Of course, Jake's tiny car gets (good, better, the best) gas mileage of all.

   9. I do get (good, better, best) gas mileage now that I have new tires.

  10. These days, gas mileage is (important, more important, most important) than it used to be.

Exercise 5

Label all of the adjectives (adj) and adverbs (adv) in the following sentences. Mark the ones you are sure of; then check your answers and find the ones you missed.

   1. I took a very unusual art class over the summer.

   2. The intriguing title of the class was "Frame-Loom Tapestry."

   3. We created small colorful tapestries on a wooden frame.

   4. We started with four wooden stretcher bars, two long ones and two short ones.

5. Then we carefully joined them at the corners to make a rectangular frame.

6. Next, we wound white cotton string around the frame lengthwise.

7. We finally had the basis for our tapestries.

8. We took brightly colored yarns and fabric strips and wove them between the strings.

9. I was very happy with the results.

10. My first tapestry looked like a beautiful sunset.

PROOFREADING EXERCISE

Correct the five errors in the use of adjectives and adverbs in the following student paragraph. Then try to label all of the adjectives (adj) and adverbs (adv) in the paragraph for practice.

I didn't do very good in my last year of high school. I feel badly whenever I think of it. I skipped my classes and turned in messy work. My teachers warned me about my negative attitude, but I was real stubborn. Now that I am a college student, I am even stubborner. I go to every class and do my best. Now, success is only my goal.

SENTENCE WRITING

Write a short paragraph (five to seven sentences) describing your favorite class in grade school or high school. Then go back through the paragraph and label your single-word adjectives and adverbs.

Contractions

When two words are shortened into one, the result is called a *contraction*:

is not ·····➤ isn't   you have ·····➤ you've

An apostrophe marks the spot where the letter or letters are left out in most contractions:

I am	I'm
I have	I've
I shall, I will	I'll
I would	I'd
you are	you're
you have	you've
you will	you'll
she is, she has	she's
he is, he has	he's
it is, it has	it's
we are	we're
we have	we've
we will, we shall	we'll
they are	they're
they have	they've
are not	aren't
cannot	can't
do not	don't
does not	doesn't
have not	haven't
let us	let's
who is, who has	who's
where is	where's
were not	weren't

would not	wouldn't
could not	couldn't
should not	shouldn't
would have	would've
could have	could've
should have	should've
that is	that's
there is	there's
what is	what's

Remember that one contraction does not follow this rule: *will not* becomes *won't*.

In all other contractions that you're likely to use, the apostrophe goes exactly where the letter or letters are left out. Note especially that *it's, they're, who's,* and *you're* are contractions. Use them when you mean *two* words. (See p. 48 for more about the possessive forms—*its, their, whose,* and *your*—which *don't* need apostrophes.)

E X E R C I S E S

Add the missing apostrophes to the contractions in the following sentences. A few of the sentences do not include any contractions. Be sure to correct each exercise before going on to the next so you'll catch your mistakes early.

Exercise 1

1. Theres a house in China thats famous in the world of architecture for what it doesnt have.

2. Its called "The Suitcase House" because it doesnt seem to have any rooms.

3. At least the rooms arent there above the floor.

4. If you were standing inside the house, youd see just an empty rectangular space with a shiny wooden floor.

5. The rooms are all there, but theyre hidden beneath the floor.

6. The Suitcase House's floor is unique; its actually a patchwork of lifting panels.

7. Underneath each panel is a room that you cant get to unless you lift up the panel in the floor.

8. When you want to cook your dinner, you lift up the panel for the kitchen.

9. When you dont need the kitchen any more, you close the panel, and its gone.

10. If youre interested, you can rent the Suitcase House and see it for yourself.

Source: Residential Architect Magazine, September 1, 2004

Exercise 2

1. Theres a new kind of addiction to be worried about.

2. Experts call it "infomania," and its having an impact on people's lives.

3. If someones addicted to e-mail, cell phone calls, and text messages, that person suffers from infomania.

4. That persons not alone.

5. A recent study shows that around sixty percent of us have at least a mild case of infomania.

6. If theres a computer around, well check our e-mail, even if were in the middle of a meeting or some other important activity.

7. Well check our messages when we should be resting at home or on vacation.

8. The results of the study showed that theres a price to be paid.

9. People lose approximately 10 points of their IQ scores if theyre distracted by e-mails and phone calls.

10. Thats double the amount of a decline in intelligence than if they were smoking marijuana.

Source: BBC News, April 22, 2005

Exercise 3

1. My friends and I needed some extra money for a trip wed planned, so we decided to have a group yard sale.

2. I didnt think that Id find very many items to sell in my own house.

3. But I couldnt believe how much stuff I discovered that I hadnt ever used.

4. There wasnt any reason to hang onto an old exercise bicycle, for instance.

5. And I knew I didnt want to keep the cat-shaped clock that hung in my room when I was a kid.

6. My parents werent willing to part with the clock, though; I guess theyre more sentimental than I am right now.

7. It isnt easy to get rid of some things, and my friends didnt have any better luck with their parents than Id had.

8. Still, since there were so many of us, we ended up with a yard full of merchandise.

9. We spent the weekend selling a cup here and a bike there until wed made over three hundred dollars.

10. Now were convinced that without our yard-sale profits, we couldnt have had such a fun-filled trip.

Exercise 4

1. Charles F. Brannock is someone whos not as well-known as the machine he invented.

2. Im sure you remember having your foot measured at some point in your life.

3. Youre in a shoe store, and the salesperson wants to sell you a shoe that fits perfectly.

4. So the clerk grabs a metal device thats behind the counter and plops it on the floor.

5. Its a silver and black metal tray, ruler, and vise all in one.

6. My parents wouldnt let anyone sell us a pair of shoes when I was young unless wed been measured using one of these contraptions.

7. Theyre called Brannock Devices, named for Charles F. Brannock, the man who invented them.

8. He got the idea while he was still in college and working in his father's shoe store, where he noticed that the wooden stick they used to measure customers' feet wasnt practical.

9. Brannock spent countless hours in his dorm room designing a metal device thats able to measure three parts of a person's foot at once.

10. The Brannock Device is still used and manufactured today, and its design hasnt been greatly altered since its original patent in 1928.

Source: Invention & Technology, Summer 2000

Exercise 5

1. Every semester, theres a blood drive at my school, and usually I tell myself Im too busy to participate.

2. But this time, Ive decided to give blood with a couple of my friends.

3. Weve all wanted to donate before, but individually we havent had the nerve.

4. Well visit the "bloodmobile" together and support each other if any of us cant do it.

5. My friend Carla has donated before, so shes the one weve asked about how it feels.

6. She described the whole process and assured us that its easy and painless.

7. First, a volunteer asks us some questions and takes a small blood sample from one of our earlobes to see if we are or arent able to give blood.

8. Once were cleared to donate, well be asked to lie down and have one of our arms prepared for the actual donation.

9. Thats the part Ill be dreading, but Carla says its just the first stick that stings a little.

10. After that, she says that theres no sensation at all except the satisfaction of helping with such a worthy cause.

PROOFREADING EXERCISE

Correct the ten errors in this student paragraph. They could be from any of the areas we have studied so far.

Ive heard about a Web site created to allow people to share there books with complete strangers. Its called BookCrossing.com, and when your finished reading a book, it can be past on to a knew reader just by leaving it on a park bench, at a cafe, or wherever you like. Before you pass it on, you just register the book on the Web site, get its ID number, and tell wear you're going to leave it. Then you place a note or a sticker in the book with a identification number and the Web address telling the person whose going to find it what to do next. This way, people can keep track of the books they decide to "release into the wild," which is how the Web site phrases it. The best part about "bookcrossing" is that it's anonymous, and its free!

Source: Book, March/April 2002

SENTENCE WRITING

Doing exercises will help you learn a rule, but even more helpful is using the rule in writing. Write ten sentences using contractions. You might write about the types of recycling that you and your friends or family take part in, or you can choose your own subject.

Possessives

Words that clarify ownership are called *possessives*. The trick in writing possessives is to ask the question "Who (or what) does the item belong to?" Modern usage has made *who* acceptable when it begins a question. More correctly, of course, the phrasing should be "*Whom* does the item belong to?" or even "*To whom* does the item belong?"

In any case, if the answer to this question does not end in *s* (as in *player, person, people, children, month*), simply add an *apostrophe* and *s* to show the possessive. Look at the first five examples in the chart below.

However, if the answer to the question already ends in *s* (as in *players and Brahms*), add only an apostrophe after the *s* to show the possessive. See these two examples in the chart and say them aloud to hear that their sound does not need to change when made possessive.

Finally, some *s*-ending words need another sound to make the possessive clear. If you need another *s* sound when you *say* the possessive (for example, *the office of my boss* becomes *my boss's office*), add the apostrophe and another *s* to show the added sound.

a player (uniform)	Whom does the uniform belong to?	a player	Add *'s*	a player's uniform
a person (clothes)	Whom do the clothes belong to?	a person	Add *'s*	a person's clothes
people (clothes)	Whom do the clothes belong to?	people	Add *'s*	people's clothes
children (games)	Whom do the games belong to?	children	Add *'s*	children's games
a month (pay)	What does the pay belong to?	a month	Add *'s*	a month's pay
players (uniforms)	Whom do the uniforms belong to?	players	Add *'*	players' uniforms
Brahms (Lullaby)	Whom does the Lullaby belong to?	Brahms	Add *'*	Brahms' Lullaby
my boss (office)	Whom does the office belong to?	my boss	Add *'s*	my boss's office

The trick of asking "Whom does the item belong to?" will always work, but you must ask the question every time. Remember that the key word is *belong*. If you ask the question another way, you may get an answer that won't help you. Also, notice that the trick does not depend on whether the answer is *singular* or *plural*, but on whether it ends in *s* or not.

TO MAKE A POSSESSIVE

1. Ask "Whom (or what) does the item belong to?"
2. If the answer doesn't end in *s*, add an *apostrophe* and *s*.
3. If the answer already ends in *s*, add just an *apostrophe* or an *apostrophe* and *s* if you need an extra sound to show the possessive (as in *boss's office*).

EXERCISES

Follow the directions carefully for each of the following exercises. Because possessives can be tricky, we include explanations in some exercises to help you understand them better.

Exercise 1

Cover the right column and see if you can write the following possessives correctly. Ask the question "Whom (or what) does the item belong to?" each time. Don't look at the answer before you try!

1. the jury (reaction)   _____   the jury's reaction

2. an umpire (decision)   _____   an umpire's decision

3. Jess (remarks)   _____   Jess's (or Jess') remarks

4. Alice (company)   _____   Alice's company

5. the Porters (cat)   _____   the Porters' cat

6. Ms. Tobias (car)   _____   Ms. Tobias's car

7. parents (values)   _____   parents' values

8. a butterfly (wings)   _____   a butterfly's wings

9. two butterflies (wings)   _____   two butterflies' wings

10. a novel (success)   _____   a novel's success

(Sometimes you may have a choice when the word ends in *s*. *Jess's remarks* may be written *Jess' remarks*. Whether you want your reader to say it with or without an extra *s* sound, be consistent when given such choices.)

CAUTION—Don't assume that every word that ends in *s* is a possessive. The *s* may indicate more than one of something, a plural noun. Make sure the word actually possesses something before you add an apostrophe.

A few commonly used words have their own possessive forms and don't need apostrophes added to them. Memorize this list:

our, ours	its
your, yours	their, theirs
his, her, hers	whose

Note particularly *its, their, whose,* and *your.* They are already possessive and don't take an apostrophe. (These words sound just like *it's, they're, who's,* and *you're,* which are *contractions* that use an apostrophe in place of their missing letters.)

Exercise 2

Cover the right column and see if you can write the required form. The answer might be a *contraction* or a *possessive.* If you miss any, go back and review the explanations.

1. (She) the best teacher I have.	She's
2. (They) remodeling next door.	They're
3. Does (you) computer work?	your
4. (Who) traveling with us?	Who's
5. My parrot enjoys (it) freedom.	its
6. (They) car needs new tires.	Their
7. (Who) shoes are those?	Whose
8. My apartment is noisy; (it) by the airport.	it's
9. (He) going to give his speech today.	He's
10. (There) some pie in the refrigerator.	There's

Exercise 3

Here's another chance to check your progress with possessives. Cover the right column again as you did in Exercises 1 and 2, and add apostrophes correctly to any possessives. Each answer is followed by an explanation.

1. My cousins spent the weekend at my parents mountain cabin.

parents' (You didn't add an apostrophe to *cousins,* did you? The cousins don't possess anything.)

2. The border guard collected all of the tourists passports.

tourists' (Whom did the passports belong to?)

3. I attended my sisters graduation.

sister's (if it is one sister) sisters' (two or more sisters)

4. Two of my friends borrowed the camp directors boat.

director's (The friends don't possess anything.)

5. Patricks salad tasted better than hers.

Patrick's (*Hers* is already possessive and doesn't take an apostrophe.)

6. After a moments rest, the dog wagged its tail again.

moment's (*Its* is already possessive and doesn't take an apostrophe.)

7. Overnight, someone covered the Smiths house with tissue.

Smiths' (The house belongs to the Smiths.)

8. Childrens shoe sizes differ from adults sizes.

children's, adults' (Did you use the "Whom do they belong to" test?)

9. The sign read, "Buses only."

No apostrophe, no possessive.

10. A toothpastes flavor affects its sales.

toothpaste's (*Its* is already possessive and doesn't take an apostrophe.)

Exercises 4 and 5

Now you're ready to add apostrophes to the possessives that follow. But be careful. *First,* make sure the word really possesses something; not every word ending in s is a possessive. *Second,* remember that certain words already have possessive forms and don't use apostrophes. *Third,* even though a word ends in s, you can't tell where the apostrophe goes until you ask the question, "Whom (or what) does the item belong to?" The apostrophe or apostrophe and s should follow the answer to that question. Check your answers after the first set.

Exercise 4

1. In July of 2005, a baby stroller saved a childs life.

2. A 7-month-old babys nanny was pushing her stroller down a street in Manhattan.

3. Suddenly, an empty buildings roof caved in, and its outer wall collapsed on top of them.

4. The nannys arm and leg were broken by falling debris.

5. Amazingly, none of the babys bones were broken.

6. The strollers frame had protected her from the debris and saved her life.

7. Due to many bystanders quick efforts, both the nanny and the baby were rescued.

8. In response to the incident, officials were flooded with parents requests for the name of that stroller.

9. Its official name is the Mountain Buggy Urban Double Stroller.

10. Understandably, that particular models sales increased as a result.

Source: New York Daily News, July 15, 2005

Exercise 5

1. Claude Monets paintings of water lilies are world famous.

2. Monet also created a series of paintings that captured the beauty of Londons bridges at the turn of the twentieth century.

3. Monet was inspired by the fogs influence on light, color, and texture.

4. He wrote about the foggy weathers positive effect on his mood and creativity.

5. Now historians and scientists know more about the unusually thick fog that hung over London at that time.

6. It was really smog—fog mixed with soot, smoke, and other pollutants.

7. Peoples health suffered so much that hundreds died each week at its worst.

8. Monet himself had lung disease.

9. The artists views of London in the fog went on tour as an exhibition in 2005.

10. The exhibit was called "Monets London."

Source: Discover, September 2005

PROOFREADING EXERCISE

Find the six errors in this student's paragraph about a problem with her car. All of the errors involve possessives.

I'm not satisfied with my cars ride; it's too rough. For instance, when a roads surface has grooves in it, the wheels get pulled in every direction. My tires treads seem too deep for ordinary city driving. Bumps and potholes usually send my passenger's heads straight into the roof. When I bought my car, I asked about it's stiff suspension and heavy-duty tires. The salesperson told me that the suspension's elements would eventually soften for a smoother ride, but they haven't. I should have known not to trust anyones words more than my own instincts.

SENTENCE WRITING

Write ten sentences using the possessive forms of the names of your family members or the names of your friends. You could write about a recent event that brought your friends or family together. Just tell the story of how the event came about and briefly what happened that day.

REVIEW OF CONTRACTIONS AND POSSESSIVES

Here are two review exercises. First, add the necessary apostrophes to the following sentences. Try to get all the correct answers.

1. Theres a popular tradition most of us celebrate on Valentines Day.

2. We give each other little candy hearts with sayings on them, such as "Im Yours," "Youre Cute," and "Be Mine."

3. Americas largest maker of these candies is Necco; thats short for New England Confectionery Company.

4. Necco calls its version of the candies "Sweethearts Brand Conversation Hearts," and Neccos sayings have only two basic requirements: theyve got to be short and "sweet."

5. The candy hearts recipe is very sweet indeed—its ninety percent sugar.

6. The companys history goes back to the mid-1800s, and at first the sayings were printed on paper and placed inside a shell-shaped candy, more like a fortune cookies design than the tiny printed hearts we buy now.

7. In 1902, the candys shape was changed to a heart, and the sayings were printed directly on the candy.

8. Necco now makes eight billion of its candy hearts each year to satisfy the countrys desire to continue the hundred-year-old tradition.

9. Stores may begin stocking boxes of conversation hearts as early as New Years Day, but statistics show that over seventy-five percent of each years boxes are purchased in the three days before Valentines Day.

10. And if a couple of boxes are left over after February 14th, theyll stay fresh for up to five years.

Second, add the necessary apostrophes to the following short student essay.

BOWLING FOR VALUES

Growing up as a child, I didnt have a set of values to live by. Neither my mother nor my father gave me any specific rules, guidelines, or beliefs to lead me through the complicated journey of childhood. My parents approach was to set me free, to allow me to experience lifes difficulties and develop my own set of values.

They were like parents taking their young child bowling for the first time. They hung their values on the pins at the end of the lane. Then they put up the gutter guards and hoped that Id hit at least a few of the values theyd lived by themselves.

If I had children today, Id be more involved in developing a set of standards for them to follow. Id adopt my mom and dads philosophy of letting them discover on their own what theyre interested in and how they feel about life. But Id let them bowl in other lanes or even in other bowling alleys. And, from the start, theyd know my thoughts on religion, politics, drugs, sex, and all the ethical questions that go along with such subjects.

Now that Im older, I wish my parents wouldve shared their values with me. Being free wasnt as comfortable as it mightve been if Id had some basic values to use as a foundation when I had tough choices to make. My childrens lives will be better, I hope. At least theyll have a base to build on or to remodel—whichever they choose.

PROGRESS TEST

This test covers everything you've studied so far. One sentence in each pair is correct. The other is incorrect. Read both sentences carefully before you decide. Then write the letter of the incorrect sentence in the blank. Try to isolate and correct the error if you can.

1. _____ **A.** My best friend is taking a film class with me.

B. We should of taken separate classes to stay focused.

2. _____ **A.** If your looking for a new place to eat lunch, try food trucks.

B. Their food is tasty, and it's not too expensive.

3. _____ **A.** A pair of sunglasses should complement a person's style.

B. Some peoples' sunglasses don't enhance their style at all.

4. _____ **A.** Big summer movies often have to many special effects.

B. Holiday movies focus more on stories than effects.

5. _____ **A.** Learning to drive was easier then I thought it would be.

B. I learned the basics from my dad and then took a few lessons.

6. _____ **A.** I received several complements on my presentation.

B. Its organization was very effective, I think.

7. _____ **A.** Our singing teacher was absent yesterday.

B. A student lead the rehearsal, and we never sounded better.

8. _____ **A.** I took my doctor's advise and signed up for a yoga class.

B. It's improving my concentration and my flexibility.

9. _____ **A.** Music effects people in different ways.

B. The music in my yoga class focuses my mind and body.

10. _____ **A.** My computer has a problem with it's DVD player.

B. It doesn't start up when I insert a DVD.

PART 2

Sentence Structure

Sentence structure refers to the way sentences are built using words, phrases, and clauses. Words are single units, and words link up in sentences to form clauses and phrases. Clauses are word groups *with* subjects and verbs, and phrases are word groups *without* subjects and verbs. Clauses are the most important because they make statements—they tell who did what (or what something is) in a sentence. Look at the following sentence for example:

We visited the Grand Canyon with our geology club over the summer.

It contains twelve words, each playing its own part in the meaning of the sentence. But which of the words together tell who did what? *We visited the Grand Canyon* is correct. That word group is a clause. Notice that *with our geology club* and *over the summer* also link up as word groups but don't include somebody (subject) doing something (verb). Instead, they are phrases to clarify *how* and *when* we visited the Grand Canyon.

Importantly, you could leave out one or both of the phrases and still have a sentence—*We visited the Grand Canyon*. However, you cannot leave the clause out. Then you would just have *With our geology club over the summer*. Remember, every sentence needs at least one clause that can stand by itself.

Learning about the structure of sentences helps you control your own. Once you know more about sentence structure, you can understand writing errors and learn how to avoid them.

Among the most common errors in writing are fragments, run-ons, and awkward phrasing.

Here are some fragments:

Wandering around the new library all afternoon.

Because I tried to handle too many responsibilities at once.

By tutoring the students in groups.

These groups of words don't make complete statements—not one has a clause that can stand by itself. Who was *wandering around the library?* What happened *because you tried to handle too many responsibilities at once?* What did someone gain *by tutoring the students in groups?* These incomplete sentence structures fail to communicate a complete thought.

In contrast, here are some run-ons:

Book prices are dropping they're still too high.

The forecast calls for rain tomorrow I think I'll drive to school.

A truck parked in front of my driveway and it made me late for work.

Unlike fragments, run-ons make complete statements, but the trouble is they make *two* complete statements; the first *runs on* to—or runs *into*—the second. Without the help of proper punctuation, the reader has to go back and find a break between the two ideas.

So fragments don't make any complete statements, and run-ons make too many complete statements without punctuating them. Another problem occurs when the phrasing in a sentence just doesn't make sense.

Here are a few sentences with awkward phrasing:

The problem from my grades started to end.

It was a great time at my sister's graduation.

She won me at chess every time we played.

Try to find the word groups that show who did what—that is, the clauses (*The problem started, It was,* and *She won*). Now try to put the clauses and phrases together to form a precise meaning. It's difficult, isn't it? You'll see that many of the words don't work together, such as *problem from my grades, started to end, it was a great time at,* and *won me at chess*. These sentences don't communicate clearly due to awkward phrasing.

Fragments, run-ons, and awkward phrasing confuse the reader. If you can learn to avoid these and other sentence structure errors, your writing will be stronger and easier to understand. Unfortunately, there is no quick, effortless way to strengthen your sentence structure. First, you need to understand how clear sentences are built. Then you can eliminate common errors in your own writing.

This section will describe areas of sentence structure one at a time and then explain how to avoid errors associated with the different areas. For instance, we start by helping you find subjects and verbs and understand dependent clauses; then we show you how to correct fragments. You can go through the whole section yourself to learn all of the concepts and structures. Or your teacher may assign only parts based on errors the class is making.

Finding Subjects and Verbs

The most important words in sentences are those that make up its independent clause—the subject and the verb. When you write a sentence, you write about a noun or pronoun (a person, place, thing, or idea). That's the *subject*. Then you write what the subject *does* or *is*. That's the *verb*.

Lightning strikes.

The word *Lightning* is the thing you are writing about. It's the subject, and we'll underline all subjects once. *Strikes* tells what the subject does. It shows the action in the sentence. It's the verb, and we'll underline all of them twice. Most sentences do not include only two words (the subject and the verb). However, these two words still make up the core of the sentence even if other words and phrases are included with them.

Lightning strikes back and forth from the clouds to the ground very quickly.

It often strikes people on golf courses or in boats.

When many words appear in sentences, the subject and verb can be harder to find. Because the verb often shows action, it's easier to spot than the subject. Therefore, always look for it first. For example, take this sentence:

The neighborhood cat folded its paws under its chest.

Which word shows the action? The action word is folded. It's the verb, so we'll underline it twice. Now ask yourself who or what folded? The answer is cat. That's the subject, so we'll underline it once.

Study the following sentences until you understand how to pick out subjects and verbs:

The college celebrates its fiftieth anniversary tomorrow. (Which word shows the action? The action word is celebrates. It's the verb, so we'll underline it twice. Who or what celebrates? The college does. It's the subject. We'll underline it once.)

The team members shared several boxes of chocolates. (Which word shows the action? Shared shows the action. Who or what shared? Members shared.)

Internet users crowd the popular services. (Which word shows the action? The verb is crowd. Who or what crowd? Users crowd.)

Often the verb doesn't show action but links the subject with a description of what the subject *is, was,* or *will be.* Learn to spot such linking verbs—*is, am, are, was, were, has been, seem, feel, appear, become, look.* . . . (For more information on linking verbs, see the discussion of sentence patterns on p. 133).

> Marshall is a neon artist. (First spot the verb is. Then ask who or what is? Marshall is.)

> The sandwiches in the cafeteria look stale. (First spot the verb look. Then ask who or what look? Sandwiches look.)

Sometimes the subject comes after the verb, especially when a word like *there* or *here* begins the sentence without being a real subject.

> In the audience were two reviewers from the *Times*. (Who or what were in the audience? Two reviewers from the *Times* were in the audience.)

> There was a fortune-teller at the carnival. (Who or what was there? A fortune-teller was there at the carnival.)

> There were name tags for all the participants. (Who or what were there? Name tags were there for all the participants.)

> Here are two examples. (Who or what are here? The examples are here.)

NOTE—Remember that *there* and *here* (as used in the last three sentences) are not subjects. They simply point to something.

When a sentence is a command, it may appear to be missing a subject. However, an unwritten *you* is understood by the reader.

> Fill in all spaces on the form. (You fill in all spaces on the form.) Place flap A into slot B. (You place flap A into slot B.)

> Make an appointment for Tuesday. (You make an appointment for Tuesday.)

A sentence may have more than one subject.

> Toys and memorabilia from the 1950s–1990s are valuable collectibles.

> Celebrity dolls, board games, and even cereal boxes from those decades sell for high prices online.

A sentence may also have more than one verb.

Water boils at a certain temperature and freezes at another.

The ice tray fell out of my hand, skidded across the floor, and landed under the table.

E X E R C I S E S

Identify the subjects and verbs in the following sentences. Remember to start by double-underlining the verb(s), then single-underlining the subject(s). When you finish each exercise, compare your markings carefully with the answers. Refer back to the explanations and examples whenever necessary.

Exercise 1

1. Harold Lloyd became a star of comic films during the silent era of Hollywood.

2. In a fun twist, his character's name in many of his films was also Harold.

3. Harold worked in Hollywood at the same time as Charlie Chaplin and Buster Keaton.

4. One accessory distinguished Harold from the others: a pair of round eyeglasses.

5. The glasses had no lenses but fit his face and suited his character perfectly.

6. A suit and a straw hat completed Harold's simple yet effective costume.

7. Unlike Chaplin and Keaton's clownish characters, Harold looked like an ordinary young man but was physically ready for anything—from great fun to a good fight.

8. Harold performed incredible stunts in spite of a hand injury from an explosion early in his career.

9. In his most famous film, *Safety Last!*, Harold climbed a building and dangled dangerously from its clock.

10. Luckily, Harold Lloyd's movies are now available on DVD for the enjoyment of future generations.

Exercise 2

1. Travelers often carry food and other products from one country to another.
2. They ride trains or take planes to their new destinations.
3. Customs officials check passengers for illegal foods or other contraband.
4. Sometimes, customs officers catch smugglers of very unusual items.
5. One woman from Australia made the news recently.
6. There were two odd things about her skirt.
7. It looked very puffy and made a sloshing noise.
8. Customs officers found fifty-one live tropical fish in an apron under her skirt.
9. The apron had special pockets and held fifteen plastic bags.
10. Officials arrested the woman and confiscated her cargo.

Source: UnderwaterTimes.com, June 6, 2005

Exercise 3

1. Chris Lindland had a simple idea.
2. He used an ordinary fabric in an extraordinary way.
3. Lindland invented "Cordarounds."
4. Cordarounds are corduroy pants with a twist.
5. The corduroy ridges go across instead of down the pant legs.
6. These new pants have their own Web site.
7. The Web site is, predictably, cordarounds.com.
8. There are different colors and styles of Cordarounds.
9. They cost a little more than regular corduroy pants.
10. Lindland sells other new styles of clothes on his Web site.

Exercise 4

1. Cats are extremely loyal and determined pets.
2. They form strong attachments to their families.
3. One cat recently showed her love for the Sampson family very clearly.
4. The Sampsons made a temporary move and took Skittles, the cat, with them.
5. The Sampsons and Skittles spent several months 350 miles away from home.
6. Before the end of their stay, Skittles disappeared.
7. The family returned home without their beloved cat and considered her lost.
8. Seven months later, there was a surprise on their doorstep.
9. Skittles somehow navigated her way home but barely survived the 350-mile trip.
10. This incredible story proves the loyalty and determination of cats.

Source: Current Science, May 3, 2002

Exercise 5

1. There are a number of world-famous trees in California.
2. One of them is the oldest tree on the planet.
3. This tree lives somewhere in Inyo National Forest.
4. The type of tree is a bristlecone pine.
5. Scientists call it the Methuselah Tree.
6. They place its age at five thousand years.
7. The soil and temperatures around it seem too poor for a tree's health.
8. But the Methuselah Tree and its neighbors obviously thrive in such conditions.
9. Due to its importance, the Methuselah Tree's exact location is a secret.
10. Such important natural specimens need protection.

Source: Current Science, May 3, 2002

PARAGRAPH EXERCISE

Identify the subjects and verbs in the following excerpt about an important moment in film history from *The Knowledge Book: Everything You Need to Know to Get by in the 21st Century* by National Geographic. Remember to start by double underlining the verb(s), then single underlining their subject(s). Check your answers often, and refer to the explanations and examples whenever necessary. Note that film titles in this excerpt are in quotation marks. See page 188 for more about punctuating titles; standard practice in academic writing is to underline or italicize movie titles.

The 1960s and 1970s: Renewal through Independence

The golden age of cinema was over. A new generation of filmmakers . . . emerged on the scene during this period of crisis.

Worldwide Awakening

Everywhere there was a renewal of film and cinema. In Latin America, the Brazilian Glauber Rocha provided the impetus for *Cinema Novo* with his cinema as political allegories. In the U.S., a group of young directors, actresses, and actors responded to the creative standstill of the large studios—the first [were] Dennis Hopper and Peter Fonda with their naively pessimistic interpretation of the American Dream in "Easy Rider" (1969). George Lucas ("THX 1138," 1970) and Steven Spielberg ("Duel," 1971) made their debut. Martin Scorsese ("Mean Streets," 1973; "Taxi Driver," 1976; "Raging Bull," 1980) and Francis Ford Coppola ("The Conversation," 1974; "The Godfather," 1972; "Apocalypse Now," 1979) directed their best films. The decade of "New Hollywood" was a stroke of luck for cinema and the film industry.

SENTENCE WRITING

Write ten sentences about any subject—your favorite color or season, for instance. Keeping your subject matter simple in these sentence writing exercises will make it easier to find your sentence structures later. After you have written your sentences, go back and underline your subjects once and your verbs twice.

Locating Prepositional Phrases

Prepositional phrases are among the easiest structures in English to learn. Remember that a phrase is just a group of related words (at least two) without a subject and a verb. And don't let a term like *prepositional* scare you. If you look in the middle of that long word, you'll find a familiar one—*position*. In English, we tell the *positions* of people and things in sentences using prepositional phrases.

Look at the following sentence with its prepositional phrases in parentheses:

Our trip (to the desert) will begin (at 6:00) (in the morning) (on Friday).

One phrase tells *where* the trip will take us (*to the desert*), and three phrases tell *when* the trip will begin (*at 6:00, in the morning,* and *on Friday*). Most prepositional phrases show the position of someone or something in *space* or in *time*.

Here is a list of some prepositions that can show positions in *space*:

to	across	next to	against
at	through	inside	under
in	beyond	between	beneath
on	among	above	around
by	near	behind	past
over	with	from	below

Here are some prepositions that can show positions in *time* (note some repeats):

at	for	past	within
by	after	until	since
in	before	during	throughout

These lists include only individual words, *not phrases*. Remember, a preposition must be followed by a noun or pronoun object—a person, place, thing, or idea—to create *a prepositional phrase*. Notice that as the preposition changes in the prepositional phrases below, the balloon's position in relation to the object, *the clouds*, changes completely.

The hot-air balloon floated *above the clouds.*
below the clouds.
within the clouds.
between the clouds.
past the clouds.
near the clouds.

Now notice how these other prepositions similarly affect the time of its landing:

The balloon landed *before 3:30.*

> *at precisely 3:30.*
> *after 3:30.*
> *before the thunderstorm.*
> *during the thunderstorm.*
> *after the thunderstorm.*

NOTE—A few words—*of, as,* and *like*—are prepositions that do not fit neatly into either the space or time category, yet they are very common prepositions (book *of essays*, note *of apology*, type *of bicycle*; act *as a substitute*, use *as an example*, testified *as an expert*; sounds *like a computer*, acts *like a sedative*, moves *like an athlete*).

By locating prepositional phrases, you will be able to find subjects and verbs more easily. For example, you might have difficulty finding the subject and verb in a long sentence like this:

During the rainy season, one of the windows in the attic leaked at all four of its corners.

But if you put parentheses around all the prepositional phrases like this

(During the rainy season), one (of the windows) (in the attic) leaked (at all four) (of its corners).

then you have only two words left—the subject and the verb. Even in short sentences like the following, you might pick the wrong word as the subject if you don't put parentheses around the prepositional phrases first.

A box (of books) arrived (with a return address) (from Italy).

The mood (around campus) is cheerful today.

NOTE—Don't mistake *to* plus a verb for a prepositional phrase. Special forms of verbals always start with *to,* but they are not prepositional phrases (see p. 123). For example, in the sentence "I like to take the train to school," *to take* is a verbal, not a prepositional phrase. However, *to school* is a prepositional phrase because it begins with a preposition (to), ends with a noun (school), and shows position in space.

E X E R C I S E S

Put parentheses around the prepositional phrases in the following sentences. Be sure to start with the preposition itself (*in, on, to, at, of* . . .) and include the word or words that go with it (*in the morning, on our sidewalk, to Hawaii* . . .). Then underline the sentences' subjects once and verbs twice. Remember that the subject and verb in a sentence are never inside prepositional phrases, so if you locate the prepositional phrases *first,* the subjects and verbs will be much easier to find. Check your answers for each exercise before continuing to the next.

Exercise 1

1. Roald Dahl is the author of *Charlie and the Chocolate Factory.*

2. In his youth, Dahl had two memorable experiences with sweets.

3. One of them involved the owner of a candy store.

4. Dahl and his young friends had a bad relationship with this particular woman.

5. On one visit to her store, Dahl put a dead mouse into one of the candy jars behind her back.

6. The woman later went to his school and demanded his punishment.

7. He and his friends received several lashes from a cane in her presence.

8. During his later childhood years, Dahl became a taste-tester for the Cadbury chocolate company.

9. Cadbury sent him and other schoolchildren boxes of sweets to evaluate.

10. Dahl tried each candy and made a list of his reactions and recommendations.

Source: Sweets: A History of Candy (Bloomsbury, 2002)

Exercise 2

1. A killer whale at MarineLand in Canada actually invented his own stunt.

2. After feeding time, gulls often ate the leftover fish on the surface of the water.

3. One orca found a way to benefit from the gulls' habit.

4. He filled his mouth with fish chunks and squirted them on top of the water.

5. Then he sank beneath the surface and waited for a gull.

6. The whale caught the gull and had it for dessert.

7. This whale then taught his new trick to some of the other whales.

8. One main aspect of the whales' behavior fascinated scientists.

9. These whales taught the trick to themselves and to each other without human guidance.

10. Luckily, cameras captured all of the learning on film for study in the future.

Source: Science News, August 20, 2005

Exercise 3

1. My family and I live in a house at the top of a hilly neighborhood in Los Angeles.

2. On weekday mornings, nearly everyone drives down the steep winding roads to their jobs or to school.

3. In the evenings, they all come back up the hill to be with their families.

4. For the rest of the day, we see only an occasional delivery van or compact school bus.

5. But on Saturdays and Sundays, there is a different set of drivers on our roads.

6. On those two days, tourists in minivans and prospective home buyers in convertibles cram our narrow streets.

7. For this reason, most of the neighborhood residents stay at home on weekends.

8. Frequently, drivers unfamiliar with the twists and turns of the roads in this area cause accidents.

9. The expression "Sunday driver" really means something to those of us on the hill.

10. In fact, even "Saturday drivers" are a nuisance for us.

Exercise 4

1. Most of us remember playing with Frisbees in our front yards in the early evenings and at parks or beaches on weekend afternoons.

2. Fred Morrison invented the original flat Frisbee for the Wham-O toy company in the 1950s.

3. Ed Headrick, designer of the professional Frisbee, passed away at his home in California in August of 2002.

4. Working at Wham-O in the 1960s, Headrick improved the performance of the existing Frisbee with the addition of ridges in the surface of the disc.

5. Headrick's improvements led to increased sales of his "professional model" Frisbee and to the popularity of Frisbee tournaments.

6. After Headrick's redesign, Wham-O sold 100 million of the flying discs.

7. Headrick also invented the game of disc golf.

8. Like regular golf but with discs, the game takes place on special disc golf courses like the first one at Oak Grove Park in California.

9. Before his death, Headrick asked for his ashes to be formed into memorial flying discs for select family and friends.

10. Donations from sales of the remaining memorial discs went toward the establishment of a museum on the history of the Frisbee and disc golf.

Source: Los Angeles Times, August 14, 2002

Exercise 5

1. An engraved likeness of Pocahontas, the famous Powhatan princess, is the oldest portrait on display at the National Portrait Gallery.

2. In 1607, Pocahontas—still in her early teens—single-handedly helped the British colonists in Virginia to survive.

3. Later, in 1616, Pocahontas traveled to England after her marriage to John Rolfe and after the birth of their son.

4. She visited the court of King James I and impressed the British with her knowledge of English and with her conversion to Christianity.

5. For her new first name, Pocahontas chose Rebecca.

6. During her seven-month stay in England, she became extremely ill.

7. At some point before or during her illness, Simon Van de Passe engraved her portrait on copper.

8. The portrait shows Pocahontas in a ruffled collar and fancy English clothes but with very strong Native American features.

9. Successful sales of prints from the portrait illustrate her fame abroad.

10. Pocahontas died on that trip to England at the age of twenty-two.

PARAGRAPH EXERCISE

Put parentheses around the prepositional phrases in the following excerpt from *Meet Me in St. Louis*, a book about the 1904 World's Fair by Robert Jackson:

Even the Liberty Bell came to the fair during that summer—after seventy-five thousand St. Louis school children had signed a petition requesting its visit. On June 8, the cracked bell arrived on a flat wagon pulled by a team of horses and surrounded by policemen from Philadelphia. Crowds lined the edges of the Plaza of St. Louis, hoping to get a glimpse of this famous artifact. Mayor Rolla Wells pronounced the occasion Liberty Bell Day and called off school in the city so that children could come to the fair.

SENTENCE WRITING

Write ten short sentences on different types of phones or mobile devices. Such simple descriptive topics will prompt you to write sentences with prepositional phrases: for example, "Many people use phones (with pull-out keyboards)." When you finish your sentences, put parentheses around any prepositional phrases and underline your subjects once and your verbs twice.

Understanding Dependent Clauses

All clauses are groups of related words that contain a subject and a verb. However, there are two kinds of clauses: *independent* and *dependent*. Independent clauses have a subject and a verb and make complete statements by themselves. Dependent clauses also have a subject and a verb, but these clauses don't make complete statements because of the words that begin them. Here are some of the words (conjunctions or pronouns) that can begin dependent clauses:

after	since	where
although	so that	whereas
as	than	wherever
as if	that	whether
because	though	which
before	unless	whichever
even if	until	while
even though	what	who
ever since	whatever	whom
how	when	whose
if	whenever	why

When a clause begins with one of these dependent words, it is usually a dependent clause. To see the difference between an independent and a dependent clause, look at this example of an independent clause:

We studied history together.

It has a subject (We) and a verb (studied), and it makes a complete statement. But as soon as we put one of the dependent words in front of it, the clause becomes *dependent* because it no longer makes a complete statement:

After we studied history together . . .

Although we studied history together . . .

As we studied history together . . .

Before we studied history together . . .

Since we studied history together . . .

That we studied history together . . .

When we studied history together . . .

While we studied history together . . .

Each of these dependent clauses leaves the reader expecting something more. Each would depend on another clause—an independent clause—to make it a sentence. For the rest of this discussion, we'll place a dotted line beneath dependent clauses.

After we studied history together, we went to the evening seminar.

We went to the evening seminar *after* we studied history together.

The speaker didn't know *that* we studied history together.

While we studied history together, the library became crowded.

As you can see in these examples, *when a dependent clause comes before an independent clause, it is followed by a comma.* Often the comma prevents misreading, as in the following sentence:

When we returned, our library books were on the floor.

Without a comma after *returned,* the reader would read *When we returned our library books* before realizing that this was not what the writer meant. The comma prevents misreading. Sometimes if the dependent clause is short and there is no danger of misreading, the comma can be left off, but it's safer simply to follow the rule that a dependent clause coming before an independent clause is followed by a comma. You'll learn more about the punctuation of dependent clauses on page 84, but for now just remember to use a comma when a dependent clause comes before an independent clause.

Note that a few of the dependent words (*that, who, which, what*) can do "double duty" as both the dependent word and the subject of the dependent clause:

Thelma wrote a poetry book *that* sold a thousand copies.

The manager saw *what* happened.

Sometimes the dependent clause is in the middle of the independent clause:

The book *that* sold a thousand copies was Thelma's.

The events *that* followed the parade delighted everyone.

The dependent clause can even be the subject of the entire sentence:

What you do also affects me.

How your project looks counts for ten percent of the grade.

Also note that sometimes the *that* of a dependent clause is omitted:

I know that you feel strongly about this issue.

I know you feel strongly about this issue.

Everyone received the classes *that* they wanted.

Everyone received the classes they wanted.

Of course, the word *that* doesn't always introduce a dependent clause. It may be a pronoun and serve as the subject or object of the sentence:

That was a really long movie.

We knew *that* already.

That can also be an adjective, a descriptive word telling *which one:*

That movie always makes me laugh.

We took them to *that* park last week.

E X E R C I S E S

Exercise 1

Each of the following sentences contains *one* independent and *one* dependent clause. Draw a dotted line beneath the dependent clause in each sentence. Start at the dependent word and include all the words that go with it. Remember that dependent clauses can show up in the beginning, middle, or end of a sentence.

Example: We study together whenever we meet in the library.

> **1.** When people visit Google's homepage on one evening in March each year, they are often surprised.

2. They notice immediately that the whole page is black instead of white.

3. After they look into it further, they discover the reason for the temporary color change.

4. The black page signifies that Google is a participant in Earth Hour.

5. In 2008, Google joined countless cities, companies, and individuals who turn their lights off for one hour in an international effort to encourage energy conservation.

6. People around the globe cut their electricity and live in the dark as soon as the clock strikes 8 pm in their locations.

7. When the hour is up at 9 pm, they turn the electricity back on.

8. Earth Hour is an idea that began in Australia.

9. In 2007, the first Earth Hour that the Australians celebrated occurred between 7:30 and 8:30 pm on March 31.

10. Even though some people dismiss Earth Hour as a minor event, others believe in its power as a symbol of environmental awareness.

Exercises 2–5

Follow the same directions as in Exercise 1; however, this time draw your dotted lines far below the dependent clauses. Then go back to both the independent and dependent clauses and draw a double underline beneath the verbs and a single underline beneath their subjects.

Example: We study together whenever we meet in the library.

Exercise 2

1. The world is a miserable place when you have an upset stomach.

2. Whether you get carsick, airsick, or seasick, you probably welcome any advice.

3. Motion sickness is most common when people are between the ages of seven and twelve.

4. Motion sickness happens to some people whenever the brain receives mixed messages.

5. If the inner ear feels movement but the eyes report no movement, the brain gets confused.

6. This confusion results in dizziness and the feeling that all is not well.

7. Experts suggest that you sleep well and eat lightly to avoid motion sickness.

8. When you travel by car, you should sit in the middle of the back seat and look straight out the windshield.

9. On an airplane or a boat, the best seat is one that allows a view of the clouds or horizon.

10. Whenever the queasy feeling comes, you should sip small amounts of water.

Exercise 3

1. The Breathalyzer is a machine that measures a person's blood alcohol level.

2. Police officers use the device when they suspect a drunk driver.

3. Robert F. Borkenstein was the man who invented the Breathalyzer.

4. Before Borkenstein created the portable measuring device, officers took suspects' breath samples in balloons back to a laboratory for a series of tests.

5. Borkenstein's Breathalyzer was an improvement because all testing occurred at the scene.

6. The Breathalyzer was so reliable and became so feared that one man went to extremes to avoid its results.

7. While this man waited in the back of the police car, he removed his cotton underwear and ate them.

8. He hoped that the cotton cloth would soak up all the alcohol in his system.

9. When the desperate man's case went to court, the judge acquitted him.

10. The judge's decision came after spectators in the court laughed so hard that they could not stop.

Source: Los Angeles Times, August 18, 2002

Exercise 4

1. On June 8, 1924, George Mallory and Andrew Irvine disappeared as they climbed to the top of Mount Everest.

2. Earlier, when a reporter asked Mallory why he climbed Everest, his response became legendary.

3. "Because it is there," Mallory replied.

4. No living person knows whether the two British men reached the summit of Everest before they died.

5. Nine years after Mallory and Irvine disappeared, English climbers found Irvine's ice ax.

6. In 1975, a Chinese climber spotted a body that was frozen in deep snow on the side of the mountain.

7. He kept the news secret for several years but finally told a fellow climber on the day before he died himself in an avalanche on Everest.

8. In May 1999, a team of mountaineers searched the area that the Chinese man described and found George Mallory's frozen body, still intact after seventy-five years.

9. After they took DNA samples for identification, the mountaineers buried the famous climber on the mountainside where he fell.

10. The question remains whether Mallory was on his way up or down when he met his fate.

Exercise 5

1. I read an article that described the history of all the presidents' dogs.

2. George Washington cared so much about dogs that he interrupted a battle to return a dog that belonged to a British general.

3. Abraham Lincoln, whose dog's name was actually Fido, left his loyal pet in Illinois after the Lincolns moved to the White House.

4. Teddy Roosevelt met and adopted Skip, the dog that he loved best, after the little terrier held a bear at bay in the Grand Canyon.

5. Franklin Delano Roosevelt also adored his dog Fala, another stout terrier who was so famous that a separate statue of him sits next to FDR at the Franklin Delano Roosevelt Memorial in Washington, D.C.

6. Nikita Khrushchev traveled from Russia with Pushinka, a dog that he gave to John F. Kennedy's daughter Caroline.

7. At a gas station in Texas, Lyndon Johnson's daughter Luci found a little white dog, Yuki, whom President Johnson loved to have howling contests with in the Oval Office.

8. Of course, Nixon had his famous Checkers, and George Bush Sr. had Millie, the spaniel who wrote her own best-selling book with the help of Barbara Bush.

9. And just when it seemed that all presidents prefer dogs, Bill Clinton arrived with Socks, a black-and-white cat.

10. In 2009, Barack Obama's family chose Bo, a Portuguese Water Dog, as the White House pet because one daughter is allergic to other dog breeds.

PARAGRAPH EXERCISE

Draw a broken line beneath the five dependent clauses in this paragraph from the book *Look at the Sky and Tell the Weather* by Eric Sloane, in which he explains the unique challenge of predicting the weather in New England. To find dependent clauses, remember to look for dependent words (such as *when, where, that, what, because, while, after, if . . .*) and be sure they are followed by subjects and verbs. Underline the verbs twice and their subjects once in both the independent and dependent clauses.

New England is a tightrope where the weather usually balances between warm maritime air and the periodic flows of cold continental air from the northwest. So if ever there was a place where amateur folklore weather prophets do their best work, I might suggest New England. The tightrope between the two air masses often waves and writhes, causing sunny weather in one spot while rain is only a mile or two away. You can't show that sort of thing on a weather map. A New England weather prophet just has to know his sky and wind and remember by past experience what follows which sky phenomena.

SENTENCE WRITING

Write ten sentences about your morning routine (getting ready for school, eating breakfast, driving or riding to school, etc.). Try to write sentences that contain both independent and dependent clauses. Then draw a broken line beneath your dependent clauses, underline your subjects, and double underline your verbs.

Correcting Fragments

Sometimes a group of words looks like a sentence—with a capital letter at the beginning and a period at the end—but it may be missing a subject, a verb, or both. Such incomplete sentence structures are called *fragments*. Here are a few examples:

Just raises his hand in class without thinking. (*Who* does? There is no subject.)

Pauline and her sister with the twins. (*Did* what? There is no verb.)

Plenty to do in the lab. (This fragment is missing a subject and a real verb. *To do* is a verbal, see p. 123.)

To change these fragments into sentences, we must make sure each has a subject and a real verb:

That student just raises his hand in class without thinking. (We added a subject.)

Pauline and her sister with the twins volunteered. (We added a verb.)

The tutors had plenty to do in the lab. (We added a subject and a real verb.)

Sometimes we can simply attach such a fragment to the previous sentence:

I want a fulfilling career. Teaching, for example. (fragment)

I want a fulfilling career—teaching, for example. (correction)

Or we can add a subject or a verb to the fragment and make it a complete sentence:

I want a fulfilling career. Teaching is one example. (correction)

PHRASE FRAGMENTS

By definition, phrases are word groups *without* subjects and verbs, so whenever a phrase is punctuated as a sentence, it is a fragment. Look at this example of a sentence followed by a phrase fragment beginning with *hoping* (see p. 123 for more about verbal phrases):

The actors waited outside the director's office. Hoping for a chance to audition.

We can correct this fragment by attaching it to the previous sentence:

The actors waited outside the director's office, hoping for a chance to audition.

Or we can change it to include a subject and a real verb:

> The actors waited outside the director's office. They were hoping for a chance to audition.

Here's another example of a sentence followed by a phrase fragment:

> Language classes are difficult. Especially when taken in summer school.

Here the two have been combined into one complete sentence:

> Language classes taken in summer school are especially difficult.

Or a better revision might be

> Language classes are especially difficult when taken in summer school.

Sometimes, prepositional phrases are also incorrectly punctuated as sentences. Here a series of prepositional phrases follows a sentence, but the word group is a fragment—it has no subject and verb of its own. Therefore, it needs to be corrected.

> I live a simple life. With my family on our farm in central California.

Omitting the period is one possible correction:

> I live a simple life with my family on our farm in central California.

Or it could be corrected this way:

> My family and I live a simple life on our farm in central California.

DEPENDENT CLAUSE FRAGMENTS

A dependent clause punctuated as a sentence is another kind of fragment. A sentence needs a subject, a verb, *and* a complete thought. As discussed in the previous section, a dependent clause has a subject and a verb, but it begins with a word that makes its meaning incomplete, such as *after, while, because, since, although, when, if, where, who, which,* and *that.* (See p. 69 for a longer list of these words.) To correct such fragments, we can either eliminate the word that makes the clause dependent *or* add an independent clause.

FRAGMENT

While <u>some</u> of us <u>wrote</u> in our journals.

CORRECTED

<u>Some</u> of us <u>wrote</u> in our journals.

or

While <u>some</u> of us <u>wrote</u> in our journals, the fire <u>alarm</u> <u>rang</u>.

FRAGMENT

Which <u>kept</u> me from finishing my journal entry.

CORRECTED

The fire <u>alarm</u> <u>kept</u> me from finishing my journal entry.

or

<u>I</u> <u>responded</u> to the fire alarm, *which* <u>kept</u> me from finishing my journal entry.

You might ask, are fragments ever permissible? Professional writers sometimes use fragments in books, articles, advertising, and other kinds of writing. But professional writers use these fragments intentionally, not in error. Until you're an experienced writer, it's best to write complete sentences. Especially in college writing, you should avoid using fragments.

E X E R C I S E S

Some of the following word groups are sentences, and some are fragments. The sentences include subjects and verbs and make complete statements. Write the word "correct" next to each of the sentences. Then change the fragments into sentences by making sure that each has a subject, a real verb, and a complete thought.

Exercise 1

1. Some people get tattoos on a whim.
2. Not thinking about the consequences.
3. Studies of people with tattoos reveal interesting facts.

4. Many people change their minds after being tattooed.

5. About half of the people, to be exact.

6. Removing a tattoo is not easy.

7. Involving lasers to remove the pigment in the skin.

8. Alexandrite, YAG, and ruby are the three types of lasers.

9. Used on different colors and in different combinations.

10. A good dermatologist can remove most of a tattoo with lasers.

Exercise 2

1. One of Jerry Seinfeld's props was inducted into the Smithsonian Institution.

2. It's the white pirate shirt from the famous "Puffy Shirt" episode of *Seinfeld*.

3. The shirt that Jerry had to wear on TV.

4. To help Kramer's friend, a fashion designer.

5. The shirt is now on display at the National Museum of American History.

6. Along with Dorothy's ruby slippers from *The Wizard of Oz*.

7. And other famous objects, like the original Kermit the Frog from *Sesame Street*.

8. Jerry Seinfeld spoke at the ceremony to commemorate the shirt.

9. He explained why he thought the "Puffy Shirt" episode was so funny.

10. Because the shirt had the combination of a funny design and a funny name.

Source: Smithsonian, March 2005

Exercise 3

Each pair contains one sentence and one phrase fragment. Correct each phrase fragment by attaching the phrase to the complete sentence before or after it.

1. It's almost impossible to find a parking space on or near campus. Without getting up really early.

2. Hoping for the best. I always pay my sixty dollars a year for a parking permit.

3. My car's old engine can't tolerate long periods of waiting. Stalling or backfiring every few minutes.

4. In order to get a space close to my first class. I follow anyone who is walking towards a parked car.

5. Rarely offering signs of encouragement. Students usually keep walking through the parking lots, down the street, and toward the bus stop.

6. Due to their own struggles with parking. Visitors who return to their cars sometimes offer help.

7. There is one foolproof way to ensure a perfect parking place. Getting to campus before 6:30 am.

8. Every morning, I see the early birds in their cars with their seats back. Sleeping there for hours before class.

9. Because of my late-night study habits. I can barely make it to school by 8:00 am.

10. Due to increases in enrollment. The parking problem is here to stay.

Exercise 4

Each pair contains one sentence and one dependent clause fragment. Correct each dependent clause fragment by eliminating its dependent word or by attaching the dependent clause to the independent clause before or after it.

1. We were writing our in-class essays. When suddenly the emergency bell rang.

2. Everyone in the class looked at each other first and then at the teacher. Who told us to gather up our things and follow him outside.

3. The series of short rings continued. As we left the room and noisily walked out into the parking lot beside the main building.

4. The sunlight was very warm and bright compared to the classroom's fluorescent lights. Which always make everything look more clinical than natural.

5. As we stood in a large group with students and teachers from other classes. We wondered about the reason for the alarm.

6. I have never heard an emergency alarm. That was anything but a planned drill.

7. Without the danger of injury, a party atmosphere quickly developed. Since we all got a break from our responsibilities.

8. I've noticed that the teachers seem the most at ease during these situations. Because they don't have to be in control.

9. After we students and the teachers chatted for ten minutes or so. The final bell rang to signal the end of the drill.

10. When we sat down at our desks again. The teacher asked us to continue writing our essays until the end of the hour.

Exercise 5

All of the following word groups are individual fragments punctuated as sentences. Make the necessary changes to turn each fragment into a sentence that makes sense to you. Your corrections will most likely differ from the sample answers at the back of the book. But by comparing your answers to ours, you'll see that there are many ways to correct a fragment.

1. Whenever I see a seagull up close.

2. After lunch on Tuesdays, our club meeting in the gym.

3. After we turned in our research assignments.

4. Traveling overseas without a lot of planning.

5. The pizza arriving within thirty minutes of our call.

6. It being the hardest question on the test.

7. That people often stretch the truth.

8. Discussing the topic with the person next to you.

9. Even though "wet paint" signs were still on the walls.

10. How a series of paragraphs becomes an essay.

PROOFREADING EXERCISE

Find and correct the six fragments in the following paragraph.

We are all familiar with photos that have been digitally altered to enhance some part of the image. Whether it's a celebrity's waistline or a country's coastline. Questioning the reliability of photographs is not a new practice. One example from the early 1900s being the infamous pictures of the Cottingley Fairies. The story of these photos began in 1918 when two girls from the small English town of Cottingley took pictures of themselves surrounded by tiny dancing figures. Then insisting that the creatures in the photos were real live fairies. Caught on film in their natural habitat for the first time. Scientific tests, the girls' assurances, and people's desire to believe led many to accept that the Cottingley fairies actually existed. Even Sir Arthur Conan Doyle, creator of Sherlock Holmes, wrote a book called *The Coming of the Fairies*. Which he published to stress the importance of the photographs in 1920. Eventually, the girls revealed that the figures in the photographs were only drawings of fairies. And that they had destroyed the drawings and buried them after taking the pictures. *Fairy Tale: A True Story* (1997) is a popular film that is based on these events.

SENTENCE WRITING

Write ten fragments (like the ones in Exercise 5) and then revise them so that they are complete sentences. For even more good practice, exchange papers with another student and turn your classmate's ten fragments into sentences.

Correcting Run-on Sentences

A word group with a subject and a verb is a clause. As we have seen, the clause may be independent (making a complete statement and able to stand alone as a sentence), or it may be dependent (beginning with a dependent word and unable to stand alone as a sentence). When two *independent* clauses are written together without proper punctuation between them, the result is called a *run-on sentence*. Here are some examples.

World music offers a lot of variety I listen to it in my car.

I love the sound of drums therefore, bhangra is one of my favorite styles.

Run-on sentences can be corrected in one of six ways:

1. Separate the independent clauses into two sentences with a period.

World music offers a lot of variety. I listen to it in my car.

I love the sound of drums. Therefore, bhangra is one of my favorite styles.

2. Connect the two independent clauses with a semicolon alone.

World music offers a lot of variety; I listen to it in my car.

I love the sound of drums; therefore, bhangra is one of my favorite styles.

3. Connect the two independent clauses with a semicolon and a transition.

Look over the following list of connecting words (transitions):

also	however	otherwise
consequently	likewise	then
finally	moreover	therefore
furthermore	nevertheless	thus

When one of these words is used to join two independent clauses, a semicolon comes before the connecting word, and a comma usually comes after it.

Mobile devices are essential in our society; however, they are very expensive.

Earthquakes scare me; nevertheless, I live in Los Angeles.

Yasmin traveled to London; then she took the "Chunnel" to Paris.

The college recently built a large new library; thus we have more study areas.

NOTE—The use of the comma after the connecting word depends on how long the connecting word is. If it is only a short word, like *then* or *thus,* the comma is not necessary.

4. **Connect the two independent clauses with a comma and one of the following seven words (the first letters of which create the word *fanboys*, an easy way to remember them):** *for, and, nor, but, or, yet,* **or** *so.*

   Swans are beautiful birds, *and* they mate for life.

   Students may sign up for classes in person, *or* they may register online.

Each of the *fanboys* has its own meaning when used as a connecting word. For example, *so* means "as a result," and *for* means "because":

   World music offers a lot of variety, *so* I never get bored with it.

   Bhangra is one of my favorite styles, *for* I love the sound of drums.

   I applied for financial aid, *but* (or *yet*) I make too much money to receive it.

   My brother doesn't know how to drive, *nor* does he plan to learn.

Before you put a comma before a *fanboys,* be sure there are two independent clauses. Note that the first sentence that follows has two independent clauses. However, the second sentence contains just one clause with two verbs and therefore needs no comma.

   Registration begins next week, and it continues throughout the summer.

   Registration begins next week and continues throughout the summer.

5. **Add a dependent word—such as *when, since, after, while,* or *because*—to the clause used at the beginning of the sentence, and follow the dependent clause with a comma.**

   Because I enjoy acoustic guitar music, I listen to it in my car.

6. **Add a dependent word—such as *when, since, after, while,* or *because*—to the clause used at the end of the sentence (no comma necessary).**

   I listen to acoustic guitar music in my car *because* I enjoy it.

Learn these ways to join two clauses, and you'll avoid run-on sentences.

SIX WAYS TO CORRECT RUN-ON SENTENCES

Run-on: The movie had a dull plot many people left early.

1. The movie had a dull plot. Many people left early. (period)
2. The movie had a dull plot; many people left early. (semicolon)
3. The movie had a dull plot; therefore, many people left early.
   (semicolon + transition)
4. The movie had a dull plot, so many people left early.
   (comma + *fanboys*)
5. Because the movie had a dull plot, many people left early.
   (dependent clause at beginning + comma)
6. Many people left early because the movie had a dull plot.
   (dependent clause at end, no comma)

EXERCISES

Exercises 1 and 2

CORRECTING RUN-ONS WITH PUNCTUATION

Some of the following sentences are run-ons. If the sentence contains two independent clauses without proper punctuation, use one of the first four ways to correct the run-on (using punctuation only). All existing punctuation in the sentences is correct. When correcting punctuation, remember to capitalize after a period but not after a semicolon and to insert a comma only when the words *for, and, nor, but, or, yet,* or *so* are already used to join the two independent clauses.

Exercise 1

1. Mary Mallon is a famous name in American history but she is not famous for something good.
2. Most people know Mary Mallon by another name and that is "Typhoid Mary."
3. Mallon lived during the late nineteenth and early twentieth centuries.
4. At that time, there was little knowledge about disease carriers.
5. Mary Mallon was the first famous case of a healthy carrier of disease but she never believed the accusations against her.

6. Mallon, an Irish immigrant, was a cook she was also an infectious carrier of typhoid.

7. By the time the authorities discovered Mallon's problem, she had made many people ill a few of her "victims" actually died from the disease.

8. A health specialist approached Mallon and asked her for a blood sample she was outraged and attacked him with a long cooking fork.

9. Eventually, the authorities dragged Mallon into a hospital for testing but she fought them hysterically the entire time.

10. The lab tests proved Mallon's infectious status and health officials forced Mary Mallon to live on an island by herself for twenty-six years.

Source: Los Angeles Times, September 2, 2002

Exercise 2

1. Frank Epperson invented something delicious and refreshing and it comes on a stick.

2. In 1905, Epperson was an eleven-year-old boy he lived in San Francisco.

3. On the porch outside his house, he was mixing a fruity drink with a stick and forgot to put his drink away before going to bed.

4. The drink sat outside all night with the stick still in it.

5. There was a record-breaking cold snap that evening and the drink froze.

6. In the morning, Frank Epperson ate his frozen juice creation it made a big impression.

7. Epperson grew up and kept making his frozen "Epsicles" they came in seven varieties.

8. Eighteen years after that cold night, Epperson patented his invention but with a different name.

9. Epperson's kids loved their dad's treat and they always called them "pop's sicles."

10. So Popsicles were born and people have loved them ever since.

Source: Biography Magazine, July 1999

Exercises 3 and 4

CORRECTING RUN-ONS WITH DEPENDENT CLAUSES

Most of the following sentences are run-ons. Use one of the last two ways to correct run-ons, by making one or more of the clauses *dependent*. You may rephrase the sentences, but be sure to use dependent words (such as *since, when, as, after, while, because,* or the other words listed on p. 69) to begin dependent clauses and to add a comma only if the dependent clause comes first. Since various words can be used to form dependent clauses, your answers might differ from those suggested in the answers.

Exercise 3

1. I went to the orthodontist last month she told me that I needed braces.

2. I was happy I always wanted them.

3. My brother thought that I was crazy for wanting braces.

4. He wore the metal kind for five and a half years, and he hated them.

5. My dentist told me about many types of braces I wanted the invisible kind.

6. The dentist said that the invisible ones were perfect for my case she began the process.

7. She took a casting of my teeth and sent it to the invisible braces company.

8. The company made a series of sets of clear braces I will wear them for several weeks each.

9. The first set fits my teeth perfectly they are almost totally invisible.

10. I am glad that orthodontists offer this new type of braces they are just right for me.

Exercise 4

1. I've been reading about sleep in my psychology class I now know a lot more about it.

2. Sleep has five stages we usually go through all these stages many times during the night.

3. The first stage of sleep begins our muscles relax and mental activity slows down.

4. During stage one, we are still slightly awake.

5. Stage two takes us deeper than stage one we are no longer aware of our surroundings.

6. We spend about half our sleeping time in the second stage.

7. Next is stage three in it we become more and more relaxed and are very hard to awaken.

8. Stage four is the deepest in this stage we don't even hear loud noises.

9. The fifth stage of sleep is called REM (rapid eye movement) sleep our eyes move back and forth quickly behind our eyelids.

10. REM sleep is only about as deep as stage two we do all our dreaming during the REM stage.

Exercise 5

Correct the following run-on sentences using any of the methods studied in this section: adding punctuation or using dependent words to create dependent clauses. See the chart on p. 89 if you need to review the methods.

1. Boston Red Sox fans have a tradition they celebrate it at every home game without question.

2. Very few people know how the tradition began but most people don't care to know.

3. It happens in the eighth inning and everyone looks forward to it.

4. The loud speakers at Fenway Park play the song "Sweet Caroline" all of the fans sing along.

5. There is a problem with the tradition the original song has no link to Boston or baseball.

6. Neil Diamond sings the thirty-year-old song but his last name is only a baseball coincidence.

7. In the past, other teams played the song at stadiums but in 2002, Boston started playing it at every game.

8. Some people say that the tradition brought the team good luck.

9. The Red Sox won the 2004 World Series no one really expected that they would.

10. Players and teams in sports are often superstitious singing "Sweet Caroline" is a lucky charm that the fans, the players, and the management love.

Source: The Boston Globe, May 29, 2005

REVIEW OF FRAGMENTS AND RUN-ON SENTENCES

If you remember that all clauses include a subject and a verb, but only independent clauses can be punctuated as sentences (since only they can stand alone), then you will avoid fragments in your writing. And if you memorize these six ways to punctuate clauses, you will be able to avoid most punctuation errors.

PUNCTUATING CLAUSES

I am a student. I am still learning.	(two sentences)
I am a student; I am still learning.	(two independent clauses)
I am a student; therefore, I am still learning.	(two independent clauses connected by a transition such as *also, consequently,* finally, *furthermore, however, likewise, moreover, nevertheless, otherwise, then, therefore, thus*)
I am a student, so I am still learning.	(two independent clauses connected by a *fanboys: for, and, nor, but, or, yet, so*)
I am still learning *because I am a student.*	(dependent clause at end of sentence)
Because I am a student, I am still learning.	(dependent clause at beginning of sentence) Dependent words include *after, although, as, as if, because, before, even if, even though, ever since, how, if, since, so that, than, that, though, unless, until, what, whatever, when, whenever, where, whereas, wherever, whether, which, whichever, while, who, whom, whose,* and *why.*

It is essential that you study the previous chart to learn which of the italicized words transition between independent clauses and which of them create dependent clauses.

PROOFREADING EXERCISE

Rewrite the following paragraph, making the necessary changes to eliminate fragments or run-on sentences.

With the focus on cleanliness lately in advertising for soaps and household cleaning products. People are surprised to hear that we may be too clean for our own good. This phenomenon is called the "hygiene hypothesis" and recent studies support its validity. For instance, one study showing the benefits of living with two or more pets. Babies may grow up with healthier immune systems and be less allergic if they live with a dog and a cat or two dogs or two cats. The old thinking was that young children would become more allergic living with many pets but they don't. Somehow the exposure to pets and all their "dirty" habits gives youngsters much-needed defenses. Maybe as much as a seventy-five percent lower allergy risk, according to this study.

Source: Los Angeles Times, September 2, 2002

SENTENCE WRITING

Write a sample sentence of your own to demonstrate each of the six ways to correct run-on sentences by punctuating two clauses properly. You may model your sentences on the examples used in the box on page 85 or the chart on page 89.

Identifying Verb Phrases

Sometimes a verb is one word, but often the verb includes two or more words. Verbs made of more than one word are called *verb phrases*. Look at that following list of forms of the verb *speak,* for example. Most of them are verb phrases, made up of the main verb (*speak*) and one or more helping verbs.

speak	is speaking	had been speaking
speaks	am speaking	will have been speaking
spoke	are speaking	is spoken
will speak	was speaking	was spoken
has spoken	were speaking	will be spoken
have spoken	will be speaking	can speak
had spoken	has been speaking	must speak
will have spoken	have been speaking	should have spoken

Note that words certain words are not verbs, but they may be near a verb or in the middle of a verb phrase. These words usually act as adverbs—but they are never verbs:

already	ever	not	really
also	finally	now	sometimes
always	just	often	usually
probably	never	only	possibly

Jason has *never* spoken to his instructor before. He *always* speaks with other students.

Two forms of *speak—speaking* and *to speak*—look like verbs, but neither form can ever be the only verb in a sentence. No *ing* word by itself or *to* _____ form of a verb can act as the main verb of a sentence.

Jeanine speaking French. (a fragment lacking a complete verb phrase)

Jeanine has been speaking French. (a sentence with a complete verb phrase)

And no verb with *to* in front of it can ever be the real verb in a sentence.

Ted to speak in front of groups. (a fragment without a real verb)

Ted hates to speak in front of groups. (a sentence with a real verb)

These two forms, *speaking* and *to speak,* may be used as subjects or other parts of a sentence.

adj

Speaking on stage is an art. *To speak* on stage is an art. Ted had a *speaking* part in that play.

E X E R C I S E S

Double underline the verbs or verb phrases in the following sentences. For now, you do not need to mark subjects. The sentences may contain independent *and* dependent clauses, so there may be several verbs and verb phrases. (Remember that *ing* verbs alone and the *to* _____ forms of verbs are never real verbs in sentences.)

Exercise 1

1. People from all over the world entered a dog-cloning contest in June 2008.

2. The "Golden Clone Giveaway" was sponsored by BioArts International and Best Friends Again, a dog-cloning company in California.

3. BioArts had succeeded in cloning the company owner's dog, Missy, in 2007.

4. The company's Web site showed pictures of Missy and three of her clones: Mira, Chingu, and Sarang.

5. To enter the "Golden Clone Giveaway" contest, applicants submitted an application and wrote a short essay describing why their dog would be perfect to clone.

6. James Symington was chosen from all the applicants as the winner of the first "Golden Clone Giveaway."

7. Symington had written his essay about Trakr, a rescue dog who had worked at Ground Zero on 9/11 and had even found one of the last survivors in the debris.

8. For those who could afford to pay for the service, BioArts and Best Friends Again also conducted auctions for their dog-cloning procedures.

9. The five Internet auctions occurred in July 2008; each auction opened with a $100,000 starting bid.

10. After the company had successfully cloned the five dogs that were purchased in the auctions, it stopped all operations and issued a press release "Six Reasons Why We're No Longer Cloning Dogs."

Source: www.bioarts.com

Exercise 2

1. Scientists successfully cloned a dog for the first time in 2005.

2. Cloning experts had been attempting to clone a dog for many years.

3. They had had success with horses, cats, and even rats before they could clone a dog.

4. The scientists who eventually succeeded were from Seoul National University in South Korea.

5. They named the cloned dog Snuppy as a tribute to the university where the accomplishment was made, and they pronounced the name "Snoopy."

6. Of course, Snuppy could thank his "parent" dog, a three-year-old Afghan hound, for all of his great physical features.

7. Both dogs had long glossy black fur that was accentuated by identical brown markings on their paws, tails, chests, and eyebrows.

8. Unfortunately, the cloning procedure does not guarantee that the clone of a dog will share the unique features of the original dog's personality.

9. Nevertheless, now that dog cloning has been achieved, many people have shown an interest in cloning their own dogs.

10. Although some people may not be happy with just a physical copy of a beloved pet, for others, a copy is better than nothing.

Source: Science News, August 6, 2005

Exercise 3

1. I have always wondered how an Etch A Sketch works.

2. This flat TV-shaped toy has been popular since it first arrived in the 1960s.

3. Now I have learned the secrets inside this popular toy.

4. An Etch A Sketch is filled with a combination of metal powder and tiny plastic particles.

5. This mixture clings to the inside of the Etch A Sketch screen.

6. When the pointer that is connected to the two knobs moves, the tip of it "draws" lines in the powder on the back of the screen.

7. The powder at the bottom of the Etch A Sketch does not fill in these lines because it is too far away.

8. But if the Etch A Sketch is turned upside down, the powder clings to the whole underside surface of the screen and "erases" the image again.

9. Although the basic Etch A Sketch has not changed since I was a kid, it now comes in several different sizes.

10. Best of all, these great drawing devices have never needed batteries, and I hope that they never will.

Exercise 4

1. During my last semester of high school, our English teacher assigned a special paper.

2. He said that he was becoming depressed by all the bad news out there, so each of us was asked to find a piece of good news and write a short research paper about it.

3. I must admit that I had no idea how hard that assignment would be.

4. Finally, I found an article while I was reading my favorite magazine.

5. The title of the article was a pun; it was called "Grin Reaper."

6. I knew instantly that it must be just the kind of news my teacher wanted.

7. The article explained that one woman, Pam Johnson, had started a club that she named The Secret Society of Happy People.

8. She had even chosen August 8 as "Admit You're Happy Day" and had already convinced more than fifteen state governors to recognize the holiday.

9. The club and the holiday were created to support people who are happy so that the unhappy, negative people around will not bring the happy people down.

10. As I was writing my essay, I visited the Society of Happy People Web site, *www.sohp.com*, and signed my teacher up for their newsletter.

Exercise 5

1. Donald Redelmeier was sitting in front of his television a few years ago, and he was not alone.

2. He was enjoying the Academy Awards along with millions of other TV viewers.

3. Redelmeier focused on the nominees as they were waiting for the announcement of the winners' names.

4. Suddenly, he was struck by the good health and lively mannerisms of them all.

5. Redelmeier's experiences as a doctor of ordinary people did not match what he was seeing on TV.

6. He devised a study that would explore the effects of success and recognition on health.

7. He would use the winners and losers of Academy Awards as the pool of subjects for his data.

8. He wondered if Oscar winners would live longer than losers and those who had never been nominated.

9. The results of his study showed that the winners do live an average of four years longer than the losers.

10. Luckily, nominees who lose also live a few months longer than those who are not nominated, so they do get some benefits.

Source: Current Science, May 6, 2005, and *Forbes.com,* June 19, 2003

REVIEW EXERCISE

To practice finding the sentence structures we have studied so far, mark the following paragraphs from the book *Don't Try This at Home: The Physics of Hollywood Movies* by Adam Weiner. First, put parentheses around prepositional phrases; then underline verbs and verb phrases twice and their subjects once. Finally, put a broken line beneath dependent clauses. Start by marking the first paragraph and checking your answers. Remember that *ing* verbs alone and the *to* _____ forms of verbs are never real verbs in sentences, as explained on page 123. Also note that we have identified a few minor changes to the excerpt with brackets [ ] and ellipses (. . .). For more about their use, see page 228.

The Physics—Our Homemade Cloaking Device

If we were to make ourselves invisible, an observer would not see us, but would see whatever is on the other side of us. In order to do this, we would have to prevent light from reflecting off of us, and also somehow bend the light from objects behind us into the prying eyes of inquisitive observers. We would need to create a mirage.

For our purposes we will play around with a couple of optical concepts. We will redirect light in order to create a crude "cloaking device"/mirage. Maybe we won't be invisible, but at least we might confuse and irritate our adversary for a second. [First we will make] our imaginary spaceship completely black so that no light will be reflected off of its surface. Then we will try to create the mirage of the background stars and planets where an observer would be looking at the ship. We will consider applying the following methods to make our homemade optical deception: (1) surround the ship with fiber optics cables, and (2) find a way to refract light around the ship.

The fiber optics idea is pretty simple. All [that] we need to do is [to] use total internal reflection inside the cables to bend light around the ship. . . .

Will this work? Well it depends what we mean by "work." We can divert light such that we create a mirage in front of the ship, but we are going to have problems with reflections off of the exterior of the cables, and not all of the light will necessarily be totally internally reflected because it depends on the angle of the rays relative to the cables. This means [that] *we will be able to see the cables*. In addition, light rays can diffuse as they pass through the cables so that the image/mirage won't be as sharp as the original. Will we be invisible? Not really. Will it be a pretty cool effect? I think so!

Using Standard English Verbs

The next two discussions are for those who need to practice using Standard English verbs. Many of us grew up doing more speaking than writing. But in college and in the business and professional worlds, knowledge of Standard Written English is essential.

The following charts show the forms of four verbs as they are used in Standard Written English. These forms might differ from the way you use these verbs when you speak. Memorize the Standard English forms of these important verbs. The first verb (*talk*) is one of the regular verbs (verbs that all end the same way according to a pattern); most verbs in English are regular. The other three verbs charted here (*have, be,* and *do*) are irregular and are important because they are used not only as main verbs but also as helping verbs in verb phrases.

Don't go on to the exercises until you have memorized the forms of these Standard English verbs.

REGULAR VERB: TALK

PRESENT TIME		**PAST TIME**	
I		I	
you	talk	you	
we		we	talked
they		they	
he, she, it	talks	he, she, it	

IRREGULAR VERB: HAVE

PRESENT TIME		**PAST TIME**	
I		I	
you	have	you	
we		we	had
they		they	
he, she, it	has	he, she, it	

IRREGULAR VERB: BE

PRESENT TIME		PAST TIME	
I	am	I	was
you		you	
we	are	we	were
they		they	
he, she, it	is	he, she, it	was

IRREGULAR VERB: DO

PRESENT TIME		PAST TIME	
I		I	
you		you	
we	do	we	did
they		they	
he, she, it	does	he, she, it	

Sometimes you may have difficulty with the correct endings of verbs because you don't actually hear the words correctly. Note carefully the *s* sound and the *ed* sound at the end of certain words. Occasionally, the *ed* is not clearly pronounced, as in "They tri*ed* to finish their essays," but most of the time you can hear it if you listen.

Read the following sentences aloud, making sure that you exaggerate every sound.

1. He seems satisfied with his new job.

2. She likes saving money for the future.

3. It takes strength of character to control spending.

4. Todd brings salad to every party that he attends.

5. I used to know all of the state capitals.

6. They were supposed to sign both forms.

7. He recognized the suspect and excused himself from the jury.

8. The chess club sponsored Dorothy in the school's charity event.

Now read some other sentences aloud from this text, making sure that you say all the *s*'s and *ed*'s. Reading aloud and listening to others will help you use the correct verb endings automatically.

E X E R C I S E S

In these pairs of sentences, use the *present* form of the verb in the first sentence and the *past* form in the second. All the verbs follow the pattern of the regular verb *talk* except the irregular verbs *have*, *be*, and *do*. Keep referring to the charts if you're not sure which form to use. Check your answers after each set.

Exercise 1

   1. (pack)   He _____ suitcases very well. He _____ all of our suitcases for the cruise.

   2. (be)   The twins _____ never late for class in college. In high school, they _____ often late for class, and their grades suffered.

   3. (walk)   This semester, I _____ to school as often as I can. Last semester, I _____ to school about two times a week.

   4. (have)   She _____ a class in the gym building at noon. Yesterday, she _____ a cold and missed class.

   5. (need)   For the speech assignment, we _____ some index cards. For last week's in-class essay, we _____ a large blue book.

   6. (do)   Helena usually _____ her math homework every night. Last night, she _____ her English homework and fell asleep.

   7. (be)   Normally, he _____ not a shy person. However, he _____ shy in high school.

   8. (like)   I _____ the new movie in the trilogy as much as I _____ the one that came out last year.

   9. (have)   All of my friends _____ new cell phones. They all _____ old phones like mine before they upgraded them.

   10. (be)   Currently, I _____ a full-time student. I _____ a part-time student last semester.

Exercise 2

   1. (do)   You _____ too much homework every night. Last night, you _____ three hours of homework.

   2. (be)   We _____ members of the chess club now. Last year, we _____ not members of any clubs.

3. (have)   Tim currently _____ really short hair. He _____ longer hair before he joined the swim team.

4. (type)   We always _____ our paragraphs and essays in the lab. Last week, we _____ three papers there.

5. (count)   The teacher _____ the students before she takes roll. Yesterday, she _____ wrong and thought that everyone was in class.

6. (have)   I always _____ fun in the summer. Last summer, I _____ a great time in Las Vegas.

7. (open)   My little brother usually _____ his presents very quickly. Last year, he _____ his birthday presents so quickly that we couldn't match the cards with the presents.

8. (do)   She _____ the crossword puzzle in the newspaper every Sunday. Last Sunday, she even _____ the bonus puzzle.

9. (plan)   I _____ my class schedules very carefully now that I am in college. I never _____ them so carefully before.

10. (be)   I _____ finally as tall as my brother. I _____ the shortest member of my family until recently.

Exercise 3

Choose the correct Standard English verb forms.

1. I (do, does) an exercise routine every morning so that I (don't, doesn't) get out of shape again.

2. A couple of months ago, I (have, had) a bad experience after I (decide, decided) to join some friends for basketball.

3. I (was, were) on my best friend Ana's team, but I (play, played) really badly.

4. Ana (talk, talked) to me after the game.

5. She (ask, asked) me why I (was, were) so slow on the court.

6. I (was, were) really embarrassed.

7. Ana and I (was, were) in high school together, and we (was, were) even in the same P.E. class.

8. We both (enjoy, enjoyed) the track exercises the most and (like, liked) to challenge each other's stamina.

9. Then, after high school, I (start, started) my job as a clerk in an insurance office and (stop, stopped) exercising.

10. Now that I (am, is) back to a good routine, I (plan, planned) to call Ana to set up another game.

Exercise 4

Choose the correct Standard English verb forms.

1. I recently (change, changed) my career plans; now I (want, wants) to be a chef.

2. Last year, I (have, had) my mind set on becoming a kindergarten teacher.

3. I (sign, signed) up for several childhood education classes, and they all (turn, turned) out to be disappointing.

4. The class work (was, were) often too easy, and the reading assignments (was, were) too hard.

5. We (does, did) spend part of the semester working in a real kindergarten class where we (was, were) able to observe just what the teacher (does, did).

6. The teacher that I (observes, observed) (have, had) twenty-seven children to look after.

7. I (watch, watched) her as she (help, helped) them learn their numbers and letters.

8. She (have, had) her students, their parents, and the school's administration to worry about all the time.

9. I never (imagine, imagined) that a kindergarten teacher (have, had) so many responsibilities.

10. A chef (need, needs) to worry about the food and the customers, and those (is, are) responsibilities that I (is, am) ready to take.

Exercise 5

Choose the correct Standard English verb forms to show **the past**.

1. Last semester, my English teacher (assign, assigns, assigned) a fun activity.

2. We (has, have, had) one week to interview other students in the class for an essay about the personality of the group.

3. During the interviews, we (ask, asks, asked) each other questions about our hobbies, jobs, and majors.

4. I (like, likes, liked) the interviewing part of the assignment.

5. But I (do, does, did) not enjoy the writing part as much.

6. I (am, was, were) a little nervous about my essay's thesis because it (is, was, were) long and a little complicated.

7. The teacher (want, wants, wanted) us to compare the whole group to a person with a unique personality.

8. My idea (is, was, were) that the group (is, was, were) like an only child with lots of toys.

9. I (base, bases, based) my idea on the interviews that I (has, have, had) with my classmates.

10. They all (seem, seems, seemed) to want even more than they already (has, have, had).

PROOFREADING EXERCISE

In the following paragraph, correct any sentences that do not use Standard English verb forms. Use present verb forms for your corrections.

Most people believe that they has the best pets. I think that we have the cutest pet hamster in the world. Her name is Toots. The name come from the little dog that die in the movie *Lassie Come Home.* Our Toots don't look like that dog, but she have something about her that reminds us of it. The dog in the movie protect her owner from some really mean men. When the men try to beat the man who own her, Toots is so brave. She jump in front of her owner and saves him. Our hamster is small but fearless too, so her name is Toots.

SENTENCE WRITING

Write ten sentences about a pet that you have (or a friend has). Check your sentences to be sure that they use Standard English verb forms. Try exchanging papers with another student for more practice.

Using Regular and Irregular Verbs

All regular verbs end the same way in the past form and when used with helping verbs. Here is a chart showing all the forms of some *regular* verbs and the various helping verbs with which they are used.

REGULAR VERBS				
BASE FORM	**PRESENT**	**PAST**	**PAST PARTICIPLE**	***ING* FORM**
(Use after *can, may, shall, will, could, might, should, would, must, do, does, did.*)			(Use after *have, has, had.* Some can be used after forms of *be.*)	(Use after forms of *be.*)
ask	ask *(s)*	asked	asked	asking
bake	bake *(s)*	baked	baked	baking
count	count *(s)*	counted	counted	counting
dance	dance *(s)*	danced	danced	dancing
decide	decide *(s)*	decided	decided	deciding
enjoy	enjoy *(s)*	enjoyed	enjoyed	enjoying
finish	finish *(es)*	finished	finished	finishing
happen	happen *(s)*	happened	happened	happening
learn	learn *(s)*	learned	learned	learning
like	like *(s)*	liked	liked	liking
look	look *(s)*	looked	looked	looking
mend	mend *(s)*	mended	mended	mending
need	need *(s)*	needed	needed	needing
open	open *(s)*	opened	opened	opening
start	start *(s)*	started	started	starting
suppose	suppose *(s)*	supposed	supposed	supposing
tap	tap *(s)*	tapped	tapped	tapping
walk	walk *(s)*	walked	walked	walking
want	want *(s)*	wanted	wanted	wanting

NOTE—When there are several helping verbs, the one closest to the verb determines which form of the main verb should be used: They *should* finish soon; they could *have* finished an hour ago.

When do you write *ask, finish, suppose, use?* And when do you write *asked, finished, supposed, used?* Here are some rules that will help you decide.

Write *ask, finish, suppose, use* (or their *s* forms) when writing about the present time, repeated actions, or facts:

He *ask*s questions whenever he is confused.

They always *finish* their projects on time.

I *suppose* you want me to help you move.

Birds *use* leaves, twigs, and feathers to build their nests.

Write *asked, finished, supposed, used*

1. **When writing about the past:**

   He *asked* the teacher for another explanation.

   She *finished* her internship last year.

   They *supposed* that there were others bidding on that house.

   I *used* to study piano.

2. **When some form of *be* (other than the word *be* itself) comes before the word:**

   He was *asked* the most difficult questions.

   She is *finished* with her training now.

   They were *supposed* to sign at the bottom of the form.

   My essay was *used* as a sample of clear narration.

3. **When some form of *have* comes before the word:**

   The teacher has *asked* us that question before.

   She will have *finished* all of her exams by the end of May.

   I had *supposed* too much without any proof.

   We have *used* many models in my drawing class this semester.

All the verbs in the chart on page 103 are *regular*. That is, they're all formed in the same way—with an *ed* ending on the past form and on the past participle. But many verbs are irregular. Their past and past participle forms change spelling instead of just adding an *ed*. Here's a chart of some *irregular* verbs. Notice that the base, present, and *ing* forms end the same as regular verbs. Refer to this list when you aren't sure which verb form to use. Memorize all the forms you don't know.

IRREGULAR VERBS

BASE FORM	PRESENT	PAST	PAST PARTICIPLE	*ING* FORM
(Use after *can, may, shall, will, could, might, should, would, must, do, does, did.*)			(Use after *have, has, had.* Some can be used after forms of *be.*)	(Use after forms of *be.*)
be	is, am, are	was, were	been	being
become	become *(s)*	became	become	becoming
begin	begin *(s)*	began	begun	beginning
break	break *(s)*	broke	broken	breaking
bring	bring *(s)*	brought	brought	bringing
buy	buy *(s)*	bought	bought	buying
build	build *(s)*	built	built	building
catch	catch *(es)*	caught	caught	catching
choose	choose *(s)*	chose	chosen	choosing
come	come *(s)*	came	come	coming
do	do *(es)*	did	done	doing
draw	draw *(s)*	drew	drawn	drawing
drink	drink *(s)*	drank	drunk	drinking
drive	drive *(s)*	drove	driven	driving
eat	eat *(s)*	ate	eaten	eating
fall	fall *(s)*	fell	fallen	falling
feel	feel *(s)*	felt	felt	feeling
fight	fight *(s)*	fought	fought	fighting
find	find *(s)*	found	found	finding
forget	forget *(s)*	forgot	forgotten	forgetting
forgive	forgive *(s)*	forgave	forgiven	forgiving
freeze	freeze *(s)*	froze	frozen	freezing
get	get *(s)*	got	got *or* gotten	getting
give	give *(s)*	gave	given	giving
go	go *(es)*	went	gone	going
grow	grow *(s)*	grew	grown	growing
have	have *or* has	had	had	having
hear	hear *(s)*	heard	heard	hearing
hold	hold *(s)*	held	held	holding
keep	keep *(s)*	kept	kept	keeping
know	know *(s)*	knew	known	knowing
lay (to put)	lay *(s)*	laid	laid	laying

IRREGULAR VERBS (CONTINUED)

BASE FORM	PRESENT	PAST	PAST PARTICIPLE	*ING* FORM
lead (like "bead")	lead *(s)*	led	led	leading
leave	leave *(s)*	left	left	leaving
lie (to rest)	lie *(s)*	lay	lain	lying
lose	lose *(s)*	lost	lost	losing
make	make *(s)*	made	made	making
meet	meet *(s)*	met	met	meeting
pay	pay *(s)*	paid	paid	paying
read (pron. "reed")	read *(s)*	read (pron. "red")	read (pron. "red")	reading
ride	ride *(s)*	rode	ridden	riding
ring	ring *(s)*	rang	rung	ringing
rise	rise *(s)*	rose	risen	rising
run	run *(s)*	ran	run	running
say	say *(s)*	said	said	saying
see	see *(s)*	saw	seen	seeing
sell	sell *(s)*	sold	sold	selling
shake	shake *(s)*	shook	shaken	shaking
shine (give light)	shine *(s)*	shone	shone	shining
shine (polish)	shine *(s)*	shined	shined	shining
sing	sing *(s)*	sang	sung	singing
sleep	sleep *(s)*	slept	slept	sleeping
speak	speak *(s)*	spoke	spoken	speaking
spend	spend *(s)*	spent	spent	spending
stand	stand *(s)*	stood	stood	standing
steal	steal *(s)*	stole	stolen	stealing
strike	strike *(s)*	struck	struck	striking
swim	swim *(s)*	swam	swum	swimming
swing	swing *(s)*	swung	swung	swinging
take	take *(s)*	took	taken	taking
teach	teach *(es)*	taught	taught	teaching
tear	tear *(s)*	tore	torn	tearing
tell	tell *(s)*	told	told	telling
think	think *(s)*	thought	thought	thinking
throw	throw *(s)*	threw	thrown	throwing
wear	wear *(s)*	wore	worn	wearing
win	win *(s)*	won	won	winning
write	write *(s)*	wrote	written	writing

Sometimes verbs from the past participle column are used after some form of the verb *be* (or verbs that take the place of *be* like *appear, seem, look, feel, get, act, become*) to describe the subject or to say something in a passive, rather than an active, way.

She is contented.

You appear pleased. (You *are* pleased.)

He seems delighted. (He *is* delighted.)

She looked surprised. (She *was* surprised.)

I feel shaken. (I *am* shaken.)

They get bored easily. (They *are* bored easily.)

You acted concerned. (You *were* concerned.)

They were thrown out of the game. (Active: *The referee threw them out of the game.*)

We were disappointed by the news. (Active: *The news disappointed us.*)

Often these verb forms actually become adjectives (words that describe the subject); at other times they still act as part of the verb in the sentence. What you call them doesn't matter. More important is to be sure that you use the correct form from the past participle column.

E X E R C I S E S

Write the correct form of the verbs in the blanks. Refer to the charts and explanations on the preceding pages if you aren't sure which form to use after a certain helping verb. Check your answers after each exercise.

Exercise 1

1. (eat) People _____ a lot when they go to the movies.

2. (eat) I can _____ a whole bag of popcorn myself.

3. (eat) When someone else is _____ popcorn, the crunching sound drives me crazy.

4. (eat) Once I have _____ my dinner, I stay away from snacks.

5. (eat) My sister _____ a worm when she was in kindergarten.

6. (eat) My two-year-old nephew _____ everything; he is not picky.

7. (eat)   He will even _____ sushi when his parents order it at restaurants.

8. (eat)   The meal at the conference was _____ in silence.

9. (eat)   We _____ while we watched a documentary on television.

10. (eat)   If you want to pass the test, you should _____ a good breakfast.

Exercise 2

1. (buy)   My parents should _____ a new television because they _____ their current TV back in the 1990s.

2. (know)   They do not even _____ how outdated their TV is. If I _____ of a way to make it break down, I would do it.

3. (be)   That _____ the only way they would discuss getting a new TV. Unfortunately, some old television sets _____ really reliable and well-made.

4. (agree)   Both of my parents _____ that if something isn't broken, it shouldn't be replaced. Obviously, my siblings and I do not _____ with them.

5. (tell)   My brother and I have _____ them all about the great features available on the new sets. We might as well have been _____ them about spaceships.

6. (sit)   Our mom and dad will happily _____ through local broadcast-station shows and would never dream of subscribing to a cable or dish service. Once I house- _____ for my parents while they were on vacation and was extremely bored.

7. (have)   Well, at least my parents are _____ fun together. Maybe I _____ the wrong attitude.

8. (get)   Last year, I _____ a state-of-the-art TV. I may be _____ hundreds of stations now, but I'm still not satisfied.

9. (need)   In fact, I may _____ companionship much more than my parents _____ a new TV.

10. (be)   I _____ sure that my mom and dad _____ the most old-fashioned people I know, but they are also the happiest people I know.

Exercise 3

1. (take, suppose)   My friend Brenda _____ a day off last week even though she was _____ to be working.

2. (do, earn)   She _____ not feel sick exactly; she just felt that she had _____ a day of rest.

3. (call, tell, feel)   So Brenda _____ her office and _____ her boss that she did not _____ well enough to work that day.

4. (think, be)   She never _____ that she would get caught, but she _____ wrong.

5. (leave, drive, see)   Just as Brenda was _____ the house to buy some lunch, her coworker _____ by and _____ her.

6. (feel, know, tell)   She _____ such panic because she _____ that he would _____ their boss that she looked fine.

7. (try, go)   Brenda _____ to explain herself when she _____ back to the office the next day.

8. (be, undo)   The damage had _____ done, however, and nothing could _____ it.

9. (wish, take)   Now Brenda _____ that she could _____ back that day.

10. (use, call, do)   She _____ to have a great relationship with her boss, but since the day she _____ in "sick," he _____ not trust her anymore.

Exercise 4

1. (use, put)   Many people _____ a direct deposit system that _____ their salary money directly into their bank accounts.

2. (do, do)   With such a system, the employer _____ not have to issue paychecks, and employees _____ not have to cash or deposit them.

3. (transfer, spend)   The employer's computer just _____ the money to the bank's computer, and the employee can _____ it as usual after that.

4. (be, like, choose)   Direct deposit _____ almost always optional, but so many people _____ the system that most people _____ it.

5. (do, want)   My uncle _____ not trust such systems; he _____ to have complete control over his cash.

6. (trust, be)   He barely even _____ banks to keep his money safe for him, so he _____ definitely suspicious of direct deposit.

7. (imagine, make)   I can _____ him as a pioneer in an old Western movie sleeping on a mattress stuffed with all of the money he has ever _____.

8. (talk, ask, worry)   I was _____ to my uncle about money the other day, and I _____ him why he always _____ about it so much.

9. (look, say, live, understand)   He just _____ at me and _____, "If you had ever _____ without money, you would _____."

10. (wonder, be)   I _____ about my uncle's past experiences and hope that he _____ never without money again.

Exercise 5

1. (lie, fall)   I was _____ out in the sun last Sunday, and I _____ asleep.

2. (be, do)   That _____ the worst thing I could have _____.

3. (wear, shield)   I was _____ a pair of big dark sunglasses, which _____ my eyes from the light.

4. (lie, wake, realize, happen)   I must have _____ there for over an hour before I _____ up and _____ what had _____.

5. (feel, start)   At first I _____ fine, but then my skin
                              _____ to feel really tight and thin.

6. (pass, turn, begin)   As the minutes _____ , my skin _____
                              bright red, and the pain _____.

7. (describe, experience) I can't even _____ how much pain I
                              _____.

8. (be, feel, see)   Almost worse than the pain _____ the
                              embarrassment I _____ as I _____
                              my face in the mirror.

9. (look, tape, be, protect, wear)   Around my eyes, it _____ as if someone
                              had _____ the shape of white glasses
                              to my face, but that _____ just the skin
                              that had been _____ by the sunglasses
                              I was _____.

10. (have, feel)   The people at work _____ a big laugh
                              the next day at my expense, but then
                              they just _____ sorry for me.

PROGRESS TEST

This test covers everything you've studied so far. One sentence in each pair is correct. The other is incorrect. Read both sentences carefully before you decide. Then write the letter of the incorrect sentence in the blank. Try to name the error and correct it if you can.

1. _____ **A.** No one was left in the classroom except the teacher and me.

   _____ **B.** As soon as I finish the test, the bell rang.

2. _____ **A.** Textbooks available online.

   _____ **B.** They can be less expensive than the ones in stores.

3. _____ **A.** Our class took a field trip to the museum and I loved it.

   _____ **B.** I asked the teacher if I could do some extra credit there.

4. _____ **A.** My research paper will probably be late.

   _____ **B.** I should of gone to the library sooner.

5. _____ **A.** We were suppose to lock the door after class.

   _____ **B.** We forgot and had to drive back to school.

6. _____ **A.** Adam and Tracy have finished all of their school work.

   _____ **B.** Their going away for spring break, and I'm staying at home.

7. _____ **A.** The package had no official label, only a handwritten address.

   _____ **B.** We were surprise that it was delivered on time.

8. _____ **A.** In my math class, we've already took three quizzes.

   _____ **B.** We'll have six more quizzes before the final exam.

9. _____ **A.** The bus driver tried to start the bus after it stalled.

   _____ **B.** Nothing worked so we all got off the bus and waited for another one.

10. _____ **A.** Although I don't like the taste of grapefruits or lemons.

    _____ **B.** I do like cleaning products with citrus scents.

Maintaining Subject-Verb Agreement

As we have seen, the subject and verb in a sentence work together, so they must always agree. Different subjects need different forms of verbs. When the correct verb follows a subject, we call it subject-verb agreement.

The following sentences illustrate the rule that *s* verbs follow most singular subjects but not plural subjects.

One student studies.	Two students study.
The bell rings.	The bells ring.
A democracy listens to the people.	Democracies listen to the people.
One person writes the dialogue.	Many people write the dialogue.

The following sentences show how forms of the verb *be* (*is, am, are, was, were*) and helping verbs (*be, have,* and *do*) are made to agree with their subjects. We have labeled only the verbs that must agree with the subjects.

This puzzle is difficult.	These puzzles are difficult.
I am amazed.	You are amazed.
He was studying.	They were studying.
That class has been canceled.	Those classes have been canceled.
She does not want to participate.	You do not want to participate.

The following words are always singular and take an *s* verb or the irregular equivalent (*is, was, has, does*):

one	anybody	each
anyone	everybody	
everyone	nobody	
no one	somebody	
someone		

Someone feeds my dog in the morning.

Everybody was at the party.

Each does her own homework.

Remember that prepositional phrases often come between subjects and verbs. You should ignore these interrupting phrases, or you may mistake the wrong word for the subject and use a verb form that doesn't agree.

Someone from the apartments feeds my dog in the morning. (*Someone* is the subject, not *apartments*.)

Everybody on the list of celebrities was at the party. (*Everybody* is the subject, not *celebrities*.)

Each of the twins does her own homework. (*Each* is the subject, not *twins*.)

However, the words *some, any, all, none,* and *most* are exceptions to this rule of ignoring prepositional phrases. These words can be singular or plural, depending on the words that follow them in prepositional phrases. Again, we have labeled only the verbs that must agree with the subjects.

Some of the *information* is helpful.

Some of the *facts* are convincing.

Does any of the *furniture* come with the apartment?

Do any of the *chairs* and *tables* come with the apartment?

All of her *work* has been published.

All of her *poems* have been published.

None of the *jewelry* was missing.

None of the *jewels* were missing.

On July 4th, <u>most</u> of the *country* <u>celebrates</u> with a picnic or a party.

On July 4th, <u>most</u> of the *citizens* <u>celebrate</u> with a picnic or a party.

When a sentence has more than one subject joined by *and,* the subject is plural:

The <u>teacher</u> *and* the <u>tutors</u> <u>eat</u> lunch at noon.

A <u>doughnut</u> *and* a <u>bagel</u> <u>were</u> sitting on the plate.

However, when two subjects are joined by *or,* then the subject *closest* to the verb determines the verb form:

Either the <u>teacher</u> *or* the <u>tutors</u> <u>eat</u> lunch at noon.

Either the <u>tutors</u> *or* the <u>teacher</u> <u>eats</u> lunch at noon.

A <u>doughnut</u> *or* a <u>bagel</u> <u>was</u> sitting on the plate.

In most sentences, the subject comes before the verb. However, in some cases, the subject follows the verb, and subject-verb agreement needs special attention. Study the following examples:

Over the building <u>flies</u> a solitary <u>flag</u>. (flag flies)

Over the building <u>fly</u> several <u>flags</u>. (flags fly)

There <u>is</u> a good <u>reason</u> for that deadline. (reason is)

There <u>are</u> good <u>reasons</u> for that deadline. (reasons are)

E X E R C I S E S

Circle the correct verbs in parentheses to maintain subject-verb agreement in the following sentences. Remember to ignore prepositional phrases, unless the subjects are *some, any, all, none,* or *most.* Check your answers after the first exercise.

Exercise 1

1. Do you know why the skin on our fingertips (wrinkle, wrinkles) after a long shower or bath?
2. The explanation (is, are) simple.
3. All of our skin (absorb, absorbs) water.
4. The bottoms of our hands and feet (absorb, absorbs) the most water.
5. They (soak, soaks) up more water because they (has, have) the thickest layers of skin on our bodies.
6. This thick skin on our fingers (swell, swells) and (expand, expands) from the excess water.
7. Wrinkles (result, results) from the expansion of the skin covering the small surface of our fingertips.
8. The same thing (doesn't, don't) happen as quickly in sea water, however.
9. The salts and other minerals in the sea water (block, blocks) it from being absorbed.
10. So next time you (take, takes) a long bath, you will understand why your fingers and toes (get, gets) so wrinkled.

Exercise 2

1. There (is, are) new risks for kids in this technological age; these risks primarily (involve, involves) their wrists.
2. Many adults already (suffer, suffers) from carpal tunnel syndrome.
3. And now children (is, are) also coming down with similar conditions, called repetitive stress injuries (RSIs).
4. From the use of computers and video games (come, comes) unnatural body positions that (lead, leads) to health problems.
5. The child's wrists, neck, and back (start, starts) to hurt or feel numb after he or she (work, works) or (play, plays) on the computer for a long time.
6. The problem (start, starts) with computer furniture.
7. The chairs, desks, and screens (is, are) usually not at the proper height to be used comfortably by children.

8. Straining and repetition often (cause, causes) reduced circulation and even nerve damage.

9. Often RSI damage to the wrists (is, are) irreversible.

10. Experts in the field of RSI (warn, warns) parents to teach children how to avoid these injuries.

Exercise 3

1. Everyone in my drawing class (is, are) supposed to finish a drawing a week.

2. But each of us (has, have) a different way of beginning.

3. One of my classmates always (start, starts) by humming and rocking back and forth in front of his easel.

4. Another one just (put, puts) dots in the places where she (want, wants) her figures to go.

5. Jennifer, my best friend, (like, likes) to draw really light circles wherever the faces will be.

6. In the past, I (has, have) usually started by drawing a continuous line until it (look, looks) like something.

7. In other words, I (let, lets) the drawing tell me what it (want, wants) to be.

8. But Jennifer and my other classmates (has, have) taught me something.

9. It (help, helps) to have a plan; their drawings often (turn, turns) out better than mine.

10. Either they or I (am, are) right, but I don't know which it (is, are) yet.

Exercise 4

1. When most people (think, thinks) of rattlesnakes, they (picture, pictures) them in a desert environment.

2. However, there (is, are) rattlesnakes that (live, lives) in forests.

3. This type of rattlesnake (is, are) called a timber rattlesnake.

4. In wooded areas, timber rattlesnakes (encounter, encounters) chipmunks, squirrels, and birds.

5. When one of these snakes (go, goes) hunting, it (look, looks) for these animals.

6. Scientists (has, have) discovered that chipmunks, squirrels, and birds (defend, defends) themselves in an unusual way.

7. These furry and feathered creatures (tease, teases) and (taunt, taunts) the snake until it (give, gives) up and (leave, leaves).

8. Chipmunks (run, runs) in all directions and (make, makes) loud sounds.

9. A mother squirrel who (is, are) protecting her pups (flick, flicks) its tail and (kick, kicks) dirt at the snake.

10. Two of the birds (work, works) together, (swoop, swoops) down on the snake, and (pounce, pounces) on it.

Source: Science News, August 27, 2005

Exercise 5

1. A group of scientists (is, are) looking into the sensation that we (call, calls) déjà vu.

2. Déjà vu (is, are) the feeling that we (is, are) repeating an experience that (has, have) happened in exactly the same way before.

3. Part of the odd sensation (is, are) that we (is, are) aware of the illogical part of déjà vu while it (is, are) happening.

4. Scientists (has, have) developed a new profile of a person who (is, are) likely to experience this particular sensation.

5. People who (is, are) most prone to déjà vu (is, are) between fifteen and twenty-five years old.

6. Regardless of age, however, anyone who (experience, experiences) déjà vu probably (has, have) a vivid imagination.

7. Stress and fatigue (is, are) often factors because the mind (function, functions) differently under these conditions.

8. Education level and income also (determine, determines) a person's susceptibility to déjà vu.

9. The phenomenon of déjà vu (seem, seems) to require an open mind.

10. Since political leanings (affect, affects) open-mindedness, liberals (tend, tends) to have more déjà vu experiences than conservatives.

Source: Psychology Today, March/April 2005

PROOFREADING EXERCISE

Find and correct the ten subject-verb agreement errors in the following paragraph.

I exercise in a large park near my house several times a week. The fresh air and pretty scenery refreshes me and make me happy. There is several paths I can follow each day. One of my favorite walks go up a steep hill and down through a grove of ferns. The droplets of water on the ferns splashes on me as I brush past them. Then the path open into a grassy area that take my breath away sometimes. The late afternoon sunlight shine through the branches of a few large trees, and it create beautiful shadows on top of the grass. Another of the paths goes straight between a row of tall, narrow trees. The trunks of the trees is smooth, but their leafy tops sways in the wind because they are so high. I love my afternoon walks in the park.

SENTENCE WRITING

Write ten sentences in which you describe the shoes you are wearing. Have fun writing about their smallest details! Use verbs in the present time. Then go back over your sentences—underline your subjects once, underline your verbs twice, and be sure they agree. Exchange papers with another student and check each other's subject-verb agreement.

Avoiding Shifts in Time

People often worry about using different time frames in writing. Let common sense guide you. If you begin writing a paper in past time, don't shift back and forth to the present unnecessarily; and if you begin in the present, don't shift to the past without good reason. In the following paragraph, the writer starts in the present and then shifts to the past, then shifts again to the present:

> In the novel *To Kill a Mockingbird,* Jean Louise Finch is a little girl who lives in the South with her father, Atticus, and her brother, Jem. Everybody in town calls Jean Louise "Scout" as a nickname. When Atticus, a lawyer, defended a black man against the charges of a white woman, some of their neighbors turned against him. Scout protected her father by appealing to the humanity of one member of the angry mob. In this chapter, five-year-old Scout turns out to be stronger than a group of adult men.

All the verbs should be in the present:

> In the novel *To Kill a Mockingbird,* Jean Louise Finch is a little girl who lives in the South with her father, Atticus, and her brother, Jem. Everybody in town calls Jean Louise "Scout" as a nickname. When Atticus, a lawyer, defends a black man against the charges of a white woman, some of their neighbors turn against him. Scout protects her father by appealing to the humanity of one member of the angry mob. In this chapter, five-year-old Scout turns out to be stronger than a group of adult men.

This sample paragraph discusses only the events that happen within the novel's plot, so it needs to maintain one time frame—the present, which we use to write about literature and repeated actions.

However, sometimes you will write about the present, the past, and even the future together. Then it may be necessary to use these different time frames within the same paragraph, each for its own reason. For example, if you were to give biographical information about Harper Lee, author of *To Kill a Mockingbird,* within a discussion of the novel and its influence, you might need to use all three time frames:

> Harper Lee grew up in Alabama, and she based elements in the book on experiences from her childhood. Like the character Atticus, Lee's father was a lawyer. She wrote the novel in his law offices. *To Kill a Mockingbird* is Harper Lee's most famous work, and it received the Pulitzer Prize for fiction in 1961. Lee's book turned fifty years old in the year 2010. It deals with the effects of prejudice unforgivingly, and it will always remain one of the most moving and compassionate novels in American literature.

The previous paragraph uses past (*grew, based, was, wrote, received, turned*), present (*is, deals*), and future (*will remain*) in the same paragraph without committing the error of unnecessary shifting. A shift in time occurs when the writer changes time frames *inconsistently* or *for no reason,* confusing the reader (as in the first example given).

PROOFREADING EXERCISES

Which of the following student paragraphs shift *unnecessarily* back and forth between time frames? In those that do, change the verbs to maintain one time frame, thus making the entire paragraph read smoothly. One of the paragraphs is correct, even though it includes multiple time frames, because those time frames make sense.

1. Plastic surgery helps many people look better and feel better about themselves. Of course, there were stories of unnecessary surgeries and even heartbreaking mistakes. People could make their own decisions about whether plastic surgery was right for them. Dogs, however, can't communicate what they want. Nevertheless, some people took their dogs in for cosmetic surgeries, such as tummy tucks and face-lifts. Just like humans, dogs sometimes needed surgery to correct painful or unhealthy conditions. A dog with a low-hanging tummy could get an infection from scratches that were caused by rocks on the ground. And another dog may need a face-lift to help it stay clean when it eats. Animal lovers were worried that some canine plastic surgeries were done without good reasons.

Source: Newsweek, March 21, 2005

2. I watched a documentary on the Leaning Tower of Pisa last night. I was amazed to find out that the tower began leaning before it was even finished. Workers over several centuries adjusted their materials as they built the tower to compensate for its increasing angle. That's why the tower is actually shaped a little like a banana. I'm surprised that the famous landmark is still standing after everything people have done to it since it was finished. In the 1930s, for instance, Mussolini thought that it should be straightened. So he had workers drill holes in the foundation and pour tons of concrete beneath it. Others tried digging out the earth around the sunken part. But that just caused flooding because they went below the soil's water table. The narrator of the documentary said that every time anyone tries to correct the tower, it leans a little more to the south. Most recently, scientists have used special drilling techniques to extract enough soil deep beneath the tower to reverse its angle a little. This most recent correction may add as much as three hundred years to the life of the Leaning Tower of Pisa.

3. I really enjoyed my winter break this year. It was too short, of course, but I make the most of the time I had. My extended family had a reunion at my aunt's house in St. Louis. I didn't pack enough coats and sweaters, but the loving atmosphere keeps me warm. Once I'm back in the same house with my cousins, we goofed off just the way we used to when we were kids. One night my four closest cousins and I stay up after everyone else is in bed. We played board games and ate buttery popcorn and got the game pieces all greasy just like the old days. Overall, my trip to St. Louis with its late-night game marathon is the highlight of my winter vacation.

Recognizing Verbal Phrases

You know from the discussion on p. 91 that a verb phrase is made up of a main verb and at least one helping verb. But some forms of verbs can be used not as real verbs but as some other part of speech in a sentence. Verbs put to other uses are called *verbals*.

A verbal can be a noun acting as a subject:

Skiing is my favorite sport. (*Skiing* is a noun. Here, it is the subject of the sentence, not the verb. The real verb in the sentence is *is*.)

A verbal can be a noun acting as an object:

I like *to ski* during the winter. (*To ski* is a noun object; it is *what I like*. I could similarly write, "I like *cocoa* during the winter." The real verb in both sentences is *like*, and the two objects are *to ski*, a verbal as a noun, and *cocoa*, a regular noun.)

A verbal can be an adjective:

My *bruised* ankle healed quickly. (*Bruised* is an adjective that describes the noun, ankle. The real verb in the sentence is *healed*.)

A verbal can also be an adverb:

My ankle swelled, *doubling* in size. (*Doubling* is an adverb, adding to the verb *swelled*.)

Verbals link up with other words to form *verbal phrases*. To see the difference between a real verb phrase and a verbal phrase, look at these two sentences:

I was bowling with my best friends. (*Bowling* is the main verb in a verb phrase. Along with the helping verb *was*, it shows the action of the sentence.)

I enjoyed *bowling* with my best friends. (Here the real verb is *enjoyed*. *Bowling* is not the verb; it is the object, and it links up with a prepositional phrase to form a verbal phrase—*bowling with my best friends*—which is the whole activity I enjoyed.)

THREE KINDS OF VERBALS

1. *ing* verbs used without helping verbs (*running, thinking, baking . . .*)
2. verbs that follow *to* ___ (*to walk, to eat, to cause . . .*)
3. verb forms that often end in *ed, en,* or *t* (*tossed, spoken, burnt . . .*)

Look at the following sentences using the boxed examples in verbal phrases:

Running two miles a day is great exercise. (real verb = is)

She spent two hours *thinking of a title for her essay.* (real verb = spent)

We had such fun *baking those cherry vanilla cupcakes.* (real verb = had)

I like *to walk around the zoo by myself.* (real verb = like)

To eat exotic foods takes courage. (real verb = takes)

They actually wanted *to cause an argument.* (real verb = wanted)

Tossed in a salad, artichoke hearts add zesty flavor. (real verb = add)

Spoken in Spanish, the dialogue sounds even more beautiful.
(real verb = sounds)

Our peach trees, partially *burnt in the wild fire,* recovered quickly.
(real verb = recovered)

E X E R C I S E S

Each of the following sentences contains at least one verbal or verbal phrase. Double underline the real verbs or verb phrases and put brackets around the verbals and verbal phrases. Remember to locate the verbals first (*running, wounded, to sleep . . .*) and include any word(s) that go with them (*running a race, wounded in the fight, to sleep all night*). Real verbs will never be inside verbal phrases. Check your answers after the first set before going on to the next.

Exercise 1

1. Mark Twain lived to become one of the most admired Americans of his time.

2. Traveling across the U.S. and to countries around the world, Twain formed unwavering opinions, both favorable and unfavorable, of the people and places he visited.

3. Twain began to write his autobiography in the last years before he died in 1910.

4. Hoping to be honest and thorough, he decided to dictate his thoughts as they struck him.

5. However, he knew that it might be impossible to be as honest as he wanted to be.

6. Being truthful meant including statements that could hurt or upset the people that he knew, and he knew almost everyone.

7. Twain thought of a way to avoid causing that potential pain or embarrassment.

8. He decided not to publish his autobiography until 100 years after his death.

9. In that way, Twain did not need to hold back any of his strong opinions.

10. In 2010, the first volume of *The Autobiography of Mark Twain* was finally released, making it one of the most anticipated books of all time.

Exercise 2

1. The idea of home-schooling children has become more popular recently.

2. Many parents have decided to teach kids themselves instead of sending them to public or private school.

3. There are many different reasons to choose home-schooling.

4. In Hollywood, for instance, child actors often must use home-schooling due to their schedules.

5. The home-schooling option allows for one of their parents, or a special teacher, to continue to instruct them on the set.

6. Other parents simply want to be directly involved in their child's learning.

7. Many school districts have special independent study "schools," offering parents the structure and materials that they need to provide an appropriate curriculum on their own.

8. Children do all of their reading and writing at home, with their parents guiding them along the way.

9. The family meets with the independent study school's teacher regularly to go over the child's work and to clarify any points of confusion.

10. Many parents would like to have the time to home-school their children.

Exercise 3

1. Finding the exact origin of the game of poker is probably impossible.

2. Some think that it started as a game played in China around a thousand years ago.

3. Others have a theory placing its origins in an ancient Persian game that involves using twenty-five cards with five suits.

4. Poker also has similarities to the game "poque," played by the French when they colonized New Orleans in the 1700s.

5. Betting and bluffing were both aspects of poque.

6. So was a deck of cards containing the four suits used in modern poker: diamonds, hearts, spades, and clubs.

7. In the 1800s, Jonathan H. Green wrote about a pastime called the "cheating game."

8. He observed that people traveling down the Mississippi river enjoyed this card game.

9. Green used the name "poker" for the first time to identify it.

10. Since human beings have always loved games, tracing the history of one game can be difficult.

Source: Poker (Top That! Publishing, 2004)

Exercise 4

1. Some travelers want to know how to behave in other countries.

2. *Behave Yourself!* is a book written to help such people.

3. It outlines what to do and what not to do in different countries around the world.

4. In Austria, for example, cutting your food with a fork is more polite than cutting it with a knife.

5. In Egypt, nodding the head upward—not shaking the head from side to side—means "no."

6. In the Netherlands, complimenting people about their clothes is not a good idea.

7. An Italian diner will fold lettuce into a bite-size piece with the fork and knife instead of cutting it.

8. A common mistake that people make in many countries is to stand with their hands on their hips.

9. This posture and pointing at anything with the fingers are thought to be very rude and even threatening.

10. Travelers should study any country before visiting it in order to avoid confusing or offending anyone.

Exercise 5

1. John Steinbeck, author of *The Grapes of Wrath,* was the first native of California to receive the Nobel Prize for literature.

2. Calling his hometown of Salinas "Lettuceberg," Steinbeck's writing made the area famous.

3. At the time, not everyone liked the attention brought by his portrayals of life in *Cannery Row* and other works.

4. Steinbeck's father was the treasurer of Monterey County for ten years, working also for the Spreckels company.

5. John Steinbeck tried to find satisfaction in his birthplace, enrolling in and quitting his studies at Stanford University many times.

6. Finally, Steinbeck moved to New York, distancing himself from his California roots.

7. Steinbeck won the Nobel Prize in 1962, revealing the literary world's esteem for his work.

8. Not writing anything of the caliber of the Salinas stories while living in New York, Steinbeck did return to California before he died in 1968.

9. In 1972, the Salinas library changed its name, to be known thereafter as the John Steinbeck Library.

10. And the house Steinbeck was born in became a restaurant and then a full-fledged museum chronicling the life of Salinas' most celebrated citizen.

Source: California People (Peregrine Smith, 1982)

PARAGRAPH EXERCISE

Double underline the real verbs and verb phrases and put brackets around the verbals and verbal phrases in the following excerpt from John Waller's *The Dancing Plague: The Strange, True Story of an Extraordinary Illness*. In his book, Waller "seeks to explain why hundreds of people lapsed into a state of frantic delirium" that caused them to dance uncontrollably for "days or even weeks." In this paragraph, he describes the first recorded case that began on July 14, 1518:

Somewhere amid the narrow lanes, the congested wharves, the stables, workshops, forges, and fairs of the medieval city of Strasbourg, Frau Troffea stepped outside and began to dance. So far as we can tell no music was playing and she showed no signs of joy as her skirts flew up around her rapidly moving legs. To the consternation of her husband, she went on dancing throughout the day. And as the shadows lenghtened and the sun set behind the city's half-timbered houses, it became clear that Frau Troffea simply could not stop. Only after many hours of crazed motion did she collapse from exhaustion. Bathed in sweat and twitching, she finally sank into a brief restorative sleep. Then, a few hours later, she resumed her solitary jig. Through much of the following day she went on, fatigue rendering her movements increasingly violent and erratic. Once again, exhaustion prevailed and a weary sleep took hold.

SENTENCE WRITING

Write ten sentences that contain verbal phrases. Use the ten verbals listed here to begin your verbal phrases: *shopping, earning, giving, wearing, to drive, to sew, to talk, given, baked, built.* The last three are particularly difficult to use as verbals. You will find sample sentences in the Answers section. But first, try to write your own so that you can compare the two.

Correcting Misplaced or Dangling Modifiers

When you modify something, you change whatever it is, usually by adding to it. You might modify a car, for example, by adding special tires. In English, words, phrases, and clauses are *modifiers* when they add extra information to part of a sentence. To do its job properly, a modifier should be in the right spot—as close to the word it describes as possible. If you put new tires on the roof of the car instead of where they belong, they would be misplaced. In the following sentence, the modifier is too far away from the word it modifies to make sense. It is a misplaced modifier:

Swinging through the trees, Jonathan watched the monkeys at the zoo.

Was it *Jonathan* who was swinging through the trees? That's what the sentence says because the modifying phrase *Swinging through the trees* is next to *Jonathan*. It should be next to *monkeys* in order for the monkeys to be swinging through the trees.

At the zoo, Jonathan watched the monkeys, swinging through the trees.

The next example includes no word for the phrase *At the age of eight* to modify:

At the age of eight, my family finally bought a dog.

Obviously, the family was not eight when it bought a dog. Nor was the dog eight. The modifier *At the age of eight* is a dangling modifier with no word to attach itself to, no word for it to modify. You can get rid of a dangling modifier by turning it into a dependent clause with a clear subject and verb. (See p. 69 for a discussion of dependent clauses.)

When I was eight, my family finally bought a dog.

Now the meaning of the sentence is clear. Here's another dangling modifier:

After a two-hour nap, the train pulled into the station.

Can you identify the dangling modifier? You are correct if you think it is *After a two-hour nap*. Did the train take a two-hour nap? Who did? Here is a correction:

After a two-hour nap, I awoke just as the train pulled into the station.

EXERCISES

Carefully rephrase any of the following sentences that contain misplaced or dangling modifiers. Note that many misplaced and dangling modifiers sound comical because of the confusion about what's happening in the sentence. Some sentences are correct.

Exercise 1

1. I found a cell phone walking up the stairs.
2. Full of surprises, we loved that play and want to see it again.
3. The tires need to be replaced on his car.
4. Scribbled quickly, I could not read the phone number.
5. The parking structure on the south side of campus is nearly empty.
6. With outdated functions and styling, I need to upgrade my cell phone.
7. After taking several photographs, the shadows on the trees disappeared.
8. He filled out his application with a ballpoint pen.
9. Finishing his calculations, my accountant told me what my tax refund would be.
10. After talking to the doctor, his ear started to feel better.

Exercise 2

1. Distracted by the crowd, the officer tried to write a report.
2. When I was twelve, I bought my first share of stock.
3. She kicked her mother in the store by accident.
4. The inspector found a few termites searching outside the house.
5. Mixing the paints together, we made the color we wanted.
6. I couldn't wait to taste the food waiting in line at the new restaurant.
7. The garage is too small to hold both of our cars.
8. At the age of sixteen, the State of California offers a test to get out of high school early.
9. As the deadline for admission approached, I gathered all of my transcripts.
10. I have found many unique gift ideas shopping on the Internet.

Exercise 3

1. Lying under the table for a week, they finally found their lost credit card.
2. She located the door to the auditorium walking down the hall.
3. They bought a hammer at the hardware store.
4. After taking an aspirin, my doctor told me to drink extra water.

5. He always brings a calculator to school in his backpack.

6. Our mail carrier tripped and fell on a crack in the sidewalk.

7. Arguing nonstop, the road trip was not as much fun as we hoped it would be.

8. Now that she has finished her math classes, she can focus on her major.

9. Seeing her new granddaughter's picture for the first time, our mother cried.

10. Smiling nicely at everyone, the students immediately liked their substitute teacher.

Exercise 4

1. Getting a headache from the fumes, the ferry finally made it across the river.

2. Full of empty calories, that carnival sold the best cotton candy I'd ever tasted.

3. Two months after moving, our old apartment is still empty.

4. She promised to return the library books in her e-mail message.

5. The students took the notes sitting in small groups.

6. Before saying goodnight, the porch light burned out.

7. Decorated beautifully, our hostess showed us her favorite room.

8. Scampering along the baseboards of the cabin, I saw a tiny gray mouse.

9. Trying to open my car door with a hanger, I stared at the keys dangling from the ignition.

10. All along the highway, volunteers planted trees wearing special T-shirts.

Exercise 5

1. Feeling the excitement of the first day of school, my backpack was left behind.

2. Full of explosions, we saw the new movie that everyone is talking about.

3. My cousins and I always wrapped our gifts in our pajamas on the night before the holiday.

4. Practicing for an hour a day, his tennis has improved.

5. The price of gasoline fluctuates, rising and falling several times a year.

6. Sitting on the beach all day, I made a decision.

7. They discovered a new trail hiking in the nearby mountains.

8. She felt the pressure of trying to get good grades from her parents.

9. I enjoy traveling to new places with my friends and even my family.

10. Written in green ink, the teacher's comments seemed positive even when pointing out a problem.

PROOFREADING EXERCISE

Find and correct any misplaced or dangling modifiers in the following paragraphs.

A man in Edinburgh, Scotland, has invented a device, hoping to become famous and wealthy. The device is a variation on the center-mounted brake light used in the design of many new cars, located just above the trunk and visible from behind. Instead of just a solid red brake light, however, this invention displays words to other drivers written in bold, red-lighted letters.

With simplicity in mind, the vocabulary the inventor gave the machine is limited to three words: "Sorry," "Thanks," and "Help." After making an aggressive lane change, the machine could apologize for us. Or after being allowed to go ahead of someone, the device could offer thanks to the considerate person responsible. Of course, at the sight of the "Help" display, we could summon fellow citizens for assistance.

And there is no need to worry about operating the device while driving. With three easy-to-reach buttons, the messages can be activated without taking our eyes off the road.

SENTENCE WRITING

Write five sentences that contain misplaced or dangling modifiers; then revise those sentences to put the modifiers where they belong. Use the examples in the explanations as models. For more practice, exchange sentences with another student and correct each other's misplaced or dangling modifiers.

Following Sentence Patterns

Sentences are built according to a few basic patterns. For proof, rearrange each of the following sets of words to form a complete statement (not a question):

apples a ate raccoon the

classes have many together taken we

your in am partner I lab the

school was to she walking

in wonderful you look scrubs

There are only one or two possible combinations for each due to English sentence patterns. Either *A raccoon ate the apples,* or *The apples ate a raccoon,* and so on. But in each case, the verb or verb phrase makes its way to the middle of the statement, and the nouns and pronouns take their places as subjects and objects.

To understand sentence patterns, you need to know that every verb performs one of three jobs. Note that the focus is on the *double-underlined* verbs below.

The Three Jobs of Verbs

1. Verbs can show actions:

A raccoon ate the apples.

We have taken many classes together.

She was walking to school.

2. Verbs can link subjects with nouns, pronouns, or adjectives that describe them:

I am your partner in the lab.

You look wonderful in scrubs.

3. Verbs can help other verbs form verb phrases:

We have taken many classes together. (Without the help of *have,* the main verb would be *take* or *took.*)

She was walking to school. (Without *was,* the main verb would be *walked.*)

Look at these sentences for more examples:

Mel grabbed a scholarship application. (The verb *grabbed* shows Mel's action.)

His pen was empty. (The verb *was* links *pen* with its description as *empty*.)

Mel had been waiting for his grades. (The verbs *had* and *been* help the main verb *waiting* in a verb phrase.)

Knowing the three jobs a verb can perform will help you gain an understanding of the three basic sentence patterns:

SUBJECT + ACTION VERB + OBJECT PATTERN

Some action verbs must be followed by an object (a person, place, thing, or idea) that receives the action.

<pre>
     S   AV   Obj
</pre>
Sylvia completed her degree. (*Sylvia completed* makes no sense unless it is followed by the object that she completed—*her degree*.)

SUBJECT + ACTION VERB (+ NO OBJECT) PATTERN

At other times, the action verb itself completes the meaning and needs no object after it.

<pre>
    S   AV
</pre>
She celebrated at home with her family. (*She celebrated* makes sense alone. It does not need the two prepositional phrases—*at home* and *with her family*, which simply tell where and how she celebrated.)

SUBJECT + LINKING VERB + DESCRIPTION PATTERN

A special kind of verb that does *not* show an action is called a *linking verb*. The linking verb acts like an equal sign in a sentence: "I am student" means "I = a student" means "A student = I." These verbs link the subject with a word that describes the subject. The description can be a noun, a pronoun, or an adjective. Learn to recognize the most common linking verbs: *is, am, are, was, were, seem, feel, appear, become, look*—even *taste* and *smell* can be linking verbs at times.

<pre>
    S   LV   Desc
</pre>
Sylvia is a natural writer. (*Sylvia* equals *a natural writer*.)

<pre>
    S   LV   Desc
</pre>
Sylvia seems very happy. (*Very happy* describes *Sylvia*.)

NOTE—You learned on page 91 that a verb phrase includes a main verb and its helping verbs. Note that helping verbs can be used in any of the sentence patterns.

       S   AV

Sylvia is moving to Seattle. (Here the verb *is* does not link Sylvia with a description but helps the verb *moving,* which is an action verb with no object followed by a prepositional phrase—*to Seattle.*)

The following chart outlines the patterns using short sentences that you could memorize:

THREE BASIC SENTENCE PATTERNS

S + AV + Obj

Students eat   pizza.

S + AV + (no object)

They relax (with their friends).

S + LV + Desc

They are music majors.

They look creative.

These are the basic patterns for most of the clauses used in English sentences. Knowing them can help you control your sentences and improve your phrasing.

E X E R C I S E S

First, put parentheses around any prepositional phrases. Next, underline the verbs or verb phrases twice and their subjects once. Then mark the correct sentence pattern above the words: S + AV + Obj, S + AV, or S + LV + Desc. Remember that the patterns *never* mix or overlap. For example, you won't find "She took tall," which mixes an action verb (AV) with a description of the subject (Desc). But if there are two clauses, each one may have a different pattern. Check your answers after the first exercise.

Exercise 1

1. Sleep is an important part of life.

2. Animals and humans use sleep as a vacation for their brains and bodies.

3. Some facts about sleep might surprise people.

4. Large animals require less sleep than small animals do.

5. A typical cat will sleep for twelve hours in a day.

6. An ordinary elephant will sleep for only three hours.

7. Smaller animals use their brains and bodies at higher rates.

8. Therefore, they need many hours of sleep.

9. The reverse is true for large animals.

10. Humans fall between cats and elephants for their sleep requirements.

Exercise 2

1. Many people get migraine headaches.

2. These headaches can be extremely painful.

3. People with migraines may also suffer from nausea and dizziness.

4. Migraine sufferers avoid bright lights and loud sounds.

5. These sensations cause a different kind of discomfort.

6. Some medicines reduce the pain of migraine headaches.

7. Other drugs help with the additional symptoms.

8. No migraine treatment is perfect for everyone.

9. Scientists have been studying migraine headaches for years.

10. A cure for migraines is long overdue.

Exercise 3

1. Horatio Greenough was a sculptor in the 1800s.

2. Greenough created a controversial statue of George Washington.

3. The statue weighed twelve tons, but its weight was not the reason for the controversy.

4. The controversial aspect of the statue involved Washington's clothes.

5. The statue portrayed Washington in a toga-like garment.

6. His stomach, chest, and arms were bare and very muscular.

7. One part of the toga draped over the statue's raised right arm.

8. The bare-chested statue of Washington stood in the rotunda of the Capitol for only three years.

9. Officials moved the statue many times.

10. In 1962, it arrived in its final home at the American History Museum.

Source: Smithsonian, February 2005

Exercise 4

1. Cakes can be plain or fancy.

2. Most grocery stores and almost all bakeries sell cakes.

3. They range in price depending on size, occasion, and amount of decoration.

4. A cake with a "Happy Birthday" inscription will usually cost thirty to fifty dollars.

5. Wedding cakes, however, are often very expensive.

6. An elaborate wedding cake may cost several hundred or even a thousand dollars.

7. The multilayered traditional white wedding cake still seems the most popular kind.

8. These delicate structures need special care during transportation.

9. Some couples order two or more smaller cakes for the occasion.

10. People sometimes save a slice or section of their wedding cake as a memento.

Exercise 5

1. In 1998, Sotheby's auction house sold a piece of sixty-year-old wedding cake for an amazing price.

2. It had belonged to the Duke and Duchess of Windsor.

3. On June 3, 1937, the famous couple married in France.

4. On the day of their wedding, they put a piece of cake in a pink box and tied a pink bow around it.

5. They identified its contents as "a piece of our wedding cake"; they initialed and dated the box, and they kept it as a memento for the rest of their lives.

6. This couple's relationship, which began in the 1930s, was one of the most famous love affairs in history.

7. The Duke of Windsor gave up the throne of England to be with Wallis Simpson, the woman that he loved.

8. Unfortunately, she was a divorced American woman and could not, therefore, marry the king of England, so he abdicated.

9. The pre-auction estimate for the box containing the piece of their wedding cake was five hundred to a thousand dollars.

10. When the gavel came down, the high bid by a couple from San Francisco was $29,900.

PARAGRAPH EXERCISE

Label the sentence patterns in the following paragraph from the book *The First Men on the Moon: The Story of Apollo 11*, by David M. Harland. It helps to put parentheses around prepositional phrases first to isolate them from the words that make up the sentence patterns—the subjects, the verbs, and any objects after action verbs or any descriptive words after linking verbs (*is, was, were, seem, appear,* and so on). This paragraph describes Neil Armstrong's first moments on the moon.

Armstrong released his grip on the handrail of the ladder and

stepped fully off the foot pad. Walter Cronkite proudly told his CBS audience

that a 38-year-old American was now standing on the surface of the Moon.

When Armstrong scraped his foot across the surface, he noticed that the dark powdery material coated his overshoe. "The surface is fine and powdery. I can kick it up loosely with my toe. It adheres in fine layers like powdery charcoal to the sole and sides of my boots." Although his boots only slightly impressed the surface, the material preserved the imprint of his boots very well. "I only go in a small fraction of an inch—maybe one-eighth of an inch—but I can see the prints of my boots and the treads in the fine, sandy particles."

SENTENCE WRITING

Write ten sentences describing the weather today and your feelings about it. Keep your sentences short to allow clear sentence patterns to develop naturally. Then go back and label the sentence patterns you have used.

Avoiding Clichés, Awkward Phrasing, and Wordiness

CLICHÉS

A cliché is an expression that has been used so often it has lost its originality and effectiveness. Whoever first referred to the most important result of something as "the bottom line" had thought of an original way to express it, but today that expression is worn out. Most of us use an occasional cliché in speaking, but clichés have no place in writing. The good writer thinks up fresh new ways to express ideas.

Here are a few clichés. Add some more to the list.

too little too late

older but wiser

last but not least

in this day and age

different as night and day

out of this world

white as a ghost

sick as a dog

tried and true

at the top of their lungs

the thrill of victory

one in a million

busy as a bee

easier said than done

better late than never

Clichés lack freshness because the reader always knows what's coming next. Can you complete these expressions?

the agony of . . .

breathe a sigh of . . .

lend a helping . . .

odds and . . .

raining cats and . . .

as American as . . .

been there . . .

worth its weight . . .

Clichés are expressions that too many people use. Try to avoid them in your writing.

AWKWARD PHRASING

Another problem—awkward phrasing—comes from writing sentence structures that *no one* else would use because they break basic sentence patterns, omit necessary words, or use words incorrectly. Like clichés, awkward sentences might *sound* acceptable when spoken, but as polished writing, they are usually unacceptable.

AWKWARD

There should be great efforts in terms of the communication between teachers and their students.

CORRECTED

Teachers and their students must communicate.

AWKWARD

During the experiment, the use of key principles was essential to ensure the success of it.

CORRECTED

The experiment was a success. *or* We performed the experiment carefully.

AWKWARD

My favorite in the movie was when the guy with the ball ran the wrong way all the way across the field.

CORRECTED

In my favorite scene, the receiver ran across the field in the wrong direction.

WORDINESS

Good writing is concise writing. Don't use ten words if you can say it better in five. "In today's society" isn't as effective as "today," and it's a cliché. "At this point in time" could be "presently" or "now."

Another kind of wordiness comes from saying something twice. There's no need to write "in the month of August" or "9 a.m. in the morning" or "my personal opinion." August *is* a month, 9 a.m. *is* morning, and anyone's opinion *is* personal. All you need to write is "in August," "9 a.m.," and "my opinion."

Still another kind of wordiness comes from using expressions that add nothing to the meaning of the sentence. "The point is that we can't afford it" says no more than "We can't afford it."

Here is a sample wordy sentence:

The construction company actually worked on that particular building for a period of six months.

And here it is after eliminating wordiness:

The construction company worked on that building for six months.

Wordy Writing	Concise Writing
advance planning	planning
an unexpected surprise	a surprise
ask a question	ask
at a later date	later
basic fundamentals	fundamentals
green in color	green
but nevertheless	but (or nevertheless)
combine together	combine
completely empty	empty
down below	below
each and every	each (or every)
end result	result
fewer in number	fewer
free gift	gift
in order to	to
in spite of the fact that	although
just exactly	exactly
large in size	large
new innovation	innovation
on a regular basis	regularly
past history	history
rectangular in shape	rectangular
refer back	refer
repeat again	repeat
serious crisis	crisis
sufficient enough	sufficient (or enough)
there in person	there
two different kinds	two kinds
very unique	unique

PROOFREADING EXERCISES

The following student paragraphs contain examples of clichés, awkward phrasing, and wordiness. Revise the paragraphs so that they are concise examples of Standard Written English. When you're done, compare your revisions with the sample answers.

1. If I had to tell about my favorite class from high school, I would have to say that it was the cooking class that I took in tenth grade. The really great part of the class was that it was an independent study, and I got to choose my own meals to learn to cook and then eat. The assignments were all the same: do some research on a meal from a particular country or culture. Then buy all the ingredients for that meal, and learn to cook that meal. In order to get a grade for the assignments, I had to bring in a plate full of that food to my teacher, and then I would be graded on the meal and on my report about making it.

2. *While You Were Sleeping* is one of my favorite movies. It comes on TV at the holidays because it takes place in the snow, and there are a lot of holiday parties and celebrations in it. The whole story revolves around a case of mistaken identity when Sandra Bullock's character saves a man's life who gets injured at the train station where she works. He goes into a coma, and she pretends to be his fiancée for about a week while he is unconscious. After she becomes close to his whole family, and especially his brother, the man that she thought she liked suddenly wakes up from his coma. Eventually, everybody realizes that her character really should be with the brother, and it all ends up happily ever after.

3. Full-grown people weren't the only things that ancient civilizations made mummies out of. They also made mummies out of children who died and out of animals, too. Making mummies was a way of helping them enter into the next world, and it was done to show respect. One mummy of an Eskimo baby was found in Greenland. It dated back to the 1400s, and it was wrapped up in beautiful fur to protect it from the cold. In Egypt, archeologists discovered the mummies of everything from cats to crocodiles, cows, baboons, and birds. In Alaska, a mummy was found of a huge bison that the experts thought was over 35,000 years old. The bison was perfectly preserved, and it still had a big lion's tooth in its neck, which showed how it probably died.

Source: Kids Discover, June 2005

Correcting for Parallel Structure

Your writing will be clearer and more memorable if you use parallel structure. That is, when you write two pieces of information or any kind of list, put the items in similar form. Look at this sentence, for example:

My favorite movies are comedies, romantic, and sci-fi fantasies.

The sentence lacks parallel structure. The second item in the list, an adjective, doesn't match the other two, which are nouns. Now look at this sentence:

My favorite movies are comedies, love stories, and sci-fi fantasies.

Here the items are parallel; they are all nouns. Or you could write the following:

I like movies that make me laugh, that make me cry, and that take me away.

Again the sentence has parallel structure because all three items in the list are dependent clauses. Here are some more examples. Note how much easier it is to read the sentences with parallel structure.

WITHOUT PARALLEL STRUCTURE	WITH PARALLEL STRUCTURE
I like hiking, skiing, and to go for a sail.	I like hiking, skiing, and sailing. (all *"ing"* verbals)
The office has run out of pens, paper, ink cartridges, and we need more toner, too.	The office needs more pens, paper, ink cartridges, and toner. (all nouns)
They decided that they needed a change, that they could afford a new house, and wanted to move to Arizona.	They decided that they needed a change, that they could afford a new house, and that they wanted to move to Arizona. (all dependent clauses)

The parts of an outline should always be parallel. Following are two brief outlines about food irradiation. The parts of the outline on the *left* are not parallel. The first subtopic (I.) is a question; the other (II.) is just a noun. And the supporting points (A., B., C.) are written as nouns, verbs, and even clauses. The parts of the outline on the *right* are parallel. Both subtopics (I. and II.) are plural nouns, and all details (A., B., C.) are action verbs followed by objects.

NOT PARALLEL	PARALLEL
Food Irradiation	Food Irradiation
I. How is it good?	I. Benefits
A. Longer shelf life	A. Extends shelf life
B. Using fewer pesticides	B. Requires fewer pesticides
C. Kills bacteria	C. Kills bacteria
II. Concerns	II. Concerns
A. Nutritional value	A. Lowers nutritional value
B. Consumers are worried	B. Alarms consumers
C. Workers' safety	C. Endangers workers

Using parallel structure will make your writing more effective. Note the parallelism in these well-known quotations:

A place for everything and everything in its place.

Isabella Mary Beeton

Ask not what your country can do for you; ask what you can do for your country.

John F. Kennedy

We hold these truths to be self-evident, that all men are created equal, that they are endowed by their creator with certain unalienable rights, that among these are Life, Liberty, and the pursuit of Happiness.

Thomas Jefferson

EXERCISES

In the following exercises, rephrase any sentences that do not contain parallel structures.

Exercise 1

1. Preparing for emergencies involves two steps: planning for anything and to gather certain supplies.

2. When planning for emergencies, ask yourself the following questions.

3. What kinds of emergencies have occurred or might occur in your area?

4. Where would you go, and what method of transportation would you use to get there?

5. Have you made a list of phone contacts within the area and outside it, too?

6. Do the adults, teenagers, and do the children in the family carry those phone numbers with them?

7. Are the most important supplies ready at hand, including water, food, flashlight, radio, and are there batteries as well?

8. Have you assembled your own first-aid kit, or maybe you have bought a ready-made one?

9. Do you stay prepared by reading and understanding your important insurance policies; also, do you remember to update them?

10. By planning for anything and if you stock up on the right supplies, you can prepare yourself and your family for emergencies.

Exercise 2

1. I have read about many foods that can help people stay healthy, and a longer life may result from eating them.

2. Eating whole wheat bread benefits the brain, and energy can increase, too.

3. Apples contain ingredients to aid memory, keeping lungs healthy, and preventing cancer.

4. Kidney beans can reduce cholesterol, give someone more energy, and make moods more stable.

5. Oranges fight inflammation and the losing of eyesight.

6. Substances found in fish can prevent heart problems and depression, as well as high cholesterol.

7. Milk boosts the nervous system and also helps to postpone aging.

8. Antioxidants in red grapes benefit the heart, protect the brain, and can keep people from getting cancer.

9. Red peppers can decrease the risk of strokes or heart attacks.

10. By eating these foods, people can live longer, stay stronger, and they can be very happy.

Source: Psychology Today, July/August 2005

Exercise 3

1. I like coffee, and tea is good, too.

2. I've heard that coffee is bad for you, but drinking tea is good.

3. It must not be the caffeine that's bad because coffee has caffeine and so does tea.

4. I heard one expert say that it's the other chemicals in the coffee and tea that make the difference in health benefits.

5. All teas are supposed to be healthy, but the healthiest is supposed to be green tea.

6. Unfortunately, green tea is the only type of tea I don't like.

7. I love orange pekoe tea with tons of milk and a ton of sugar too.

8. I was really surprised to find out that all tea leaves come from the same plant.

9. I know that all coffee comes from coffee beans, but it shocked me to find out that green tea and orange pekoe are both made with leaves from the *Camellia sinensis* plant.

10. Maybe I'll give green tea another try since it could improve my health.

Exercise 4

1. I was washing my car two weeks ago, and that's when I noticed a few bees buzzing around the roof of my garage.

2. I didn't worry about it at the time, but it was something that I should have worried about.

3. As I drove into my driveway a week later, a whole swarm of bees flew up and down in front of my windshield.

4. The swarm wasn't that big, but the bees flying tightly together looked really frightening.

5. They flew in a pattern as if they were riding on a roller coaster or almost like waves.

6. I was glad that my wife and kids were away for the weekend.

7. There was nothing I could do but to wait in my car until they went away.

8. Finally, the bees flew straight up into the air and then disappeared.

9. Once inside my house, I opened the phone book and started to call a bee expert.

10. The bees had made a hive out of part of my garage roof, the expert said, but once I replace the lumber in that area, I should not be bothered with bees anymore.

Exercise 5

Revise the following sentences to make them a list of clear suggestions using parallel structures. You may want to add transitions like *first* and *finally* to help make the steps clear.

1. Experts give the following tips to get the most out of a visit to the doctor.

2. Avoid getting frustrated after a long wait in the reception area or if you have to wait a long time in the exam room.

3. You should always answer the doctor's questions first; then asking the doctor your own questions might be a good idea.

4. It's smart to inquire about a referral to a specialist if you think you need one.

5. Finding out if there are other treatments besides the one the doctor first recommends can't hurt.

6. Ask about any tests that the doctor orders, and you might wonder what the results mean, so you probably want to get in touch with the doctor after the results come back.

7. Prescriptions are often given quickly and with little explanation, so ask about side effects and optional medicines if one doesn't work.

8. When discussing these things with your doctor, try not to be nervous.

9. The final step is to be prepared to wait in a long line at the pharmacy.

10. If you follow these suggestions when visiting a doctor, you will be more informed and also you can feel involved in your own treatment.

PROOFREADING EXERCISE

Proofread the following paragraph about William Shakespeare, and revise it to correct any errors in parallel structure.

The world knows relatively little about the life of William Shakespeare. Stanley Wells' book *Is It True What They Say about Shakespeare?* addresses the questions that people continue to have about the famous poet and playwright. Because of Shakespeare's talent and the reputation that his works have earned, everyone wants to know when he was born, the schools he went to, his travels, who his friends or lovers were, the way he looked, as well as the method and date he wrote each of his poems and plays. Wells starts with the basic question, "Is it true that . . .?" Throughout the book, he identifies commonly held beliefs about Shakespeare, discusses the historical evidence, and then he judges each belief to be "true," "untrue," or something in between. Wells even examines the numerous theories that someone else wrote the works of Shakespeare, but there is no evidence that he finds strong enough to convince him of their validity.

SENTENCE WRITING

Write ten sentences that use parallel structure in a list or a pair of objects, actions, locations, or ideas. You may choose your own subject or describe a process that involves several steps to complete.

Using Pronouns

Nouns name people, places, things, and ideas—such as *students, school, computers,* and *literacy.* Pronouns take the place of nouns to avoid repetition and to clarify meaning. The pronouns *they* or *them* could replace *students* and *computers*; the pronoun *it* could replace *school* and *literacy.* Personal pronouns that replace people's names or descriptions vary depending on gender and number.

Of the many kinds of pronouns, the personal pronouns cause the most difficulty because they often include two ways of identifying the same person (or people), but only one form is correct in a given situation:

SUBJECT GROUP	OBJECT GROUP
I	me
we	us
you	you
he	him
she	her
they	them
it	it

Use a pronoun from the Subject Group in two instances:

1. Before a verb as a subject:

> *He* is my cousin. (*He* is the subject of the verb *is.*)
>
> *He* is older than *I.* (Here the meaning is not written out in full. It means "*He* is older than *I* am." *I* is the subject of the verb *am.*)

Whenever you see *than* to compare two items in a sentence, ask yourself whether a verb has been left off the end of the sentence. Add the verb, and you'll automatically use the correct pronoun. In both speaking and writing, always add the verb. Instead of incorrectly saying, "She's taller than *me*," say, "She's taller than *I am.*" Then you will use the correct pronoun.

2. After a linking verb (is, am, are, was, were) as a pronoun that renames the subject:

> The ones who should apologize are *we.* (*We* are *the ones who should apologize.* Therefore, the pronoun from the Subject Group is used.)
>
> The winner of the lottery was *she.* (*She* was *the winner of the lottery.* Therefore, the pronoun from the Subject Group is used.)

Modern usage allows some exceptions to this rule, however. For example, *It's me* or *It is her* (instead of the grammatically correct *It is I* and *It is she*) may be common in spoken English.

Use pronouns from the Object Group for all other purposes. In the following sentence, *me* is not the subject, nor does it rename the subject. It is the object of a preposition; therefore, it comes from the Object Group.

My boss went to lunch with Jenny and *me*.

A good way to tell whether to use a pronoun from the Subject Group or the Object Group is to leave out any extra name (and the word *and*). By leaving out *Jenny and,* you will say, *My boss went to lunch with me.* You would never say, *My boss went to lunch with I.*

My father and *I* play chess on Sundays. (*I* play chess on Sundays.)

She and her friends rented a movie. (*She* rented a movie.)

It is up to *us* students to find a solution. (It is up to *us* to find a solution.)

The coach asked Craig and *me* to carry the trophy. (Coach asked *me* to carry the trophy.)

PRONOUN AGREEMENT

Just as subjects and verbs must agree, pronouns should agree with the words they refer to. If the word referred to is singular, the pronoun should be singular. If the noun referred to is plural, the pronoun should be plural.

Each classroom has its own chalkboard.

The pronoun *its* refers to the singular noun *classroom* and therefore is singular.

Both classrooms have their own chalkboards.

The pronoun *their* refers to the plural noun *classrooms* and therefore is plural.

The same rules that we use to maintain the agreement of subjects and verbs also apply to pronoun agreement. For instance, ignore any prepositional phrases that come between the word and the pronoun that takes its place.

That *box* of supplies arrived with a huge dent in *its* side.

Boxes of supplies often arrive with huge dents in *their* sides.

The *player* with the best concentration usually beats *her* opponent.

Players with the best concentration usually beat *their* opponents.

When a pronoun refers to more than one word joined by *and,* the pronoun is plural:

> The *teacher* and the *tutors* eat *their* lunches at noon.
>
> *Joshua* and *Kendra* ate lunch in *their* usual spots at the table.

However, when a pronoun refers to more than one word joined by *or,* then the word closest to the pronoun determines its form:

> Either the teacher or the *tutors* eat *their* lunches in the classroom.
>
> Either the tutors or the *teacher* eats *his* lunch in the classroom.

It is tempting to avoid gender bias by using pairs of pronouns that include both singular forms—*he or she, his or her, him or her.* The results are often wordy and awkward:

> As an actor, *he or she* must share *his or her* emotions with an audience.
>
> If anybody calls, tell *him or her* that I'll be back soon.
>
> Somebody left *his or her* cell phone in the classroom.

Here are a few ways to eliminate gender bias and wordiness *without* using pairs of pronouns:

> As actors, *they* must share *their* emotions with an audience. (use plurals)
>
> Tell *anybody* who calls that I'll be back soon. (use general pronouns)
>
> Somebody left *a* cell phone in the classroom. (use articles—*a, an, the*)

E X E R C I S E S

Exercise 1

Circle the correct pronoun or pair of pronouns. Remember the trick of leaving out the extra name to help you decide which pronouns to use. (Note: The pairs of pronouns in this exercise refer to two *different* people, so both pronouns are necessary. However, the method of using plurals to avoid wordiness could be applied to your answers for practice. *She and I* enjoyed the opera = *We* enjoyed the opera.)

1. My stepmother and (I, me) went to the opera last night.

2. She usually enjoys the opera more than (I, me).

3. This time, however, (she and I, her and me) both enjoyed it.

4. Since I am less familiar with opera than (she, her), I usually don't like it as much.

5. Every time (she and I, her and me) have seen an opera before, she has chosen what to see and where to sit.

6. The one who made the choices this time was (I, me).

7. I may not know as much about opera as (she, her), but I sure picked a winner.

8. The singers seemed to be performing especially for (she and I, her and me).

9. Opera may never mean as much to me as it does to (she, her), but I am learning to appreciate it.

10. In the future, perhaps my stepmother will leave all the decisions of what to see and where to sit up to the box office and (I, me).

Exercises 2-5

Circle the correct pronoun or pair of pronouns. If the correct answer is *he or she*, *his or her*, or *him or her*, revise the sentence to avoid gender bias *and* wordiness (as explained on p. 153). Check your answers as you go through the exercise.

1. I live a long way from the city center and don't own a car, so I use public transportation and rely on (its, their) stability.

2. Based on my experiences, I'd say the city's system of buses has (its, their) problems.

3. Each of the bus routes that I travel on my way to work falls behind (its, their) own schedule.

4. Many of the other passengers also transfer on (his or her, their) way to work.

5. One day last week, each of the passengers had to gather (his or her, their) belongings and leave the bus, even though it had not reached a scheduled stop.

6. Both the driver and the mechanic who came to fix the bus offered (his, their) apologies for making us late.

7. Once the bus was fixed, the passengers were allowed to bring (his or her, their) things back on board.

8. Everyone did (his or her, their) best to hide (his or her, their) annoyance from the driver because he had been so nice.

9. As every passenger stepped off the bus at the end of the line, the driver thanked (him or her, them) for (his or her, their) patience and understanding.

10. Sometimes it is the people within a system that makes (it, them) work after all.

Exercise 3

1. The teacher gave my classmates and (I, me) very specific instructions for the essay.

2. My brother was surprised to learn that Bruce Lee was taller than (he, him).

3. (She and he, Her and him) are working on the same topic for their speeches.

4. Each of the dentists received (his or her, their) gift bags full of toothbrushes and dental floss.

5. Mobile phone companies are usually very competitive in (its, their) pricing.

6. I confess that the person responsible for ordering those flowers was (I, me).

7. Everyone in the audience had (his or her, their) opinion of the performances and expressed it with (his or her, their) applause.

8. Only the jury knows all of the factors involved in (its, their) decision.

9. No one understands your feelings better (I, me).

10. I talked to my academic counselor; it was (she, her) who called this morning.

Exercise 4

1. My friend asked, "Are you taking as many classes as (I, me) this semester?"

2. When it comes to organic farming methods, no one knows more than (she, her).

3. At work, I always answer the phone correctly by saying, "This is (she, her)" when someone asks, "May I speak to the manager?"

4. A little boy and girl were opening (his or her, their) presents when you arrived.

5. We asked the parking enforcement office to waive (its, their) fees for the event.

6. Everyone must use (his or her, their) own password to enter the network.

7. Purchase orders can be signed by my boss or (I, me).

8. The winners of the scholarships were Justin and (she, her).

9. Those two actors have given the best performance of (his or her, their) lives.

10. The judge sent the lawyers and (we, us) jurors a message.

Exercise 5

1. The university representative gave my friends and (I, me) a brochure of the campus.

2. Each of the students will buy (his or her, their) own materials for the jewelry class.

3. The top players in last year's poker tournament have finished (his or her, their) first game in this year's competition.

4. I can't remember—was it you or (I, me) who asked for a raise first?

5. Due to the holiday, everyone was allowed to turn (his or her, their) essay in late.

6. It was (she, her) who loaned him the money for a vacation.

7. There is no one more interested in bats and other flying creatures than (he, him).

8. You and (I, me) drive the same kind of car, but mine is an automatic.

9. I can't believe that the tutors helped you and (I, me) for over an hour.

10. According to Max and (she, her), the deadline for applications is today.

PROOFREADING EXERCISE

The following paragraph contains errors in the use of pronouns. Find and correct the errors.

My daughter and me drove up the coast to visit a little zoo I had heard about. It was a hundred miles and took about two hours. Once her and I arrived, we saw the petting zoo area and wanted to pet the baby animals, but they wouldn't let us. They said that it was the baby animals' resting time, so we couldn't pet them. Then we got to the farm animals. There was a prize-winning hog that was as big as a couch when it was lying down. My daughter liked the hog best of all, and as she and I drove home in the car, it was all she could talk about.

SENTENCE WRITING

Write ten sentences in which you compare yourself to someone else in terms of athletic ability or creativity. Then check that your pronouns are grammatically correct and that they agree with the words they replace.

Avoiding Shifts in Person

To understand what "person" means when using pronouns, imagine a conversation between three people. The *first* person would speak using "I." That person would call the *second* person "you." And when those two talked of a *third* person, they would use "he, she, or they." Here are more personal pronouns arranged by person:

First person—*I, me, my, we, us, our, mine*

Second person—*you, your, yours*

Third person—*he, him, his, she, her, they, them, their, one, anyone, it, its*

Although it is possible (and at times necessary) to use all three groups of pronouns in a paper, most writers try not to shift from one group to another without a good reason. Such errors are called shifts in person.

The following paragraph includes unnecessary shifts in person:

Few people know how to manage *their* time. *We* don't need to be efficiency experts to realize that *everyone* could get a lot more done by budgeting *his* or *her* time more wisely. Nor do *you* need to work very hard to become more organized.

To correct the shifts in person, you could use only *first-person* pronouns:

Few of *us* know how to manage *our* time. *We* don't need to be efficiency experts to realize that *we* could get a lot more done by budgeting *our* time more wisely. Nor do *we* need to work very hard to become more organized.

Or you could address the reader directly and use only *second-person* pronouns:

You are not alone if you don't know how to manage *your* time. *You* don't need to be an efficiency expert to realize that *you* could get a lot more done by budgeting *your* time more wisely. Nor do *you* need to work very hard to become more organized.

Finally, you could correct the shifts by using only *third-person* pronouns:

Few people know how to manage *their* time. *One* does not need to be an efficiency expert to realize that *everyone* could get a lot more done by budgeting *his* or *her* time more wisely. Nor does *anyone* need to work very hard to become more organized. (Note that "*his* or *her*" could then be deleted to avoid using this wordy pair of pronouns. See p. 153.)

PROOFREADING EXERCISES

Which of the following student paragraphs shift *unnecessarily* between first, second, and third person? In those that do, revise the sentences to eliminate such shifting. One of the paragraphs is already correct.

1. Americans have always had more than we actually need. Americans have gotten used to having as much food, water, and clothes as they want. Our restaurants throw away plates and plates of food every day. If you don't want something, you throw it in the trash. But a lot of people have started to think differently. Recycling doesn't just involve aluminum cans and plastic bottles. Americans can recycle food, water, and clothes if we think more creatively and responsibly than they've been doing in the past. You can change the society's view of recycling by just doing it.

2. My friends took me out to dinner for my birthday last week. We went to the new restaurant on the corner that allows its customers to grill their own food right at the table. As soon as we sat down, one of the servers came to our table and asked us if we had been there before. We told her that it was our first time, and she explained the process. It was all new to us. The servers kept bringing out plates of raw chicken, beef, and vegetables, and we kept throwing the food on our little grill and eating it as fast as we could. The dipping sauces were especially delicious, and the atmosphere at the new restaurant was exciting and unique.

3. If I had a choice to live in the city or the country, I would choose the city. I would choose the city because you are surrounded by other people there, and it feels friendly. The country is too quiet. There is dirt everywhere, flies flying around in the sky, bugs—which I hate—crawling on the floor inside and out. The city is a place where the lights are always on. Yes, you deal with pollution, smog, and crowds, but it just feels like home to me. A city house can be any size, shape, and color.

All the houses in the country look the same to me. No matter who you are, you have a white house and a big red barn. I have to admit that I have only been to the country a couple of times to visit my relatives, but the city would have to be the place for me.

REVIEW OF SENTENCE STRUCTURE ERRORS

One sentence in each pair contains an error. Read both sentences carefully before you decide. Then write the letter of the *incorrect* sentence in the blank. Try to name the error and correct it if you can. You may find any of these errors:

awk	awkward phrasing
cliché	overused expression
dm	dangling modifier
frag	fragment
mm	misplaced modifier
pro	incorrect pronoun
pro agr	pronoun agreement
ro	run-on sentence
shift	shift in time or person
s-v agr	subject-verb agreement error
verb	incorrect verb form
wordy	wordiness
//	not parallel

1. _____ **A.** My friend Debbie and I had a great trip to Las Vegas.

   _____ **B.** We saw two shows by Cirque du Soleil, made several trips to the buffet, and we also won some money at the roulette table.

2. _____ **A.** A huge stack of textbooks were blocking the main aisle of the campus bookstore.

   _____ **B.** All of them were science and history books.

3. _____ **A.** As the teacher entered the classroom on the first day, she takes out an instant camera.

   _____ **B.** She used it to take pictures of us to help her memorize our names.

4. _____ **A.** The tutors in the Writing Center have been very helpful.

   _____ **B.** They've taught my classmates and I how to proofread more effectively.

5. _____ **A.** If students apply for financial aid in the middle of a school year.

   _____ **B.** They might not receive money in time to pay their registration and tuition fees.

6. _____ **A.** All of my friends are better gamblers than me.

_____ **B.** I'm lucky to break even; they usually bring home extra winnings.

7. _____ **A.** Each of the referees had given a different signal.

_____ **B.** The fans were confused and so were the players.

8. _____ **A.** I am interested in business it was my original choice of major.

_____ **B.** However, after taking classes in business, I have lost interest in it.

9. _____ **A.** I had a conference with my drawing teacher in her office.

_____ **B.** She told me that perspective was what I needed to learn.

10. _____ **A.** Hanging from the clock in the classroom, we could see electrical wires that looked dangerous.

_____ **B.** The teacher called the facilities office, and two technicians arrived to check the wires.

11. _____ **A.** The thing that I hate more than anything else is when I buy a used book and discover later that it is totally full of someone else's notes and markings.

_____ **B.** Whenever I do buy a used book, I check it very carefully.

12. _____ **A.** I can never relax or have fun anymore.

_____ **B.** It seems as though I am working 24/7.

13. _____ **A.** My family gave my sister a perfect surprise party.

_____ **B.** Mom, Dad, aunts, uncles, cousins, and brothers—we all surprised her, jumping out of closets and from behind furniture.

14. _____ **A.** Some kind of loud noise interrupted class yesterday.

_____ **B.** Everyone was holding their hands over their ears.

15. _____ **A.** At the age of seven, Jake's family moved to my neighborhood.

_____ **B.** He has been my best friend ever since.

PROOFREADING EXERCISE

Find and correct the sentence structure errors in the following essay.

Mother Tells All

The most memorable lessons I have learned about myself have come from my own children. A mother is always on display she has nowhere to hide. And children are like parrots. Whatever they hear her say will be repeated again. If I change my mind about anything, you can be sure they will repeat back every word I uttered out of my mouth.

For example, last summer I told my kids that I was going to go to an exercise class and lose about forty pounds. Well, I lost some of the weight, and I did go to that exercise class. But as soon as I lost weight, I felt empty like a balloon losing air. I felt that I did not want to lose any more weight or do exercise anymore. I thought that my children would accept what I had decided.

When I stopped, the first thing one of my sons said was, "Mom, you need to go back to exercise class." Then they all started telling me what to eat all the time and I felt horrible about it. I had given up these things because I wanted to, but my words were still being repeated to me like an alarm clock going off without stopping. Finally, my kids ran out of steam and got bored with the idea of my losing weight. Once in a while, one of them still make a joke about my "attempt" to lose weight it hurts me that they don't understand.

The lesson that I have learned from this experience is that, if I am not planning on finishing something, I won't tell my children about it. They will never let me forget.

Punctuation and Capital Letters

Period, Question Mark, Exclamation Point, Semicolon, Colon, Dash

Every mark of punctuation should help the reader. Here are the rules for six marks of punctuation. The first three (. ? !) you have known for a long time and probably have no trouble with. The rule about semicolons you learned when you studied independent clauses and the ways to correct run-on sentences (pp. 83–85). The rules about the colon and the dash may be less familiar.

Put a period (.) at the end of a sentence that makes a statement and after most abbreviations.

> The heavy rain caused many traffic delays. (statement)
>
> Oct.   Tues.   in.   pgs.   ft.   Ave.   est.   inc. (abbreviations)

Put a question mark (?) after a direct question but not after an indirect one.

> Do you know if we can use our notes during the test? (direct question)
>
> I wonder if we can use our notes during the test. (indirect question)

In sentences with quotation marks, put the question mark *outside* the quote marks if the sentence itself is a question but *inside* if the quotation or title is a question.

> Did you actually say, "I quit"? (sentence is a question)
>
> I asked my boss, "Do you want me to quit?" (quotation is a question)
>
> She always sings "Do You Know the Way to San Jose?" (title is a question)

Put an exclamation point (!) after an expression to emphasize it or to show loud sounds or strong emotions. This mark is used mostly in dialogue and informal correspondence. The same rule about using quotation marks with question marks applies to using them with exclamation points.

Let's go to a movie later. I need to escape from reality!

We finally memorized Robert Frost's poem "The Road Not Taken"!

Someone in the hallway yelled, "I can't believe I got an A!"

Put a semicolon (;) between two independent clauses in a sentence unless they are joined by one of the connecting words called *fanboys* (*for, and, nor, but, or, yet, so*).

My mother cosigned for a loan; now I have my own car.

Teaching is not a glamorous job; however, people will always need teachers.

To be sure that you are using a semicolon correctly, see if a period and capital letter can be used in its place. If they can, you are putting the semicolon in the right spot.

My mother cosigned for a loan. Now I have my own car.

Teaching is not a glamorous job. However, people will always need teachers.

Put a colon (:) after a complete statement that introduces one of the following elements: a name, a list, a quotation, or an explanation.

The company announced its Employee-of-the-Month: Lee Jones. (The complete statement before the colon introduces the name that follows it.)

That truck comes in the following colors: red, black, blue, and silver. (The complete statement before the colon introduces the list that follows it.)

That truck comes in red, black, blue, and silver. (*The truck comes in* is not a complete statement, so the sentence should not include a colon.)

Thoreau had this to say about time: "Time is but the stream I go a-fishing in." (The complete statement before the colon introduces the quotation that follows it.)

Thoreau said, "Time is but the stream I go a-fishing in." (The signal phrase *Thoreau said* leads directly into the quotation; therefore, no colon—just a comma—comes between them. See p. 227 for more about signal phrases.)

Use dashes (—) to isolate inserted information, to signal an abrupt change of thought, or to emphasize what follows. Dashes are always optional, and they can be used to replace commas, semicolons, and colons.

Lee Jones—the Employee-of-the-Month—gets his own special parking space.

I found out today—or was it yesterday?—that I have inherited a fortune.

We have exciting news for you—we're moving!

EXERCISES

Exercises 1 and 2

Add to these sentences the necessary end punctuation (periods, question marks, and exclamation points). The semicolons, colons, dashes, and commas used within the sentences are correct and do not need to be changed. Pay close attention to them, however, to help with Exercises 3–5.

Exercise 1

1. Have you noticed that light bulbs don't last as long as they used to

2. Some seem to burn out after only a month or two

3. Would you believe that one light bulb has lasted for 110 years

4. Well, it's true—believe it or not

5. At a fire station in Livermore, California, the same bulb has been burning since 1901

6. The now famous light bulb is treated like a celebrity by the firefighters

7. They are proud of its history, and who wouldn't be

8. The famous bulb doesn't get cleaned or covered by any type of shade; no one wants to risk damaging it or making it burn out after so many years

9. The Livermore Light Bulb, as it's called, has even made it into the *Guinness Book of World Records* as the longest running light bulb

10. Anyone who wants to see this famous bulb in action can visit its 24-hour webcam online

Source: www.centennialbulb.org

Exercise 2

1. Have you heard of the phenomenon known as a "milky sea"

2. Sailors throughout history have described this eerie condition

3. A milky sea occurs when ocean water turns almost completely white

4. What accounts for this milky color

5. It is due to huge amounts of bacteria that glow with white light

6. Until recently, no one had photographs or other visual proof of this condition

7. In 1995, however, people took the first pictures of a milky sea off the coast of Somalia

8. Scientists later reviewed satellite images from the same period and discovered their own startling documentation that milky seas exist

9. The satellite photos clearly showed a long glowing white stretch of ocean water

10. It was the size of the state of Connecticut

Source: Science News, October 1, 2005

Exercises 3 and 4

Add any necessary semicolons, colons, and dashes to these sentences. The commas and end punctuation do not need to be changed. Some sentences are correct.

Exercise 3

1. People can learn foreign languages in several new ways these days by practicing with a partner, by studying on long plane flights, and by listening to foreign news on the radio or watching movies in other languages.

2. The Internet allows people especially those who want to learn a language to correspond easily with people from other countries.

3. The exchange goes something like this one person wants to know French he contacts a person in France who wants to learn English.

4. The two exchange emails then, as they correct each other's phrasing, they learn more about the other's language.

5. Certain audio programs and books have been designed for one purpose to offer airline passengers a quick course in a foreign language.

6. Portable music devices usually hold book-length works therefore, these in-flight language programs are easy to use.

7. The third new way to become more fluent in a foreign language is to listen to radio and film programs in another language.

8. It's easy to find foreign news sites on the Internet these radio programs feature reporters who speak clearly and use many common phrases.

9. There is a variation that anyone with a DVD player can use most DVD menus include the option of listening to the movie dubbed in another language.

10. In this way, movies can be even more entertaining they can also be more educational.

Exercise 4

1. Nancy Cartwright is a well-known actress on television however, we never see her when she is acting.

2. Cartwright is famous for playing one part the voice of Bart Simpson.

3. Besides her career as the most mischievous Simpson, Cartwright is married and has children of her own a son and a daughter.

4. Wouldn't it be strange to have a mother with Bart Simpson's voice?

5. Cartwright admits that she made her own share of trouble in school.

6. But the similarities between her and her famous character end there.

7. Bart is a boy Cartwright is obviously a woman.

8. Bart is perpetually ten years old Cartwright is in her fifties.

9. It's no surprise that Cartwright is very popular with fans.

10. When they yell for her to "Do Bart! Do Bart!" she declines by saying "No way, man!"

Exercise 5

Add the necessary periods, question marks, exclamation points, semicolons, colons, and dashes. Any commas are correct and do not need to be changed.

1. What do math and origami Japanese paper folding have to do with each other

2. Erik Demaine and other origami mathematicians would answer, "Everything"

3. If you have never heard of the field of origami mathematics, you're not alone

4. Origami math is a relatively new field back in 2003, Demaine won a "genius" award partly due to his work with origami and its applications in many fields

5. The MacArthur Foundation awarded Demaine more than just the title "genius" it awarded him half a million dollars

6. At twenty, Demaine was hired as a professor by the Massachusetts Institute of Technology he became the youngest professor MIT has ever had

7. Erik Demaine has his father to thank for much of his education Martin Demaine home-schooled Erik as the two of them traveled around North America

8. Erik was always intensely interested in academic subjects during his travels, he and his father would consult university professors whenever Erik had questions that no one else could answer

9. Erik Demaine continues to investigate one area in particular the single-cut problem

10. This problem involves folding a piece of paper then making one cut the result can be anything from a swan to a star, a unicorn, or any letter of the alphabet

Source: New York Times, February 15, 2005

PROOFREADING EXERCISE

Find and correct the punctuation errors in this student paragraph. All of the errors involve periods, question marks, exclamation points, semicolons, colons, and dashes. Any commas used within the sentences are correct and should not be changed.

The ingredients you will need for a lemon meringue pie are: lemon juice, eggs, sugar, cornstarch, flour, butter, water, and salt. First, you combine flour, salt, butter, and water for the crust and bake until lightly brown then you mix and cook the lemon juice, egg yolks, sugar, cornstarch, butter, and water for the filling. Once the filling is poured into the cooked crust; you whip the meringue. Meringue is made of egg whites and sugar! Pile the meringue on top of the lemon filling; place the pie in the hot oven for a few minutes, and you'll have the best lemon meringue pie you've ever tasted.

SENTENCE WRITING

Write ten sentences of your own that use periods, question marks, exclamation points, semicolons, colons, and dashes correctly. Imitate the sentences used in the explanations or in Exercise 1.

Comma Rules 1, 2, and 3

Commas and other punctuation marks guide the reader through your sentence structures in the same way that signs guide drivers on the highway. Imagine what effects misplaced or incorrect road signs would have. From now on, try not to use any comma without a good reason for it.

Among all of the uses of commas, six are most important. If you learn these six rules, your writing will improve. You have already read about the first rule on pages 84–85.

1. **Put a comma before *for, and, nor, but, or, yet, so* (remember these seven words as the *fanboys*) when they connect two independent clauses.**

    We all brought our essays to class, and the teacher congratulated us.

    My math book will be very expensive, so I'll look for a good deal online.

If you use a comma without a *fanboys* between two independent clauses, the result is an error called a ***comma splice.***

    Dogs are people's best friends, people are cats' best friends. (comma splice)

    Dogs are people's best friends, *and* people are cats' best friends. (corrected)

Before using a comma, be sure one of the *fanboys* actually connects two independent clauses and not just two words or phrases. The following sentence contains only one independent clause with two verbs. Because no subject follows the *fanboys*, the sentence does not require a comma:

    My <u>dog</u> <u>curled</u> up under my chair and <u>waited</u> for me to finish my essay.

Now compare the previous sentence with this one that does require a comma:

    My <u>cat</u> <u>was</u> hungry, and <u>she</u> <u>meowed</u> for me to finish my essay.

2. **Use a comma to separate items in a series, date, or address.**

    Students in literature classes read short stories, poems, and plays.

    Today I walked to school, biked to work, and took a train to the movies.

Occasionally, writers leave out the comma before the *and* connecting the last two items in a series, but it is needed to separate all of the items equally.

If a date or address is used in a sentence, put a comma after every item, including the last.

    My father was born on August 19, 1961, in Mesa, Arizona, and grew up there.

    Shelby lived in Lima, Peru, for two years.

When only the month and year are used in a date, no commas are needed.

> My aunt graduated from Yale in May 2009.

3. **Put a comma after an introductory word, phrase, or dependent clause that begins a sentence and before a tag question or comment that ends it.**

> Finally, he was able to get through to his insurance company. (introductory word)

> During her last performance, the actress fell and broke her leg. (introductory phrase)

> Whenever I finish my homework, I feel satisfied. (introductory dependent clause)

> The new chairs aren't very comfortable, are they? (tag question)

> My professor said he needed to ruminate, whatever that means. (tag comment)

E X E R C I S E S

Add commas to the following sentences according to the comma rule stated in the directions for each exercise. Any other punctuation already in the sentences is correct. Check your answers after the first set.

Exercise 1

Add commas according to Comma Rule 1. Put a comma before a *fanboys* when it connects two independent clauses. Some sentences may be correct.

1. An unusual 400-year-old mechanical clock went up for auction in 2007 and someone paid $135,000 for it.

2. The clock is made of brass covered in gold but that's not what makes it valuable.

3. The clock's value lies in its unique design for it's shaped like a skull resting on top of two crossed bones.

4. To view the time, a person must lift the skullcap but the clock might scare the person away in the process.

5. The clock's automated workings bring the skull to life in an eerie way every hour.

6. Through a timed movement that takes several minutes, the skull opens its jaw slowly and completely and then suddenly bites shut!

7. If this action weren't scary enough, two gilded snakes pop out of the skull's eyes in an alternating pattern.

8. The effect of the opening jaw and the slithering snakes is almost too much to take.

9. This golden skull clock is definitely not for everyone yet it is intriguing.

10. It may have been created four centuries ago but it looks like a prop from a modern horror movie or graphic novel.

Source: The Watchismo Times, October 26, 2007

Exercise 2

Add commas according to Comma Rule 2. Use a comma to separate three or more items in a series. If an address or date is used, put a comma after each item, including the last. Some sentences may not need any commas.

1. I graduated from high school on June 25 2006 in San Antonio Texas.

2. I was lucky to have an English teacher in high school who was young enthusiastic and highly motivated.

3. We read essays stories poems and research articles in her class.

4. One time we read a short play chose parts to memorize and gave a performance of it in front of the whole school.

5. One of my favorite of Ms. Kern's assignments was the complaint letter that she asked us to write.

6. She was trying to teach us how to follow directions how to explain something clearly and how to think about what she called our "tone of voice" when we wrote.

7. We had to write a real letter of complaint about a product a service or an experience that was unsatisfactory to us.

8. Then we sent a copy of our letter to the company's business address to our home address and to Ms. Kern's school address.

9. Ms. Kern assured us that we would receive a response from the company if we explained our complaint well asked for a reasonable solution and used an appropriate tone.

10. In the big envelope from my company was a letter of apology a bumper sticker and an impressive discount coupon to use at any of the company's stores.

Exercise 3

Add commas according to Comma Rule 3. Put a comma after introductory expressions and before any tag comments or questions.

1. Most people don't know how coffee is decaffeinated do you?

2. Although there are three methods used to decaffeinate coffee one of them is the most popular.

3. The most popular method is called water processing drawing the caffeine from the coffee beans into a water solution and removing most of it.

4. After going through the natural water processing method the coffee may be a little less flavorful.

5. To decaffeinate coffee another way manufacturers add a chemical solution to the beans and then steam them to remove the leftover chemicals.

6. Compared to the water processing method the chemical method is more "scientific" and removes more of the caffeine.

7. Finally there is the method that infuses coffee beans with carbon dioxide gas to get rid of the caffeine.

8. Since carbon dioxide is plentiful and nontoxic this process is also popular.

9. Even though the carbon dioxide method is the most expensive of the three ways to decaffeinate coffee it also removes the most caffeine.

10. Whenever I drink a cup of decaf in the future I'll wonder which method was used to remove the caffeine.

Exercise 4

Add commas according to the first three comma rules.

1. When the government issued the Susan B. Anthony dollar coin on July 2 1979 it met with some disapproval.

2. People didn't dislike the person on the coin but they did dislike the size and color of the coin.

3. It was nearly the same size as a quarter had a rough edge like a quarter's and was the same color as a quarter.

4. It differed from a quarter in that it was faceted around the face was lighter in weight and was worth four times as much.

5. Due to these problems the Susan B. Anthony dollar was discontinued and in January 2000 the government issued a new golden dollar.

6. Like the Anthony dollar the new coin portrayed the image of a famous American woman.

7. She was the young Native American guide and interpreter for the Lewis and Clark expedition and her name was Sacagawea.

8. Although the Sacagawea dollar was roughly the same size as the Anthony dollar it had a smooth wide edge and its gold color made it easy to distinguish from a quarter.

9. Sacagawea's journey included hardship suffering and illness but it also revealed her incredible knowledge courage and strength.

10. However because the Sacagawea dollar coins were not popular either the government decided to issue dollar coins with U.S. presidents on them.

Exercise 5

Add commas according to the first three comma rules.

1. In the past people believed that emeralds held magical powers.

2. They were supposed to cure disease lengthen life and protect innocence.

3. Part of their appeal was their rarity for emeralds are even rarer than diamonds.

4. Geologists have been mystified by emeralds because they are produced through a unique process the blending of chromium vanadium and beryllium.

5. These substances almost never occur together except in emeralds.

6. In South Africa Pakistan and Brazil emeralds were created by intrusions of granite millions of years ago.

7. These areas are known for their beautiful gems but emeralds from Colombia are the largest greenest and most sparkling of all.

8. In Colombia the makeup of the sedimentary rock accounts for the difference.

9. Instead of the granite found in other emerald-rich countries the predominant substance in Colombia is black shale.

10. Even though emeralds can be synthesized a real one always contains a trapped bit of fluid and jewelers call this tiny imperfection a "garden."

PROOFREADING EXERCISE

Apply the first three comma rules to the following paragraph:

I couldn't believe it but there I was in the pilot's seat of an airplane. I had casually signed up for a course in flying at the aviation school and hadn't expected to start flying right away. The instructor told me what to do and I did it. When I turned the stick to the right the plane turned right. When I turned it to the left the plane went left. Actually it was very similar to driving a car. Most of my practice involved landing bringing the plane in softly and safely. After many hours of supervised flying my time to solo came and I was really excited. I covered the checklist on the ground took off without any problems and landed like a professional. On May 8 2010 I became a licensed pilot so now I can pursue my dream of being a private pilot for a rock star.

SENTENCE WRITING

Combine the following sets of sentences in different ways using all of the first three comma rules. You may need to reorder the details and change the phrasing. Sample responses are provided in the Answers section.

I like to watch golf and baseball.

I love to play hockey and soccer.

Tutors will not correct a student's paper.

They will explain how to clarify ideas.

They will explain how to add stronger details.

They will explain how to improve organization.

Meg and Charlie bought their first car.

They bought a big car.

The dealer gave them a good price.

They should have thought more about gas mileage.

Now they spend over two hundred dollars a month on gas.

Comma Rules 4, 5, and 6

The next three comma rules all involve using pairs of commas to enclose what you might call "scoopable" elements. Scoopable elements are extra words, phrases, and clauses that can be scooped out of the middle of a sentence because they are not necessary to understand its meaning. Notice that the comma **(,)** is shaped somewhat like the tip of an ice cream scoop. Let this similarity help you remember to use commas to enclose *scoopable* elements. Two commas are used as they are here**,** one before and one after**,** to show where scoopable elements begin and end.

4. Put commas around the name of a person spoken to.

> Did you know, Danielle, that you left your backpack at the library?
>
> We regret to inform you, Mr. Davis, that your policy has been canceled.

5. Put commas around expressions that interrupt the flow of the sentence (such as *however, moreover, therefore, of course, by the way, on the other hand, I believe,* or *I think*).

> I know, of course, that I have missed the deadline.
>
> They will try, therefore, to use the rest of their time wisely.
>
> Today's exam, I think, was only a practice test.

Read the previous examples *aloud,* and you'll hear how these expressions surrounded by commas interrupt the flow of the sentence. Sometimes such expressions flow smoothly into the sentence and don't need commas around them.

> Of course he checked to see if there were any rooms available.
>
> We therefore decided to stay out of it.
>
> I think you made the right decision.

Remember that, when a word like *however* comes between two independent clauses, you should put a semicolon before it. (See p. 83.) It should also have a comma after it, following Comma Rule 3, to show that *however* introduces the second independent clause. (See p. 173.)

> The bus was late; *however,* we still made it to the museum before it closed.
>
> I am improving my study habits; *furthermore,* I am getting better grades.
>
> She was interested in journalism; *therefore,* she took a job at a local newspaper.
>
> I spent hours studying for the test; *finally,* I felt prepared.

Thus, you've seen a word like *however* used in three ways:

1. as a "scoopable" word that interrupts the flow of the sentence (needs commas around it)

2. as a word that flows smoothly within the sentence (needs no punctuation)

3. as a connecting word between two independent clauses (needs a semicolon before and a comma after it)

6. Put commas around additional information that is not needed in a sentence.

Certain additional information is "scoopable" and should be surrounded by commas. Look at the following sentence that includes additional information about its subject:

Maxine Taylor, who organized the fund-raiser, will introduce the candidates.

The clause *who organized the fund-raiser* is extra information in the sentence. Without it, we still know exactly who the sentence is about and what she is going to do: "Maxine Taylor will introduce the candidates." Therefore, the additional information is surrounded by commas to show that it is scoopable. Now read the following sentence:

The person who organized the fund-raiser will introduce the candidates.

The clause *who organized the fund-raiser* is not extra but necessary in this sentence. Without it, the subject would be unclear: "The person will introduce the candidates." The reader would not know *which person*. The clause *who organized the fund-raiser* is not scoopable, so there are no commas around it. Here's another example:

Avatar, James Cameron's film, was nominated for Best Picture.

The additional information *James Cameron's film* is scoopable. It could be left out without making the subject unclear: "*Avatar* was nominated for Best Picture." Therefore, two commas surround the scoopable information to show that it could be taken out. But here is the same sentence with the information reversed:

James Cameron's film *Avatar* was nominated for Best Picture.

In this sentence, the title of the movie is not additional, but necessary. Without it, the sentence would read, "James Cameron's film was nominated for Best Picture." The reader would not know which of Cameron's many films was nominated for Best Picture. Therefore, *Avatar* is not scoopable, and commas should not be used around it.

E X E R C I S E S

Surround any "scoopable" elements with commas according to Comma Rules 4, 5, and 6. Any commas already in the sentences follow Comma Rules 1, 2, and 3. Some sentences may be correct. Check your answers after the first set.

Exercise 1

1. The writing teacher Ms. Gonzales has published several of her own short stories.

2. The Ms. Gonzales who teaches writing is not the Ms. Gonzales who teaches history.

3. My daughter's friend Harry doesn't get along with her best friend Jenny.

4. My daughter's best friend Jenny doesn't get along with one of her other friends Harry.

5. The tiger which is a beautiful and powerful animal symbolizes freedom.

6. The tiger that was born in September is already on display at the zoo.

7. The students who helped set up the chairs were allowed to sit in the front row.

8. Kim and Teresa who helped set up the chairs were allowed to sit in the front row.

9. My car which had a tracking device was easy to find when it was stolen.

10. A car that has a tracking device is easier to find if it's stolen.

Exercise 2

1. We trust of course that people who get their driver's licenses know how to drive.

2. Of course, we trust that people who get their driver's licenses know how to drive.

3. The people who test drivers for their licenses make the streets safer for all of us.

4. Mr. Kraft who tests drivers for their licenses makes the streets safer for all of us.

5. We may therefore understand when we fail the driving test ourselves.

6. Therefore, we may understand when we fail the driving test ourselves.

7. The driver's seat we know is a place of tremendous responsibility.

8. We know that the driver's seat is a place of tremendous responsibility.

9. We believe that no one should take that responsibility lightly.

10. No one we believe should take that responsibility lightly.

Exercise 3

1. This year's Feast of Lanterns in Pacific Grove I think was better than last year's.

2. I think this year's Feast of Lanterns in Pacific Grove was better than last year's.

3. The weather was certainly perfect this year.

4. Certainly, the weather was perfect this year.

5. The people who decorated their houses with lanterns were the unsung heroes of the weeklong festival.

6. Laurie and Jane who decorated their houses with lanterns were among the unsung heroes of the weeklong festival.

7. The people who organized the Pet Parade did a great job; there were plenty of costumes and animals, and the children had lots of fun.

8. Adrienne and Andrea two volunteers at the Pet Parade were also dancers in the ballet.

9. The salads at the Feast of Salads I have to say were better last year.

10. I have to say that the salads at the Feast of Salads were better last year.

Exercise 4

1. Arthur S. Heineman a California architect designed and built the world's first motel in the mid-1920s.

2. He chose the perfect location the city of San Luis Obispo which was midway between Los Angeles and San Francisco.

3. Heineman an insightful man of business understood the need for inexpensive drive-in accommodations on long motor vehicle trips.

4. Hotels which required reservations and offered only high-priced rooms within one large structure just didn't fulfill the needs of motorists.

5. Heineman envisioned his "Motor Hotel" or Mo-Tel as a place where the parking spaces for the cars were right next to separate bungalow-style apartments for the passengers.

6. Heineman's idea was so new that when he put up his "Motel" sign several residents of the area told him to fire the sign's painter who couldn't even spell the word *hotel*.

7. Heineman had the sign painter place a hyphen between *Mo* and *Tel* to inform the public of a new kind of resting place.

8. Heineman's Milestone Mo-Tel the world's first motel opened in San Luis Obispo in 1925.

9. Before Heineman's company the Milestone Interstate Corporation could successfully trademark the name "Mo-Tel," other builders adopted the style and made *motel* a generic term.

10. Some of the original Milestone Mo-Tel building now called the Motel Inn still stands on the road between L.A. and San Francisco.

Source: Westways, May/June 2000

Exercise 5

1. I bought a book *The Story of the "Titanic"* because I am interested in famous events in history.

2. This book written by Frank O. Braynard is a collection of postcards about the ill-fated ocean liner.

3. The book's postcards four on each page can be pulled apart and mailed like regular ones.

4. The postcards have images of *Titanic*-related people, places, and events on one side.

5. The blank sides where messages and addresses go include brief captions of the images on the front of the cards.

6. The book's actual content the part written by Braynard offers a brief history of each image relating to the *Titanic*.

7. One of my favorite cards shows the ship's captain Edward Smith and its builder Lord Pirrie standing on the deck of the *Titanic* before it set sail.

8. Another card is a photograph of *Titanic* passengers on board the *Carpathia* the ship that rescued many survivors.

9. There is also a picture of two small children survivors themselves who lost their father in the disaster but were later reunited with their mother.

10. The most interesting card a photo of the ship's gymnasium shows that one of the pieces of exercise equipment for the passengers was a rowing machine.

PROOFREADING EXERCISE

Surround any "scoopable" elements in the following paragraph with commas according to Comma Rules 4, 5, and 6.

Do you know Ryan that there is a one-unit library class that begins next week? It's called Library 1 Introduction to the Library and we have to sign up for it before Friday. The librarians who teach it will give us an orientation and a series of assignment sheets. Then as we finish the assignments at our own pace we will turn them in to the librarians for credit. Ms. Kim the librarian that I spoke with said that we will learn really valuable library skills. These skills such as finding books or articles in our library and using the Internet to access other databases are the ones universities will expect us to know. I therefore plan to take this class, and you I hope will take it with me.

SENTENCE WRITING

Combine the following sets of sentences in different ways according to Comma Rules 4, 5, and 6. Try to combine each set in a way that needs commas and in a way that doesn't need commas. In other words, try to make an element "scoopable" in one sentence and not "scoopable" in another. You may reorder the details and change the phrasing as you wish. Sample responses are provided in the Answers.

Samantha Jones is a great boss.

A great boss recognizes hard work and rewards dedicated employees.

I believe that we should do something.

We should start a savings account.

A savings account will help us prepare for financial emergencies.

My roommate got a job in the bookstore.

Her name is Leslie.

The job allows her to get good discounts on books.

REVIEW OF THE COMMA

SIX COMMA RULES

1. Put a comma before a *fanboys (for, and, nor, but, or, yet, so)* when it connects two independent clauses.
2. Put a comma between three or more items in a series.
3. Put a comma after an introductory expression or before a tag comment or question at the end.
4. Put commas around the name of a person spoken to.
5. Put commas around words like *however* or *therefore* when they interrupt a sentence.
6. Put commas around unnecessary, additional ("scoopable") information.

COMMA REVIEW EXERCISE

Add the missing commas, and identify which one of the six comma rules applies in the brackets at the *end* of each sentence. Each of the six sentences illustrates a different rule.

I am writing you this note Monica to ask you to do me a favor. [ ] Before you leave for work today would you take the pizza dough out of the freezer? [ ] I plan to get started on the salads soups and desserts as soon as I wake up. [ ] I will be so busy however that I might forget to thaw out the dough. [ ] It's the first time I've cooked all the food for pizza night by myself and I want everything to be perfect. [ ] The big round pizza pan the one that is in the cupboard above the refrigerator will be the best place to keep the dough as it thaws. [ ]

Thanks for your help.

SENTENCE WRITING

Write at least one sentence of your own to demonstrate each of the six comma rules. You could write the six sentences in the form of a note to a friend, like the one in the Comma Review Exercise. Be sure to think of a new situation that the note could explain. Exchange notes with a classmate and check each other's commas.

Quotation Marks and Underlining/*Italics*

Put quotation marks around any direct quotation (the exact words of a speaker or writer) but not around a paraphrase or an indirect quotation. For a full discussion of the methods for "Choosing and Using Quotations," see pages 226–230.

In his first speech as president, Franklin D. Roosevelt said the famous words, "the only thing we have to fear is fear itself." (a direct quotation)

In his first speech as president, Franklin D. Roosevelt reassured the nation and told people not to be afraid. (a paraphrase)

The officer said, "Please show me your driver's license." (a direct quotation)

The officer asked to see my driver's license. (an indirect quotation)

If the writer or speaker continues for more than one sentence, use quotation marks before and after the whole quotation.

She said, "One of your brake lights is out. You need to take care of the problem right away."

If the quotation begins the sentence, the words telling who is speaking (called the signal phrase) are set off with a comma unless the quotation ends with a question mark or an exclamation point. See page 227 for more about signal phrases.

"I didn't even know it was broken," I said.

"Do you have any questions?" she asked.

"You mean I can go!" I answered excitedly.

"Yes," she said, "consider this just a warning."

Notice that most of the previous quotations begin with a capital letter. But when a quotation is interrupted by the signal phrase, the second part doesn't begin with a capital letter unless the second part is a new sentence.

"If you knew how much time I spent on the essay," the student explained, "you would give me an A."

"An artist might work on a painting for years," the teacher replied. "That doesn't mean that the result will be a masterpiece."

Put quotation marks around the titles of essays, articles, poems, songs, short stories, TV episodes, and other short works.

We read George Orwell's essay "A Hanging" in my speech class.

I couldn't sleep after I read "The Lottery," a short story by Shirley Jackson.

My favorite Woodie Guthrie song is "This Land Is Your Land."

Jerry Seinfeld's troubles in "The Puffy Shirt" episode are some of the funniest moments in TV history.

When handwriting, underline titles of longer works: books, newspapers, magazines, plays, albums or CDs, Web sites, movies or DVDs, and TV or radio series.

The Host is a novel by Stephanie Meyer, author of the Twilight series.

I read about the latest discovery of dinosaur footprints on CNN.com.

Many people found the series finale of Lost to be very satisfying.

My mother listens to The Writer's Almanac radio program every morning.

Italicize instead of underlining when you have access to a computer. Be consistent throughout any paper in which you use underlining or italics.

The Host is a novel by Stephanie Meyer, author of the *Twilight* series.

I read about the latest discovery of dinosaur footprints on *CNN.com*.

Many people found the series finale of *Lost* to be very satisfying.

My mother listens to *The Writer's Almanac* radio program every morning.

E X E R C I S E S

Correctly punctuate quotations and titles in the following sentences by adding quotation marks or underlining/*italics*.

Exercise 1

1. Marks is the title of a poem by Linda Pastan.
2. I'll never understand what No news is good news means.
3. The student asked the librarian, Can you help me find an article on spontaneous human combustion?
4. Whatever happened to The Book of Lists?
5. My Antonia is the title of one of Willa Cather's most famous novels.

6. Let's begin, the relaxation expert said, by closing our eyes and imagining ourselves in an empty theater.

7. Television series like Frontier House and Colonial House have made PBS a real competitor for reality-TV-hungry audiences.

8. I can't keep this a secret anymore, my neighbor told me. Your son has a tattoo that he hasn't shown you yet.

9. Phil Gordon's Little Green Book is the whole title of his book, and the subtitle is Lessons and Teachings in No Limit Texas Hold'em.

10. I was shocked when my high school English teacher told us, Most of Shakespeare's stories came from other sources; he just dramatized them better than anyone else did.

Exercise 2

1. Emilie Buchwald once noted, Children are made readers on the laps of their parents.

2. Have you read Mark Twain's book The Adventures of Tom Sawyer?

3. I took a deep breath when my counselor asked, How many math classes have you had?

4. Let's start that again! shouted the dance teacher.

5. Last night we watched the Beatles' movie Help! on DVD.

6. Books, wrote Jonathan Swift, are the children of the brain.

7. Voltaire stated in A Philosophical Dictionary that Tears are the silent language of grief.

8. Why do dentists ask questions like How are you? as soon as they start working on your teeth?

9. Time is the only incorruptible judge is just one translation of Creon's line from the Greek play Oedipus Rex.

10. My favorite essay that we have read this semester has to be The Pie by Gary Soto.

Exercise 3

1. Do you need any help with your homework? my father asked.

2. In William Zinsser's book On Writing Well, he explains that Readers want the person who is talking to them to sound genuine.

3. Sigmund Freud had this to say about the intensity of a particular dream: The dream is far shorter than the thoughts which it replaces.

4. Cat People and The Curse of the Cat People are two movies about people who turn into panther-like cats.

5. All for love, and nothing for reward is a famous quotation by Edmund Spenser.

6. Forrest Gump made many sayings famous, but Life is like a box of chocolates is the most memorable.

7. My teacher wrote Well done! at the top of my essay.

8. Poker expert Phil Gordon admits that Everyone makes mistakes. A bad poker player, he adds, will make the same mistake over and over again.

9. Donna asked, What time is the meeting?

10. My family subscribes to The New Yorker, and we all enjoy reading it.

Exercise 4

1. Alfred Tonnelle defined art this way: The artist does not see things as they are, but as he is.

2. I found a vintage children's book called Baby Island at the thrift store; it was a fascinating story.

3. A Russian proverb says, When money speaks, the truth is silent.

4. When someone suggested that Walt Disney run for mayor of Los Angeles following the success of Disneyland, Disney declined, saying, I'm already king.

5. About trying new foods, Swift said, It was a bold man who first ate an oyster.

6. Mark Twain noted about California, It's a great place to live, but I wouldn't want to visit there.

7. There is a French expression *L'amour est aveugle; l'amitié ferme les yeux,* which translates as follows: Love is blind; friendship closes its eyes.

8. Let's keep our voices down, the librarian said as we left the study room.

9. One of Emily Dickinson's shortest poems begins, A word is dead/When it is said/Some say.

10. Dickinson's poem ends like this: I say it just/Begins to live/That day.

Exercise 5

1. In Booker T. Washington's autobiography Up from Slavery, he describes his early dream of going to school.

2. I had no schooling whatever while I was a slave, he explains.

3. He continues, I remember on several occasions I went as far as the schoolhouse door with one of my young mistresses to carry her books.

4. Washington then describes what he saw from the doorway: several dozen boys and girls engaged in study.

5. The picture, he adds, made a deep impression upon me.

6. Washington cherished this glimpse of boys and girls engaged in study.

7. It contrasted directly with his own situation: My life had its beginning in the midst of the most miserable, desolate, and discouraging surroundings.

8. I was born, he says, in a typical log cabin, about fourteen by sixteen feet square.

9. He explains, In this cabin I lived with my mother and a brother and sister till after the Civil War, when we were all declared free.

10. As a slave at the door of his young mistress's schoolhouse, Booker T. Washington remembers, I had the feeling that to get into a schoolhouse and study in this way would be about the same as getting into paradise.

Source: Great Americans in Their Own Words (Mallard Press, 1990)

PARAGRAPH EXERCISE

Add quotation marks and underlining (*italics*) where necessary to correctly punctuate all quotations and titles included in the following paragraph.

Yesterday, I was looking through a book of quotations in the library. When I got to the section with quotes about books and reading, I noticed that the people who have been most affected by books are writers themselves. For instance, one long quotation by the popular author Amy Bloom begins, When I was little, maybe eight or nine, the books that made an enormous impression on me, and didn't fade, were The Scarlet Pimpernel, A Tale of Two Cities, and all of the Superman comic books. Then Bloom points out what these classic readings have in common: They all involve the same idea, which is someone who is ineffective and foppish on the surface but powerful and effective and mysterious and unstoppable in secret. Bloom concludes by saying, They encouraged me to develop the notion that you might appear one way but really be another. Bloom's quotation about stories with unlikely heroes makes me want to read—or write—a new one right now!

SENTENCE WRITING

Write ten sentences that list and discuss your favorite films, books, TV shows, characters' expressions, and so on. Be sure to punctuate quotations and titles correctly. Refer to the rules at the beginning of this section if necessary.

Capital Letters

1. Capitalize the first word of every sentence.

Peaches and nectarines taste best when they are cold.

Every piece of fruit is an amazing object.

2. Capitalize the first word of a sentence-length quotation.

The college president asked, "What can we do for the students today?"

"The labs tools are a little dangerous," Zoe said, "but I am always careful." (The *but* is not capitalized because it does not begin a new sentence.)

"I love my art classes," she added. "Maybe I'll change my major." (*Maybe* is capitalized because it begins a new sentence within the quoted material.)

3. Capitalize the first, last, and main words in a title. Don't capitalize prepositions (*in, of, at, with, about...*), *fanboys* (*for, and, nor, but, or, yet, so*), or articles (*a, an,* or *the*). See p. 243 for more about titles.

I found a copy of Darwin's book *The Origin of Species* at a yard sale.

Our class read the essay "How to Write a Rotten Poem with Almost No Effort."

Shakespeare in Love is a film based on the life and work of William Shakespeare.

4. Capitalize specific names of people, places, languages, and nationalities.

English	Shah Rukh Khan	Cesar Chavez
Ireland	Spanish	Hindi
Ryan White	Philadelphia	Shanghai

5. Capitalize names of months, days of the week, and special days, but not the seasons.

March	Fourth of July	spring
Monday	Valentine's Day	summer
Earth Day	Labor Day	fall

6. **Capitalize a title of relationship if it takes the place of the person's name. If *my* (or *your, her, his, our, their*) is in front of the word, a capital is not used.**

I think Mom wrote to him.	*but*	I think my mom wrote to him.
We visited Aunt Sophie.	*but*	We visited our aunt.
They spoke with Grandpa.	*but*	They spoke with their grandpa.

7. **Capitalize names of particular people or things, but not general terms.**

I admire Professor Washborne.	*but*	I admire my professor.
We saw the famous Potomac River.	*but*	We saw the famous river.
Are you from the South?	*but*	Is your house south of the mountains?
I will take Philosophy 4 and English 100.	*but*	I will take philosophy and English.
She graduated from Sutter High School.	*but*	She graduated from high school.
They live at 119 Forest St.	*but*	They live on a beautiful street.
We enjoyed the Monterey Bay Aquarium.	*but*	We enjoyed the aquarium.

EXERCISES

Add all of the necessary capital letters to the sentences that follow.

Exercise 1

1. i recently saw the movie *v for vendetta*, and i wanted to learn more about it.

2. i found out that it's based on an extensive series of comic books.

3. they were written by alan moore and illustrated by david lloyd.

4. the original episodes of *v for vendetta* were published in black and white within a british comic series called *warrior*.

5. once the series caught on in the united states, dc comics began to publish it.

6. at that time, the creators added color to the drawings.

7. the letter v in the title *v for vendetta* stands for the main character, a mysterious costumed figure who calls himself v.

8. however, many other connections between the letter v and the roman numeral 5, which is written as a v, come up throughout the story.

9. v wears a mask that people in the united kingdom refer to as a guy fawkes mask.

10. guy fawkes was an english historical figure famous for his involvement in the gunpowder plot, which failed on the fifth of november in 1605.

Exercise 2

1. j.k. rowling is a very famous british writer.

2. her harry potter novels are among the most popular books ever written.

3. the series begins with the book *harry potter and the sorcerer's stone.*

4. in england, the first book is called *harry potter and the philosopher's stone.*

5. next comes *harry potter and the chamber of secrets*, which introduces the character of tom riddle.

6. in *harry potter and the prisoner of azkaban*, everyone is trying to catch the supposed criminal named sirius black.

7. the fourth book in the series is *harry potter and the goblet of fire.*

8. harry's friends ron and hermione aggravate him in *harry potter and the order of the phoenix.*

9. readers learn more about harry's nemesis, voldemort, in *harry potter and the half-blood prince.*

10. rowling's seventh and final book finishes off the story and is called *harry potter and the deathly hallows.*

Exercise 3

1. when my art teacher asked the class to do research on frida kahlo, i knew that the name sounded familiar.

2. then i remembered that the actress salma hayek starred in the movie *frida*, which was about this mexican-born artist's life.

3. frida kahlo's paintings are all very colorful and seem extremely personal.

4. she painted mostly self-portraits, and each one makes a unique statement.

5. one of these portraits is called *my grandparents, my parents, and i.*

6. kahlo gave another one the title *the two fridas.*

7. but my favorite of kahlo's works is *self-portrait on the borderline between mexico and the united states.*

8. in an article i read in *smithsonian* magazine, kahlo's mother explains that after frida was severely injured in a bus accident, she started painting.

9. kahlo's mother set up a mirror near her daughter's bed so that frida could use herself as a model.

10. in the *smithsonian* article from the november 2002 issue, kahlo is quoted as saying, "i never painted dreams. i painted my own reality."

Exercise 4

1. hidden beneath the church of st. martin-in-the-fields in london is a great little place to have lunch.

2. it's called the café in the crypt, and you enter it down a small staircase just off trafalgar square.

3. the café is literally in a crypt, the church's resting place for the departed.

4. the food is served cafeteria-style: soups, stews, sandwiches, and salads.

5. you grab a tray at the end of the counter and load it up with food as you slide it toward the cash register.

6. although the café is dark, the vaulted ceilings make it comfortable, and you can just make out the messages carved into the flat tombstones that cover the floor beneath your table.

7. one of london's newspapers ranked the café in the crypt high on its list of the "50 best places to meet in london."

8. the café in the crypt can even be reserved for private parties.

9. the café has its own gallery, called—what else?—the gallery in the crypt.

10. so if you're ever in london visiting historic trafalgar square, don't forget to look for that little stairway and grab a bite at the café in the crypt.

Source: www.stmartin-in-the-fields.org

Exercise 5

1. my mom and dad love old movie musicals.

2. that makes it easy to shop for them at christmas and other gift-giving occasions.

3. for mom's birthday last year, i gave her the video of gilbert and sullivan's comic opera *the pirates of penzance.*

4. it isn't even that old; it has kevin kline in it as the character called the pirate king.

5. i watched the movie with her, and i enjoyed the story of a band of pirates who are too nice for their own good.

6. actually, it is funnier than i thought it would be, and kevin kline sings and dances really well!

7. dad likes musicals, too, and i bought him tickets to see the revival of *chicago* on stage a few years ago.

8. he loves all those big production numbers and the synchronized choreography.

9. thanks to baz luhrmann and others, movie musicals made a comeback.

10. *moulin rouge* and the film version of *chicago* are just two examples.

REVIEW OF PUNCTUATION AND CAPITAL LETTERS

Punctuate these sentences. They include all the rules for punctuation and capitalization you have learned. Check your answers carefully. Sentences may require several pieces of punctuation or capital letters.

1. the alamo is the most popular historical site in texas

2. have you ever seen the first episode of the simpsons

3. the thompsons have remodeled their garage and now their daughter uses it as an apartment

4. how much will the midterm affect our grades the nervous student asked

5. we have refunded your money ms jones and will be sending you a confirmation letter

6. one of the teachers who visited the library left a textbook on the checkout counter

7. the united parcel service better known as ups was hiring on campus yesterday

8. even though i am enjoying my latin class i wish i had taken chinese instead

9. you always remember the date of my birthday march 20 but you forget your own

10. pink is a calming color but not if its hot pink

11. pam martha justin and luke left class early to practice their presentation in the hallway

12. finding a good deal for a new car online takes time patience and luck

13. my friend is reading a shakespeare play in her womens studies class

14. i wonder how much my history of textiles book will cost

15. in 2008 bill gates stepped down as the ceo of microsoft now he focuses on his charity the bill & melinda gates foundation

COMPREHENSIVE TEST

In these sentences, you'll find all the errors that have been discussed in the entire text. Try to name the error in the blank before each sentence, and then correct the error if you can. You may find any of the following errors:

adj	incorrect adjective
adv	incorrect adverb
apos	apostrophe
awk	awkward phrasing
c	comma needed
cap	capitalization
cliché	overused expression
cs	comma splice
dm	dangling modifier
frag	fragment
mm	misplaced modifier
p	punctuation
pro	incorrect pronoun
pro agr	pronoun agreement
ro	run-on sentence
shift	shift in time or person
sp	misspelled word
s-v agr	subject-verb agreement
verb	incorrect verb form
wordy	wordiness
ww	wrong word
//	not parallel

A perfect—or almost perfect—score will mean you've mastered the first part of the text.

1. _____ The twins spent their summer vacation at a computer camp and they loved it.

2. _____ Either the employees or the company have to take a cut in earnings.

3. _____ My counselor's advise has helped me so much.

4. _____ A bus full of high school students always pass me on my way to school.

5. _____ Amanda has the highest grade in the class I have the second highest.

6. _____ There are one or two questions that I have about your return policy.

7. _____ I love spring and summer; their my favorite seasons.

8. _____ The officer gave my sister and I a ticket for jaywalking.

9. _____ Camping can be fun, it can also be a nightmare.

10. _____ The students felt badly about mistreating the substitute.

11. _____ She is very creative, however, she is not a professional artist.

12. _____ I found a wrench left by a careless mechanic under the hood of my car.

13. _____ Have you read the essay called "Superman and Me," by Sherman Alexie.

14. _____ Everyone on the committee needed to cast their own separate vote.

15. _____ As we stepped outside the bright sunlight hurt our eyes.

16. _____ Some people take complements well; others don't like to hear praise.

17. _____ Your research paper uses more sources then mine, but mine has a better thesis.

18. _____ Its a perfect time of year to visit the rose garden.

19. _____ We don't know the final decision about whether our application was approved or not approved.

20. _____ The students held a debate on the proposed parking structure.

P A R T 4

Writing

What Is the Least You Should Know about Writing?

"Unlike medicine or the other sciences," William Zinsser points out, "writing has no new discoveries to spring on us. We're in no danger of reading in our morning newspaper that a breakthrough has been made in how to write [clearly]. . . . We may be given new technologies . . . to ease the burdens of composition, but on the whole we know what we need to know."

One thing is certain: people learn to write by *writing*—not by reading long discussions about writing. Therefore, the explanatory sections in Part 4 are as brief as they can be, and they include samples by both professional and student writers.

Understanding the basic structures and learning the essential skills covered in these sections will help you become a better writer.

Writing as Structure

Aside from the basics of word choice, spelling, sentence structure, and punctuation, what else do you need to understand to write better? Just as sentences are built according to accepted patterns, so are the larger "structures" in writing—paragraphs and essays, for example.

Think of writing as a system of structures, beginning small with words that connect to form phrases, clauses, and sentences. Then sentences connect to form paragraphs and essays. Each level has its own set of "blueprints." To communicate clearly in writing, words must be chosen and spelled correctly. Sentences must have a subject, a verb, and a complete thought. Paragraphs must be indented and should contain a main idea supported with sufficient detail. Essays should explore a valuable topic in several coherent paragraphs, usually including an introduction, a body, and a conclusion.

Not everyone approaches writing as structure, however. It is possible to write better without thinking about structure at all. A good place to start might be to write what you care about and to care about what you write. You can make an amazing amount of progress by simply being *genuine,* being who you are naturally. No one has to tell you to be yourself when you speak, but you might need encouragement to be yourself in your writing.

First-Person and Third-Person Approaches

You may have identified—and your professors may have pointed out—two main approaches to writing: the first-person approach (using *I, me, we, us*) and the third-person approach (using *one, he, she, it, they, them*). Note that the second-person pronoun—*you*—serves a special purpose, not commonly required in college papers. Writers use *you* to guide the reader through a process or to teach the reader how to do something, just as we use *you* in this book to teach "the least you should know about English." Unless you are writing a "how-to" paper of some kind, it's best to avoid using *you*. Let's focus, then, on first person vs. third person.

What are the benefits of the first-person approach? First-person pronouns allow you to express yourself directly ("I agree with Isaac Asimov.") and to connect with readers by including them in your observations. Here is an example from an essay about the concept of *home* on page 208: "Nesting. Why do we do it, why does it matter? Why do we care so much?" The first-person approach establishes a direct connection between the writer, the information, and the reader.

How does the third-person approach compare? The third-person point of view presents information about people and ideas more objectively. For example, you'll find this sentence in an excerpt about traffic on page 210: "So much time is spent in cars in the United States, studies show, that drivers (particularly men) have higher rates of skin cancer on their left sides. . . ." The third-person approach creates a comfortable distance between the writer, the information, and the reader.

Most writers don't consciously restrict themselves to one approach, but in some cases they do. Geoff Colvin's excerpt on page 226 and Patricia Fara's excerpt on page 233 adhere to the third-person approach because both involve biography. It is possible to use more than one approach when necessary. Professional writers often successfully blend first and third person (sometimes even first, second, and third person). See the reading about home on page 208 and the student essay about crying on page 231 for examples using a mixed point of view. Being aware of your options will help you grow as a writer.

Learning to write well is important, and confidence is the key. The Writing sections will help you build confidence, whether you are expressing your own ideas or presenting and responding to the ideas of others. Like the Sentence Structure sections, the Writing sections are best taken in order. However, each one discusses an aspect of writing that you can review on its own at any time.

Basic Structures

I. The Paragraph

A paragraph is unlike any other structure in English. It has its own visual profile: the first line is indented about five spaces, and sentences continue to fill the space between both margins until the paragraph ends (which may be in the middle of the line):

_____

_____

_____

_____

_____

_____.

As a beginning writer, you may forget to indent your paragraphs, or you may break off in the middle of a line within a paragraph, especially when writing in class. You must remember to indent whenever you begin a new paragraph and fill the space between the margins until it ends. (Note: In business writing, paragraphs are not indented but double-spaced in between.)

Defining a Paragraph

A typical paragraph develops one idea, usually phrased in a topic sentence from which all the other sentences in the paragraph radiate. The topic sentence does not need to begin the paragraph, but it most often does, and the other sentences support it with specific details. (For more on topic sentences and organizing paragraphs, see p. 220.) Paragraphs usually contain several sentences, though no set number is required. A paragraph can stand alone, but more commonly paragraphs are part of a larger composition, an essay. There are different kinds of paragraphs, based on the jobs they do.

Types of Paragraphs

SAMPLE PARAGRAPHS IN AN ESSAY

Introductory paragraphs begin essays. They provide background information about the essay's topic and usually include the thesis statement or main idea of the essay. (See p. 218 for information on how to write a thesis statement.) Here is the introductory paragraph of a student essay entitled "Really Understanding":

> I was so excited when my parents told me that I could join them in America. Four years earlier, they left China to open a Chinese fast food restaurant in Los Angeles. After my parents asked me to help them in the restaurant, I started to worry about my English because I knew only a few words that I learned in China. They told me not to worry, that I would quickly grasp the language once I heard it every day. Soon after I joined them, I made a big mistake because of my lack of English skills and my conceit. From this experience, I learned the importance of really understanding.

In this opening paragraph, the student leads up to the main idea—"the importance of really understanding"—with background information about her family's restaurant and "a big mistake" that she made.

Body paragraphs are those in the middle of essays. Each body paragraph contains a topic sentence and presents detailed information about one subtopic or idea that relates directly to the essay's thesis. (See p. 220 for more information on organizing body paragraphs.) Here are the body paragraphs of the same essay:

> My mistake happened during my second week at the restaurant. Usually my mom and I stayed in front, dishing out the food and keeping the tables clean while my father cooked in the kitchen. If I needed any help or if someone asked a question in English, my mom took care of it. However, that day my mom was sick, so she stayed home. My father and I went to work. He went straight to the kitchen, and I wiped those six square tables. By noon, my father had put big steaming trays of food on the counter. There was orange chicken, chicken with mushrooms, sweet and sour pork, kong bao chicken, and B.B.Q. pork. People came in, ordering their favorite foods.
>
> After I took care of the lunch rush, it was 2:00, but my favorite customer had not arrived. He was an old, kind, educated man who came in almost every day at 12:00. Why hadn't he come for the last two days? Was he sick? I looked at his favorite dish and started to worry about him. As I was wondering, he walked through the door. I smiled to see him. He ordered "the usual"—chicken with mushrooms and steamed rice—and sat down at the table in the left corner. I wanted to ask him why he came late to show that I cared about him, but more customers came in, and I had to serve them. They ordered all the chicken with mushrooms left in the tray, so I called to my father to cook more. The old man finished his food and walked toward me. He looked at that tray of newly cooked chicken with mushrooms for a second, and then he asked me something. I only understood the word *yesterday*. Since he had not

been in yesterday, I guessed that he said "Were you open yesterday?" I quickly answered, "Oh, yes!" He looked at me, and I could see that he didn't believe my answer, so I said "Yes" again. He just turned and walked away.

I did not understand what had happened. Two days passed, and he did not return. I thought about what he could have asked me and stared at the chicken and mushrooms for a minute. Suddenly, I realized what must have happened. He had come in two hours later than usual, at 2:00 that day, but the dish had been cooked at 12:00. Fast food cooked two hours earlier would not taste as fresh as if it were just prepared. He must have asked me "Was this *cooked* yesterday?" How could I have answered "Yes" not once but twice? He must have felt so bad about us. "He will never come back," I told myself.

Notice that each of the three body paragraphs discusses a single stage of the experience that taught her the value of really understanding.

Concluding paragraphs are the final paragraphs in essays. They bring the discussion to a close and share the writer's final thoughts on the subject. (See p. 220 for more about concluding paragraphs.) Here is the conclusion of the sample essay:

Four years have passed since then, and my favorite customer has not come back. It still bothers me. Why didn't I ask him to say the question again? If I had not been so conceited, I would have risked looking foolish for a moment. Now I am so repentant. I will never answer a question or do anything before I really understand what it means.

In this concluding paragraph, the student describes the effects of her experience—the regret and the lesson she learned.

SAMPLE OF A SINGLE-PARAGRAPH ASSIGNMENT

Single-paragraph writing assignments may be given in class or as homework. They test your understanding of the unique structure of a paragraph. They may ask you to react to a reading or to provide details about a limited topic. Here is a sample paragraph-length reaction following the class's reading of an essay called "What Is Intelligence, Anyway?" by Isaac Asimov. In his essay, Asimov explains that there are other kinds of intelligence besides just knowledge of theories and facts. This student shares Asimov's ideas about intelligence and uses personal experiences to support her reaction:

I agree with Isaac Asimov. Intelligence doesn't only belong to Nobel Prize winners. I define "intelligence" as being able to value that special skill a person has been born with. Not everyone is a math genius or a brain surgeon. For example, ask a brain surgeon to rotate the engine in a car. It isn't going to happen. To be able to take a certain skill that someone has inherited and push it to its farthest limits I would call "intelligence." Isaac Asimov's definition is similar to mine. He believes that academic questions are only correctly answered by academicians. He gives the example of a farmer. Questions on a farming test would only be correctly answered by a farmer. Not everyone has the same talent; we are all different. When I attend my math classes, I must always pay attention. If I don't, I end up struggling with what I missed. On the other hand, when I'm in my music classes, I really don't have to work hard because reading music, playing the piano, and singing all come easily to me. I see other students struggling with music the way I do with math. This is just another example of how skills and talents differ. Some people are athletic; others are brainy. Some people can sing; others can cook. It really doesn't matter what the skill might be. If it's a talent, to me that's a form of intelligence.

These shorter writing assignments help students practice presenting information within the limited structure of a paragraph. If this had been an essay-length reaction, the writer would have included more details about her own and other people's types of intelligence. And she may have wanted to quote from Asimov's essay and discuss his most important points at length.

II. The Essay

Like the paragraph, an essay has its own profile, usually including a title and several paragraphs.

Title

_____

_____

_____

_____

_____

_____.

_____

_____

_____

_____.

While the paragraph is the single building block of text used in almost all forms of writing (in essays, magazine articles, letters, novels, newspaper stories, e-mails, and so on), an essay is a larger, more complex structure.

The Five-Paragraph Essay and Beyond

The student essay analyzed on pages 204–205 illustrates the different kinds of paragraphs within essays. Many people like to include five paragraphs in an essay: an introductory paragraph, three body paragraphs, and a concluding paragraph. However, an essay can include any number of paragraphs. Three is a comfortable number of body paragraphs to start with—it is not two, which makes an essay seem like a comparison even when it isn't; and it is not four, which may be too many subtopics for the beginning writer to organize clearly.

An essay should be long enough to explore and support its topic without leaving unanswered questions in the reader's mind. As you become more comfortable with the flow of your ideas and gain confidence in your ability to express yourself, you can write longer essays. As with many skills, learning about writing begins with basic structures and then expands to include all possibilities.

Defining an Essay

There is no such thing as a typical essay. Essays may be serious or humorous, but the best of them present thought-provoking information or opinions. Try looking up the word _essay_ in a dictionary right now. Some words used to define an essay might need to be explained themselves:

An essay is _prose_ (meaning it is written in the ordinary language of sentences and paragraphs).

An essay is _nonfiction_ (meaning it deals with real people, factual information, actual opinions and events).

An essay is a *composition* (meaning it is created in parts that make up the whole, several paragraphs that explore a single topic or issue).

An essay is *personal* (meaning it shares the writer's unique perspective, even if only in the choice of topic, method of analysis, and details).

An essay is *analytical* and *instructive* (meaning it examines the workings of a subject and shares the results with the reader).

An essay may be *argumentative* (meaning it tries to convince the reader to accept an opinion or take action).

A Sample Essay

For an example of a brief piece of writing that fits the above definition, read the following essay, in which professional writer Dominique Browning explains how hard it is to define the word *home*.

Wandering Home

Every morning for weeks this spring I was awakened at five by the gentle, persistent cooing of a dove. Such a soft, lovely song, yet each day it was able to penetrate my dreams and lure me from my bed onto the balcony. I would search through the treetops for a glimpse of her until the damp chill sent me back indoors, and then finally one day I spotted her. She had built a nest on the trellis right over my door, wedged in amid a looping tangle of wisteria. I didn't dare go out onto the balcony again, for fear of disturbing her. Several days later the cooing stopped, and I suppose she became serious about laying and hatching her eggs, or why else would she sit so still and silent in her new home?

Nesting. Why do we do it, why does it matter? Why do we care so much? This has been on my mind lately, because I recently met a real wanderer, someone who is defiantly, dogmatically, devotedly nomadic. He isn't selfishly drifting; homeless by choice, he has spent the past 20 years living all over the world, doing good. Home for him is a provisional thing. I was so struck by the marked contrast to the way my friends and I have hunkered down, sent out roots, gathered treasure, gotten anchored. Maybe got stuck, who knows? I have always thought of making a home as one of those basic desires, but why should it be?

It is too easy to say home is where the heart is, where your loved ones sleep. Your loved ones can go with you, wherever you roam, and your loved ones can just as well be scattered to all corners of the world. We grow up (most of us) and ruthlessly leave behind the first homes of our childhood. And we often leave with the thought that the home we make for ourselves will be markedly different from the one made by our parents.

Some of us end up finding home in the town where we were raised. Some of us have ancestral homes, where generations of the family have been raised— places dear enough to draw everyone back. Some of us simply choose a place, or, if we are lucky, we feel the place chooses us. For some of us, a home is as large as a country—"I'm at home in France," one friend will say, or "I felt like I had come home when I got to Ireland"—and for others, a home is as small as the four walls of a room. Some of us move restlessly from house to house; others are restless within the house, rearranging the furniture, circling toward some approximation of beauty, serenity. And then some of us are so settled that our bodies creak to leave the sofa.

Maybe home is one of those subjects over which much of the world is divided: those who care about it passionately and those who don't give it a second thought. Maybe some of us are the fixed points of the compass: we're home, so others can twirl in circles around the globe. Some of us need the foundation of a home because our thoughts, dreams, emotions are constantly wheeling, wandering. And for some of us, there is the great adventure of making a home— you know, that thing about the world in a grain of sand or, dare I say, a smear of paint, a dab of plaster, the twinkle of a chandelier, the gleam of that old pearwood commode. The adamant wanderer finally confessed to having a warehouse full of stuff collected over the years, so even a nomad isn't immune to fantasies of home, however delayed the gratification of making one might turn out to be.

As for the dove: after a few quiet weeks, I noticed on the ground beneath her nest what I first took to be a bright curl of Styrofoam and of course turned out to be the fragment of an eggshell. One down. One untimely flight, one tiny lost soul. But still the dove sits, home for the time being.

Now that you have learned more about the basic structures of the paragraph and the essay, you are ready to practice the skills necessary to write them.

Writing Skills

III. WRITING IN YOUR OWN VOICE

All writing speaks on paper. And the person listening is the reader. Some beginning writers forget that writing and reading are two-way methods of communication, just like spoken conversations between two people. When you write, your reader hears you; when you read, you also listen.

When speaking, you express a personality in your choice of phrases, your movements, your tone of voice. Family and friends probably recognize your voice mail messages without your having to identify yourself. Would they also be able to recognize your writing? They would if you extended your *voice* into your writing.

Writing should not sound like talking, necessarily, but it should have a personality that comes from the way you decide to approach a topic, to develop it with details, to say it *your* way.

The beginning of this book discusses the difference between spoken English, which follows the looser patterns of speaking, and Standard Written English, which follows accepted patterns of writing. Don't think that the only way to add voice to your writing is to use the patterns of spoken English. Remember that Standard Written English does not have to be dull or sound academic. Look at this example of Standard Written English that has a distinct voice, part of the book *Traffic: Why We Drive the Way We Do (and What It Says about Us)* by Tom Vanderbilt:

Traffic has even shaped the food we eat. "One-handed convenience" is the mantra, with forkless foods like Taco Bell's hexagonal Crunchwrap Supreme, designed "to handle well in the car." I spent an afternoon in Los Angeles with an advertising executive who had, at the behest of that same restaurant chain, conducted a test, in actual traffic, of which foods were easiest to eat while driving. The main barometer of success or failure was the number of napkins used. But if food does spill, one can simply reach for Tide to Go, a penlike device for "portable stain removal," which can be purchased at one of the more than twelve hundred (and growing) CVS drugstores that feature a drive-through window. . . . Car commuting is so entrenched in daily life that National Public Radio refers to its most popular segments as "driveway moments," meaning that listeners are so riveted to a story they cannot leave their cars. . . . So much time is spent in cars in the United States, studies show, that drivers (particularly men) have higher rates of skin cancer on their left sides—look for the opposite effect in countries where people drive on the left.

Vanderbilt's examination of traffic's effect on us illustrates Standard Written English at its liveliest—from its sentence structures to its precise use of words. But more importantly, Vanderbilt's clear voice speaks to us and involves us in his fascination with traffic. You can involve your reader, too, by writing in your own voice. Here is an example of a student response to a brief assignment that asked her to describe a person who had recently made an impression on her.

Sitting at the kids' play area of my local mall one afternoon last week, I glanced over at another parent paying closer attention to his Blackberry than to his son. Enclosed in an oval-shaped ring with cushioned benches lining the edges, shoppers' kids ran around and played as their parents caught their breaths. In the middle of the play area lay an array of toys: boats, turtles, and small mounds of plastic for kids to crawl on and cylinders for them to crawl through. The workaholic looked up occasionally, making sure his son was still there. His thick brimmed glasses sat loosely on the bridge of his nose. His straight, jet-black hair was about a month overdue for a cut. In his late thirties, he was obviously concentrating more on his career and business than on his family in its youth. As I watched my own daughter run and play, I looked over to see the workaholic diligently typing away. I wasn't sure if he was checking e-mail, responding to e-mail, or updating his calendar, but his small brown eyes squinted, and this gave a pained look to his face; half deep in thought, the other half confused and stressed. Alternately leaning forward and slouching back, he caused his khaki pants to wrinkle and crease. His plaid shirt, unevenly tucked in, was held in place by an old and fading brown belt. His professional successes hadn't translated into any sense of style. Even on what might have been a rare day off, he couldn't escape the electronic leash that dominated his life. While his son grew up right in front of his eyes, his vision seemed way out of focus.

Notice that both professional and student writers can engage readers by telling stories (narration) and painting pictures with words (description). Narration and description require practice, but once you master them, you will strengthen and clarify your voice and increase interest in your writing.

Narration

Narrative writing tells the reader a story from the writer's personal experience, and since most of us like to tell stories, it is a good place to begin writing in your own voice. An effective narration allows readers to experience an event with the writer. Since we all see the world differently and feel unique emotions, the purpose of narration is to take readers with us through an experience. As a result, the writer gains a better understanding of what happened, and readers get to live other lives momentarily.

A Sample Essay

Listen to the written *voice* of this student writer sharing the story of her parent's divorce.

A Missing Part of Me

   Everyone wants a perfect family to count on at all
times. Yeah, I had all of that, but then all of a sudden,
my perfect family wasn't there anymore. My parents split
up when I was in the seventh grade. This experience was one
of the most difficult I had ever gone through. I hated that
I had to choose between going with my mom or staying with
my dad. I knew on that day that my life was going to change
forever.
   I can still remember sitting on the floor of the
closet getting my things, not knowing what to do. I had
decided to leave with my mom and my two younger brothers.
We had to gather our belongings and go stay with my Aunt
Doris. My older brother Danny had chosen to stay with my
dad. In the blink of an eye, my perfect family was gone.
   When we got to my aunt's house, it felt as if nothing
had happened. I always liked being there; it was a very
comfortable place for me. Moving in with her felt so
weird, as if it were all a dream. It all hit me again the
next morning when I woke up and realized I wasn't home.
Waking up and not being able to see my dad or Danny in
the morning was awful.
   I didn't want to show that I was sad about what had
happened. Every day seemed normal, but I could feel that
deep down inside there was a part of me missing. I tried
to keep up the same lifestyle I had before, but it was
really difficult. I did see my dad and Danny often, but
it wasn't the same anymore. I felt a big empty space
inside me, not knowing how to react to the new routine.

> "Everything happens for a reason" is a phrase many
> people say. I am thankful that I am able to visit with my
> dad whenever I want; I know people who haven't seen one
> of their parents since they split up, which is very sad.
> I think everyone should be able to spend time with both
> parents. I learned from this experience that I shouldn't
> take anything for granted. I will enjoy and appreciate
> all the time I get to spend with each of my parents. We
> never realized that the dinner we ate on the night before
> their break-up would be our last meal together as a
> family.

Description

Descriptive writing paints pictures with words that appeal to the reader's five senses—sight, sound, touch, taste, and smell. The writer of description often uses comparisons (figures of speech) to help readers picture one thing by imagining something else. For example, on page 209, Browning writes that "Some of us are the fixed points of the compass," and Vanderbilt describes the stain-remover Tide to Go as a "penlike device" in his excerpt about traffic on page 210 to help the reader *picture* the object.

In following paragraph, a student uses vivid details to bring the place she loves best to life:

> Fort Baker is located across the bay from San Francisco, almost under the Golden Gate Bridge. When I lived there as a child, nature was all I saw. Deer came onto our porch and nibbled the plants; raccoons dumped the trash cans over; skunks sprayed my brother because he poked them with a stick, and little field mice jumped out of the bread drawer at my sister when she opened it. Behind the house was a small forest of strong green trees; the dirt actually felt soft, and tall grassy plants with bright yellow flowers grew all around. I don't know the plants' real name, but my friend and I called it "sour grass." When we chewed the stems, we got a mouth full of sour juice that made our faces crinkle and our eyes water.

Here is another example of a descriptive paragraph, in which a student describes her car door's remote control device by comparing it to a robot.

MY ROBOT

My car door's remote control looks like a small robot's head. The front of it resembles a human face to me. It has two droopy eyes, a nose, and a mouth—eyes that cannot see, a nose that cannot smell, and a mouth that cannot open. It is wrapped in old shiny clear tape because its connector for a key ring is broken. The tape covers its face like an uncomfortable mask and secures the "robot" to a flat piece of leather, shaped like a bottle, which has a small chain attached to it. The chain holds my little robot like a prisoner on my key ring. My robot has a mind of its own. Like a small child, it can be capricious. Sometimes it does what I want it to do, but other times it does what it wants to do. Its brain shows that it's working by blinking a red light on its forehead. And even though my little robot looks old and tired, it usually works when I need it the most.

You may have noticed that many of the examples in this section use both narration and description. In fact, most effective writing—even a good résumé or biology lab report—calls for clear storytelling and vivid word pictures to engage the reader.

Writing Exercises

The following two exercises will help you develop your voice as a writer. For now, don't worry about topic sentences or thesis statements or any of the skills we'll teach you in the sections to come. Narration and description have their own logical structures. A narrated experience is a story with a beginning, a middle, and an end. And we describe things from top to bottom, side to side, and so on. You will find more Writing Exercises throughout this section.

Writing Exercise 1
NARRATION: FAMOUS SAYINGS

The following is a list of well-known expressions. No doubt you have had an experience that proves at least one of these to be true. Write a short essay that tells a story from your own life that relates to one of these sayings. (See if you can tell which of the sayings fit the experiences narrated in the essays "Wandering Home" on p. 208 and "A Missing Part of Me" on p. 212.) You might want to identify the expression you have chosen in your introductory paragraph. Then tell the beginning, middle, and end of the story. Be sure to use vivid details to bring the story to life. Finish with a brief concluding paragraph in which you share your final thoughts on the experience.

Life is what happens when you're busy making other plans.

Experience is the best teacher.

No two people are alike.

Absence makes the heart grow fonder.

Time heals all wounds.

Writing Exercise 2

DESCRIPTION: A VALUABLE OBJECT

Describe an object that means a lot to you. It could be a gift that you received, an object you purchased for yourself, an heirloom in your family, a memento from your childhood, or just something you carry around with you every day. Your goal is to make the reader visualize the object. Try to use details and comparisons that appeal to the reader's senses in some way. Look back at the examples for inspiration. Be sure the reader knows—from your choice of details—what the object means to you.

IV. FINDING A TOPIC

You will most often be given a topic to write about; however, when the assignment asks you to choose your own topic without any further assistance, try to go immediately to your interests.

Look to Your Interests

If the topic of your paper is something you know about and—more important—something you *care* about, then the whole process of writing will be smoother and more enjoyable for you. If you collect coins, if you can draw, or even if you just enjoy going to the movies, bring that knowledge and enthusiasm into your papers.

Take a moment to think about and jot down a few of your interests now (no matter how unrelated to school they may seem), and then save the list for use later when deciding what to write about. One student's list of interests might look like this:

buying and selling on eBay

playing poker on weekends

skiing in the mountains in winter

shopping at flea markets

Another student's list might be very different:

playing the piano

going to concerts

watching "Bollywood" movies

drawing pictures of my friends

Still another student might list the following interests:

bowling in a league

participating in my book club

traveling in the summer

buying lottery tickets

These students have listed several worthy topics for papers. And because they are personal interests, the students have the details needed to support them. With a general topic to start with, you can use several ways to gather the details you will need to support it in a paragraph or an essay.

Focused Free Writing (or Brainstorming)

Free writing is a good way to begin. When you are assigned a paper, try writing for ten minutes, putting down all your thoughts on one subject—"traveling in the summer," for example. Don't stop to think about organization, sentence structures, capitalization, or spelling—just let details flow onto the page. Free writing will help you see what material you have and will help you figure out what aspects of the subject to write about.

Here is an example:

> When my friends and I went to Sea World in San Diego last summer, we saw an amazing bird show. The birds weren't in cages or tied to perches. Instead they flew freely down out of the sky and out of windows in a phony town that surrounded the stage. And they didn't just have parrots and cockatoos like all the other bird shows I've ever seen before. In those shows the birds just did tricks for treats. But Sea World's show had eagles and falcons and really tall cranes with feathers that looked like ladies' hats on their heads. It was really amazing.

Now the result of this free writing session is certainly not ready to be typed and turned in as a paragraph. But what did become clear in it was that the student could probably compare the two types of bird shows she has seen—the species of birds used and how they were presented.

Clustering

Clustering is another way of putting ideas on paper before you begin to write an actual draft. A cluster is more visual than free writing. You could cluster the topic of "flea markets," for instance, by putting it in a circle in the center of a piece of paper and then drawing lines to new circles as ideas or details occur to you. The idea is to free your mind from the limits of sentences and paragraphs to generate pure details and ideas. When you are finished clustering, you can see where you want to go with a topic.

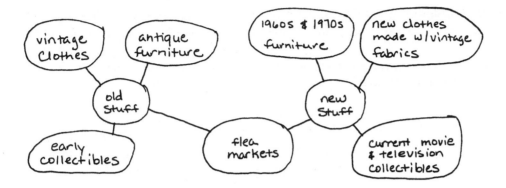

This cluster shows that the student has found two aspects of her book club that she could write about. This cluster might lead to another where the student chooses one subcategory—club members, for instance—and thinks of more details about them.

Talking with Other Students

It may help to talk to others when deciding on a topic. Many teachers divide their students into groups at the beginning of an assignment. Talking with other students helps you realize that you see things just a little differently. *Value* the difference—it will help your written voice that we discussed earlier emerge.

Writing Exercise 3
LIST YOUR INTERESTS

Make a list of four or five of your own interests. Be sure that they are as specific as the examples listed on page 215. Keep the list for later assignments.

Writing Exercise 4
DO SOME FREE WRITING

Choose one of your interests, and do some focused free writing about it. Write for ten minutes with that topic in mind but without stopping. Don't worry about anything such as spelling or sentence structures while you are free writing. The results are meant to help you find out what you have to say about the topic *before* you start to write a paper about it. Save the results for a later assignment.

Writing Exercise 5

TRY CLUSTERING IDEAS

Choose another of your interests. Put it in the center of a piece of paper, and draw a cluster of details and ideas relating to it following the sample on page 217. Take the cluster as far as it will go. Then choose one aspect to cluster again on its own. This way you will arrive at specific, interesting details and ideas—not just the first ones that come to mind. Save the results of all your efforts.

V. ORGANIZING IDEAS

Most important to keep in mind, no matter what you are writing, is the idea you want to get across to the reader. Whether you are writing a paragraph or an essay, you must have in mind a single idea that you want to express. In a paragraph, such an idea is called a *topic sentence;* in an essay it's called a *thesis statement,* but they mean the same thing—an idea you want to get across. We will begin with a discussion of thesis statements.

Thesis Statements

Let's choose one of the student interests listed on page 215. "Buying and selling on eBay" is just a general topic; it doesn't make a point. What about eBay? Why do you like it? What does it do for you or for others? What point about eBay would you like to present to your reader? You might write a sentence like this:

Buying and selling on eBay is fun and educational.

This sentence is a start, but it's not focused enough to develop. You might move into more specific territory and write one of the following sentences:

I've learned a lot about business and geography by buying and selling on eBay.

or

Buyers and sellers learn a lot about business and geography through their transactions on eBay.

Now you have said something specific in two different ways. The first sentence uses the first-person pronoun *I.* The second sentence discusses "buyers" and "sellers" in general and uses *their,* a third-person pronoun, to refer to them. Some writing instructors may ask you to avoid writing in the first-person, and others may encourage you to use it. (See p. 202 for more discussion of these approaches.) Whichever approach you use, when you write in one sentence the point you want to present to your reader, you have begun writing a thesis statement.

You may have a general idea in mind when you begin to write, but the support for it will evolve as you write. You can develop your thesis in various ways, but behind whatever you write will be your ruling thought, your reason for writing a particular essay, your thesis.

For any writing assignment, after you have done some free writing or clustering to explore your topic, the next step is to write a thesis statement. As you write your thesis statement, keep two rules in mind:

1. A thesis statement must be a sentence *with a subject and a verb* (not merely a topic).

2. A thesis statement must be *an idea that you can explain or defend* (not simply a statement of fact).

Writing Exercise 6

TOPIC, FACT, OR THESIS?

Which of the following are merely topics or facts, and which are statements that you could explain or defend in an essay? In front of each one that is just a topic or a fact, write TOPIC or FACT. In front of each one that could be a thesis statement, write THESIS. Check your answers.

1. _____ I have a friend who never lets me drive her car.

2. _____ People who do not drink enough water.

3. _____ Many people are college students because their parents want them to be.

4. _____ The meaning of the word *happiness.*

5. _____ Your life can change for the better if you start doing yoga.

6. _____ Most Americans see several movies a month.

7. _____ I woke up to find graffiti on my fence again.

8. _____ The use of cell phones in cars.

9. _____ A science fiction story compared to a love story.

10. _____ Prequels are more of a fad than a step forward in moviemaking.

Writing Exercise 7

WRITE A THESIS STATEMENT

Use your free-writing or clustering results from Writing Exercises 4 and 5 (pp. 217–218) and write at least one thesis statement based on your interests. Be sure that the thesis you write is phrased as a complete thought that can be defended or explained in an essay.

Organizing an Essay

Once you have written a good thesis and explored your topic through discussion with others or by free writing and clustering, you are ready to organize your essay.

First, you need an introductory paragraph. It should catch your reader's interest, provide necessary background information, and either include or suggest your thesis statement. (See p. 204 and p. 212 for two examples of student writers' introductory paragraphs.) In your introductory paragraph, you may also list supporting points, but a more effective way is to let them unfold paragraph by paragraph rather than to give them all away in the beginning of the essay. Even if your supporting points don't appear in your introduction, your reader will easily spot them later if your paper is clearly organized.

Your second paragraph will present your *first* supporting point—everything about it and nothing more.

Your next paragraph will be about your *second* supporting point—all about it and nothing more.

Each additional paragraph will develop *another* supporting point.

Finally, you'll need a concluding paragraph. In a short paper, it isn't necessary to restate your points. Your conclusion may be brief; even a single sentence to round out the paper may do the job. Remember that the main purpose of a concluding paragraph is to bring the paper to a close by sharing your final thoughts on the subject. (See p. 205 and p. 213 for two examples of successful concluding paragraphs.)

Learning to write a brief organized essay of this kind will help you to distinguish between the parts of an essay. Then when you're ready to write a longer paper, you'll be able to organize it clearly and be more creative in its design and content.

Topic Sentences

A topic sentence does for a paragraph what a thesis statement does for an essay—it states the main idea. Like thesis statements, topic sentences must be phrased as complete thoughts to be proven or developed through the presentation of details. But the topic sentence introduces an idea or subtopic that is the right size to cover in a paragraph. The topic sentence doesn't have to be the first sentence in a paragraph. It may come at the end or even in the middle, but putting it first is most common.

Each body paragraph should contain only one main idea, and no detail or example should be in a paragraph if it doesn't support the topic sentence or help to transition from one paragraph to another. (See p. 204 and pp. 208–209 for more examples of effective body paragraphs within essays and of paragraphs alone.)

Organizing Body Paragraphs (or Single Paragraphs)

A single paragraph or a body paragraph within an essay is organized in the same way as an entire essay, only on a smaller scale. Here's the way you learned to organize an essay:

Thesis: stated or suggested in introductory paragraph

First supporting paragraph

Second supporting paragraph

Additional supporting paragraphs

Concluding paragraph

And here's the way to organize a paragraph:

Topic sentence

First supporting detail or example

Second supporting detail or example

Additional supporting details or examples

Concluding or transitional sentence

You should have several details to support each topic sentence. If you find that you have little to say after writing the topic sentence, ask yourself what details or examples will make your reader believe that the topic sentence is true for you.

Transitional Expressions

Transitional expressions within a paragraph and between paragraphs help the reader move from one detail or supporting point in an essay to the next. When first learning to organize an essay, beginning writers may start each body paragraph and every new example with a transitional expression (*first, for example, next*). These common transitions are useful and clear, but they can sound mechanical. To improve the flow of your ideas and the strength of your written voice, try to replace some of these transitions with specific phrases (*at the start of the meeting* or *in many people's minds*) or with dependent clauses (*when drivers use cell phones* or *as I approached the intersection*).

Here are some transitions that show sequence:

Previously	Next	One (example, point. . .)
Later	Then	Another (example, point. . .)
Eventually	Finally	

Here are a few to show addition:

Also	First
Furthermore	Second
In addition	Third . . .

Here are several that show comparison or contrast:

Similarly	In the same way	In comparison
However	On the other hand	In contrast

Here are those that show consequence:

Therefore	Consequently	In conclusion
As a result	In other words	

Writing Exercise 8

ADDING TRANSITIONAL EXPRESSIONS

Place appropriate expressions from the lists above into the blanks in the following paragraph to make the transitions clear. Then try to replace one or two with specific transitional phrases or clauses to improve the flow of ideas and to add interest. Compare your choices with the ones suggested in the answers.

Whenever I plan a trip that involves driving long distances, I go through the following routine. _____, I make sure that I have a recent map of the highways so that if I get lost along the way, I won't panic. _____, even if I do have a map to the city of my destination, I go online to get specific driving directions to the hotel from the highway. _____ way that I prepare is to check my car's tires and get its engine serviced, if necessary. I know how important cell phones are on long drives; _____, I never forget to bring mine. _____, before I leave my house on the day of the trip, I call the Highway Patrol hotline to see if there are any highway closures. This routine has always worked for me. _____, I would give it up for a car with its own navigation system.

Writing Exercise 9

HOW DO YOU GET READY TO WRITE?

To practice using transitions, write a paragraph about the steps you take to get ready to sit down and write a paper. Where do you go? What materials do you gather? How do you get in the right frame of mind to write? Report the steps in order, one by one, using transitional expressions from the list on page 221 wherever you see fit. Sometimes it's helpful to add humor to a process-based paragraph or essay to liven up the steps involved in an ordinary process and connect with the reader.

VI. Supporting with Details

Now you're ready to support your main idea with subtopics and specific details. That is, you'll think of ways to prove that your thesis is true. How could you convince your reader that buying and selling on eBay can teach valuable lessons about business and geography? Try adding the word "because" to the end of your thesis to generate at least three more specific statements. You might come up with something like the following:

> I've learned a lot about business and geography by buying and selling on eBay. (because)
>
> **or**
>
> Buyers and sellers learn a lot about business and geography through their transactions on eBay. (because)

1. Honesty and fairness are very important when dealing with others on eBay.

2. Active eBay members must keep accurate records and be very organized.

3. Buyers and sellers learn about shipping methods and policies around the world.

NOTE—Imagining the word *because* at the end of your thesis will help you find subtopics that are clear and parallel in their level and presentation of ideas.

Types of Support

The subtopics developing a thesis and the details presented in a paragraph are not always *reasons* (like the ones outlined in the **analysis** of buying and selling on eBay, for instance). Supporting points may take many forms based on the purpose of the essay or paragraph. Other kinds of support include the following:

> *examples* (in an **illustration**)
>
> *meanings* (in a **definition**)
>
> *steps* or *stages* (in a "how-to" paper or **process analysis**)
>
> *types* or *kinds* (in a **classification**)
>
> *personal experiences* (in any kind of writing)
>
> *facts, statistics,* and *expert opinions* (in an **argument**)
>
> *causes* and/or *effects* (in a **causal analysis**)
>
> *similarities* and/or *differences* (in a **comparison-contrast**)

Whatever form they take, supporting points should develop the main idea expressed in the thesis statement of the essay or the topic sentence of the paragraph and help prove it to be true.

A Sample Final Draft

Here is the final draft of a first-person student essay about a challenging assignment for college students. Notice how the body paragraphs map out one student's personal experience as she struggles through the process of learning to draw a self-portrait. This essay could also have presented the same stages from a third-person point of view, using "they" to "them" to refer to "art students." The result would focus more on the process of drawing a self-portrait than on one student's unique experience with the assignment.

Drawing a Blank

On the day my drawing class started to learn about self-portraits last year, each of us had to bring a mirror to class. In backpacks and purses were make-up mirrors, dressing table mirrors—large and small mirrors of every shape and kind. I was nervous about drawing a self-portrait, so I brought only a tiny plastic pocket mirror. That way if I didn't do a good job, it would be my mirror's fault. I discovered that drawing a self-portrait involves observing myself from the outside and the inside.

I had never done well on human figure drawing. First our teacher, Ms. Newman, demonstrated the proportion of a human figure; she explained that a human body measures about seven times a human head. She used a tiny piece of chalk to draw on the board while she was talking. Then she showed how to sketch the face, from eyebrows to eyes, nose, mouth, and ears. After her lecture, she told us to begin drawing our self-portraits.

We all set up our mirrors. The ceiling danced with the reflections they made as we got to work. I looked down at my little square of scratched-up plastic and started to draw gingerly on my paper. I tried to put the eyes, nose, and mouth I had seen on the paper. When I finished, I wondered, "Who the heck is this?" The drawing didn't look anything like me. I was frustrated and sank down in my chair. After a minute, I told myself, "Try again." I drew another one, and it was a little better.

But I could not really call it a self-portrait because it didn't look exactly like me.

I asked Ms. Newman for help. She glanced at my previous attempts and said, "A good self-portrait doesn't just look like you, it also shows your personality and your feeling." She did not see either of these in my other drawings. So I tried again. I borrowed my friend's big glass mirror and stared into it; I was not only looking at my face, but also deep inside my face. This time, I freely sketched the shape of my face. Then I roughly placed my eyebrows, eyes, nose, mouth, and ears. I looked into the mirror again and drew the expression I saw there.

When my portrait was finished, I wondered at the amazing work I had done. Even though it did not perfectly look like me, it really showed my personality and emotions through the contrast of light and dark. When Ms. Newman saw it, she applauded. Not only did I get an A on this project; it also became one of the strongest pieces in my portfolio. I realized that few things can be done successfully the first time. If I had given up after my first try, I would never have captured the real me.

(Note: See p. 240 for a rough draft of this essay, before its final revisions.)

Learning to support your main ideas with vivid details is perhaps the most important goal you can accomplish in this course. Many writing problems are not really writing problems but *thinking* problems. Whether you're writing a research paper or merely an answer to a test question, if you take enough time to think, you'll be able to discover a clear thesis statement and support it with paragraphs full of meaningful details.

Writing Exercise 10

WRITE AN ESSAY ON ONE OF YOUR INTERESTS

Return to the thesis statement you wrote about one of your interests for Writing Exercise 6 on p. 219. Now write a thoughtful essay about it (using either the first-person or third-person approach, see p. 202). You can explain the allure of your interest, its drawbacks or its benefits. Don't forget to include details from the free writing or clustering you may have done on the topic beforehand and to use meaningful transitional expressions.

VII. Choosing and Using Quotations

Including quotations from another writer can add dimension and depth to your paragraphs and essays. Try to think of a reading as a friendly resource, inviting you to quote from it in order to present ideas beyond your own. Remember, you're in control of what any other writer "says" in your writing by choosing what to quote and where to include quotations in your paper.

Choosing Quotations

Imagine you've been asked to read a short selection and write a response that answers the following question: "Which is more important for success, talent or hard work?" You should have no trouble using the previously discussed methods to organize your ideas about talent vs. hard work and support them with details and observations of your own. But the assignment also requires that you include quotations from the reading prompt in your response.

Let's look at the sample reading below. It's about how hard work may have contributed as much to Mozart's music as his legendary talent did. As you read this brief excerpt from Geoff Colvin's book *Talent Is Overrated*, try to spot phrases or statements that you think would be particularly quotable in a paper about talent vs. hard work. Also notice that Colvin includes a quotation to support his own ideas:

> Mozart is the ultimate example of the divine-spark theory of greatness. Composing music at age five, giving public performances as a pianist and violinist at age eight, going on to produce hundreds of works, some of which are widely regarded as ethereally great and treasures of Western culture, all in the brief time before his death at age thirty-five—if that isn't talent, and on a mammoth scale, nothing is. . . .
>
> Mozart's method of composing was not quite the wonder it was long thought to be. For nearly two hundred years many people have believed that he had a miraculous ability to compose entire major pieces in his head, after which writing them down was mere clerical work. That view was based on a famous letter in which he says as much: "the whole, though it be long, stands almost finished and complete in my mind . . . the committing to paper is done quickly enough . . . and it rarely differs on paper from what it was in my imagination."
>
> That report certainly does portray a superhuman performer. The trouble is, this letter is a forgery, as many scholars later established. Mozart did not conceive whole works in his mind, perfect and complete. Surviving manuscripts show that Mozart was constantly revising, reworking, crossing out and rewriting whole sections, jotting down fragments and putting them aside for months or years. Though it makes the results no less magnificent, he wrote music the way ordinary humans do.

One way to begin quoting effectively is to highlight the details or phrasing that you respond to the most in a reading. Be choosy. Just as you would choose ring tones or clothes to reflect your personality, you can pick particular quotations from readings to enhance the effect of your writing. Remember that quotations must reproduce the original's exact wording, so transcribe them very carefully and place them within quotation marks. (See p. 187.)

Let's say you've chosen these four sentences to quote from in your essay:

"Mozart is the ultimate example of the divine-spark theory of greatness."

"For nearly two hundred years many people have believed that he had a miraculous ability to compose entire major pieces in his head, after which writing them down was mere clerical work."

"Surviving manuscripts show that Mozart was constantly revising, reworking, crossing out and rewriting whole sections, jotting down fragments and putting them aside for months or years."

"Though it makes the results no less magnificent, he wrote music the way ordinary humans do."

Using Quotations

The next step is to cut the quotations down to a manageable size so they won't overpower your ideas.

"Mozart is the ultimate example ~~of the divine-spark theory~~ of greatness."

"For nearly two hundred years many people have believed that he had a miraculous ability to compose entire major pieces in his head~~, after which writing them down was mere clerical work~~."

"~~Surviving manuscripts show that Mozart was~~ constantly revising, reworking, crossing out and rewriting whole sections, jotting down fragments and putting them aside for months or years."

"~~Though~~ it makes the results no less magnificent, ~~he~~ wrote music the way ordinary humans do."

Read on to see how these shortened quotations can be included in the paper using signal phrases and proper punctuation to let the reader know where you've left out or changed wording from the original.

Signal Phrases and Punctuation

A quotation by itself—even if it's a complete statement such as "I have a dream"—cannot function as a sentence in your paper without a signal phrase. The job of a signal phrase is to identify the writer or source of the quotation and to provide a subject and a verb to anchor the quotation within your paper. The italicized subject and verb in the following sentence make up its signal phrase:

In his famous speech, *Martin Luther King, Jr. declares*, "I have a dream."

A **signal phrase** should include the writer's name or other identification and a strong verb like the ones listed below. Avoid relying on the verb *says* or *writes* when so many more interesting verbs like the following are available:

explains	suggests	argues	feels
points out	asserts	illustrates	adds
believes	thinks	notes	insists
claims	observes	declares	reports
acknowledges	admits	states	concludes

A signal phrase can be placed *at the beginning*, *in the middle*, or *at the end* of the quotation to add variety to your sentences. Use commas to set off signal phrases and an **ellipsis** (. . .) to show where you have cut words from full-length quoted sentences. No ellipsis is necessary when quoting only phrases from the original. If an ellipsis ends the sentence, the period makes a total of four dots:

Signal phrase at the beginning of the quotation (a comma follows the signal phrase):

Geoff Colvin believes, "Mozart is the ultimate example of . . . greatness."

Signal phrase in the middle of the quotation (commas surround the signal phrase):

"For nearly two hundred years," **Colvin explains**, "many people have believed that he had a miraculous ability to compose entire major pieces in his head. . . ."

Signal phrase at the end of the quotation (a comma comes before the signal phrase):

Mozart worked very hard, "constantly revising, reworking, crossing out and rewriting whole sections, jotting down fragments and putting them aside for months or years," **Colvin adds**.

You may have noticed that the previous examples use an ellipsis when words have been left out of the *middle* or the *end* of a shortened quote, but not the *beginning* of one. When leaving off the first words of a quotation, maintain the small letter that the quoted part begins with to show that the opening words have been cut.

When a quotation is introduced by "that," the signal phrase does *not* require a comma. Note that any change made to a quote should placed within **brackets** [ ]:

Colvin feels *that* "it makes [Mozart's] results no less magnificent. . . ."

Once you've identified the single source writer's name in previous sentences, you can include *brief* quotations without a signal phrase:

> As a music major myself, I'm glad to know that Mozart "wrote music the way ordinary humans do."

A Sample Paragraph Using Quotations

The following paragraph answers the question about talent vs. hard work and uses quotations from the reading on page 226 to support the writer's ideas and experiences:

> I always thought that talent was more important than hard work. I never tried anything for too long if I didn't have the talent to do it easily. For instance, I started learning the violin and gave up within two weeks because it didn't feel as natural for me as the guitar. After reading Geoff Colvin's information about Mozart, I wish I had tried harder. Many people think of Mozart when the word *talent* comes up. Colvin believes, "Mozart is the ultimate example of . . . greatness." Without even studying Mozart's life, everyone seems to know about his gifts. "For nearly two hundred years," Colvin explains, "many people have believed that he had a miraculous ability to compose entire major pieces in his head. . . ." However, Mozart worked very hard, "constantly revising, reworking, crossing out and rewriting whole sections, jotting down fragments and putting them aside for months or years," Colvin adds. I never pictured Mozart doing so much hard work. Colvin feels that "it makes [Mozart's] results no less magnificent. . . ." I agree with him. As a music major myself, I'm glad to know that Mozart "wrote music the way ordinary humans do." Next semester, I might give the violin one more try.

GUIDELINES FOR INCLUDING QUOTATIONS

1. Choose a sentence that you would like to quote from a reading.
2. Consider shortening the phrasing of the original sentence for clarity.
3. Put quotation marks around the other writer's words.
4. Write a signal phrase to identify the writer or source of the quotation.
5. Use a comma (or commas) to set off the signal phrase in your sentence.
6. No comma is necessary if the word "that" introduces the quotation.
7. Use brackets [ ] to identify a change made within a quotation.
8. Use an ellipsis . . . in place of words cut from the middle or end of a quoted sentence (but not when quoting just a phrase).

These methods for including quotations are not difficult to learn; with practice, they will become second nature. Understanding how to quote from a reading will help you complete more complex assignments in the future. Once you know how to include quotations from a single source effectively, you will be ready to learn how to quote from multiple readings and to document them using the Modern Language Association (MLA) format. For now, just practice the basic methods of quoting from one source.

Writing Exercise 11

WRITE A PARAGRAPH USING QUOTATIONS

Return to the essay "Wandering Home" on page 208 and find three quotations that you would like to use to support your own ideas in a short paragraph that answers the question "Why is *home* so difficult to define?" Be sure to follow the "Guidelines for Including Quotations" on page 229. Feel free to imitate the Sample Paragraph Using Quotations on page 229.

VIII. WRITING AN ARGUMENT

Writing assignments often ask you to take a stand on an issue or to share an opinion and prove that it is valid. Such writing is called *argumentation,* but it doesn't involve "fighting" or "arguing" in the sense that these words might be used in everyday life. In fact, intense emotions can weaken an argument if they are not balanced by logic and fairness. The purpose of a written argument is to convince the reader to value your opinion and possibly to agree with it.

Taking a Stand and Proving Your Point

A strong written argument fulfills three basic requirements. First, it takes a clear stand on an issue or a controversial topic. Second, it provides logical and relevant support for the writer's position. And third, it discusses the issue or topic in a fair-minded way, taking other points of view into account. Let's look at some examples by both professional and student writers.

An in-class assignment asked students to write a short essay in response to the following prompt:

> In his book <u>Crying: The Natural & Cultural History of Tears</u>, Tom Lutz explores the "universal" aspect of crying: he asks, "Why do we cry? Tears of happiness, tears of joy, the proud tears of a parent, tears of mourning, frustration, defeat—what do they have in common?" Lutz continues with his questions, "Why do certain ways of feeling make us cry and why does crying feel the way it does? How do we understand other people's weeping?" In short, he wonders, "What, exactly, do tears express?" Lutz also notes that "The historical change for men over the last century makes crying, however infrequent, the rule rather than the exception" and argues that "this is undoubtedly a good thing. To deny tears is to deny a fundamental pleasure. . . ." Considering Lutz's comments and your own experiences, do you accept crying as a valuable social activity?

In other words, is crying "a good thing"? Why, or why not? Try to convince the reader with a fair-minded approach and with many examples for support.

A Sample Argument

As you might imagine, this assignment prompted a variety of responses from student writers. In the short essay that follows, one student argues that crying is for the strong—not weak—at heart and confesses that she wishes she could cry more often:

Is Crying a Weakness or a Strength?

From time to time, all people cry. Some cry more than others, but every person alive has to have cried at least once. When most people think of crying, they associate it with pain, hurt feelings, hearts breaking, or the complete opposite—"tears of joy." Tears of joy may come from watching a child take its first steps, attending a wedding, or accomplishing a life-long dream. Now, in society tears of joy are commonly acceptable; however, tears of sadness are a different story.

Some view crying as a weakness that comes from not being able to control our reactions to pain and sorrow, similar to how most children act. When a child bumps his head, he cries. When a child can't find his toy, he cries. When his mommy won't give him a cookie or his daddy won't carry him, he cries. But as children get older, they get stronger and learn to be tough and fend for themselves. I think that this process partially explains why people are looked down on for crying. Crying is viewed as a childish thing to do, and adults should be able to just get over it.

But what about when a loved one dies, or when a person witnesses a tragedy? Under these circumstances, it is more acceptable to cry by society's standards. When 9/11 happened, the news showed hundreds of people crying, and that was totally acceptable. However, when someone loses a job and cries about it, that might be considered a weakness, especially if it is a man who is crying. Men are not supposed to show emotions, right? Wrong! Lutz explains that when a man cries, it is "undoubtedly a good thing. To deny tears is to deny a fundamental pleasure" that is extremely healthy for anyone's mental state.

I wish I could cry more. The fact is, though, I can't bring myself to tears. For some reason, it is extremely hard for me to cry. The only time that I do cry is when someone else is hurting and I can't do anything to help. The last time I cried was when my dad cried. But when I see a homeless puppy on the side of the road or when I watch <u>The Notebook</u>, a tear will never fall from my eyes. The funny thing is that I'm a very emotional person, and these things really do get to me.

I believe that crying is a good way to just let it all out. It breaks down the walls and barriers we have built and lets our emotions flow. Although crying may be viewed as a weakness, only truly strong and stable people can kick their pride in the butt and just cry until they have no more tears.

This student's in-class essay fulfills the three requirements of a strong written argument by clearly stating her position in her final paragraph, by describing many of her observations about crying to support her position, and by fairly acknowledging that some people will always view crying as a weakness.

Obviously, the student's paper would have been longer and more developed if it had been an out-of-class essay with a two- or three-week deadline. Then this student could have read Lutz's whole book and included factual support with her personal experiences. She could have interviewed fellow students and included their comments. She might have found an expert who counters her opinion about crying and written her essay as a comparison-contrast of the expert's opinions and her own.

THREE REQUIREMENTS OF A STRONG WRITTEN ARGUMENT

1. **1.** Takes a clear stand on an issue or a controversial topic.
2. **2.** Provides logical and relevant support (personal experience, opinions of experts, facts and statistics, results of interviews).
3. **3.** Discusses the issue or topic in a fair-minded way, allowing for other points of view.

Writing Exercise 12

TAKE A STAND ON GRADES

Read and carefully consider the following paragraph proposing a few changes in education:

> Education at all levels should be changed so that it is completely grade-free and noncompetitive. All letter grades should be eliminated and replaced by a pass/fail system, and scores of any kind should be provided as information only, not for the purpose of ranking. Students should also receive credit for self-study and Internet-gained knowledge and skills. Attendance and completion of assignments should be the only requirements for moving ahead in a course of study. In addition, students should be allowed to repeat courses, even after successfully completing all of the assignments, if they so choose. Students should take charge of their own educations and learn at their own pace.

Do you agree or disagree with this hypothetical proposal to eliminate grades and give students total flexibility in their studies? Take care to consider the issue from all angles. How would such profound changes affect students, teachers, parents, school officials, and the public? Then use what you've learned about argumentation to write a brief essay in which you take a stand on one side of this issue or the other. Refer to the student sample "Is Crying a Weakness or a Strength?" as a model for using relevant experiences and observations to prove your point, and remember to be fair-minded in your presentation.

Reading Longer, More Challenging Works

See if you can spot all of the elements of strong written argument in the following professional sample from the book *Scientists Anonymous: Great Stories of Women in Science,* by Patricia Fara. This biographical reading about Rachel Carson and her work as a scientist and writer may require you to look up several words in the dictionary. Notice that Fara also quotes a bit of Carson's writing to give a clear example of its impact and importance.

Although you may feel challenged by the level of writing and the references to history, politics, and sociology in this excerpt, your own feelings about gender and about the environment should make it easy for you to relate to the issues that Fara addresses in her portrayal of Rachel Carson as "The Green Pioneer."

THE GREEN PIONEER

One common form of gender prejudice is to say that women are closer to nature than men, and are therefore (supposedly) better at studying plants and animals. At first Rachel Carson (1907–64) seemed to match this stereotype—she was a superb writer who won prizes for her poetic books about the oceans and marine life. But in her mid-fifties, she wrote a very different type of book, *Silent Spring*, which accused scientists of destroying the world.

Carson loved writing, and at university in America she studied English before switching to science. After her father died she had to support her family, and she combined her twin passions—literature and marine biology—by writing information booklets for the Bureau of Fisheries. While she continued to work for the government, she also became famous for her books about the sea, which she wrote in a lyrical style as if they were poems written in prose, even though they were scientifically accurate. Carson described the environment as harmonious and beautiful, and stressed the underlying unity of nature. For example, she described how a small worm normally washed up by the tide twice a day will spontaneously follow the same pattern in an aquarium, living "out its life in this alien place, remembering in every fiber of its small green body the tidal rhythm of the distant sea."

After the Second World War, people were appalled at the devastations caused by the atomic bombs dropped on Japan, and physicists were strongly criticized. Carson increased this scepticism about science by discussing the biological sciences. She had been planning a book about the origin of life, but then she realized that scientists were destroying the natural world she loved so much. Instead of writing about the beauty of nature, she decided to write a hard-hitting book exposing the dangers of chemicals. She attacked commercial companies, condemning them for sacrificing the health of the environment in order to make more profit.

Carson collected evidence from scientific experts to prove that the environment was being ruined forever. She explained how protecting crops with insect sprays was a short-sighted policy because the lethal chemicals were killing birds and also seeping higher and higher up the food chain to harm human beings.

She lashed out at hypocrisy. Why, she asked, were so many scientists researching into insecticides? The answer, of course, was money. . . . If they refused to accept that insecticides should be banned until absolutely solid evidence of their destructive effects had been found, then it would be too late to do anything about it.

After Carson's *Silent Spring*, the old-fashioned view that studying nature was a gentle female pastime disappeared forever. The book marks the beginning of a new type of environmental writing that focuses on the potentially horrific consequences of scientific progress. Issues such as global warming and genetically modified foods are no longer restricted to academic conferences, but have become urgent political problems.

From now on, try not to avoid reading essays, articles, or books that challenge you in length or complexity. Even if you don't understand every word and reference, you'll improve as a reader and a writer and will prepare yourself to succeed in future classes that deal with information about many different subjects and schools of thought.

IX. WRITING SUMMARIES

One of the best ways to learn to read carefully and write concisely is to write summaries. A summary is a brief piece of writing (a paragraph, usually) that presents the main ideas of a reading—a book chapter, an article, a speech, or a long essay—in your own words. It does not call for any reactions, opinions, or experiences of your own for support. Summaries contain only the most important points of the original and leave everything else out. Writing summaries strengthens your reading and writing skills. You have to understand the essence of a reading, gather its supporting points, and rephrase them in your *own* words (without including quotations from the original). Here's a tip: put the original away while you make a list of its four or five "big ideas." Then you can write sentences that express those ideas and combine them in paragraph form.

A summary, by definition, should always be much shorter than the original. Writing something *short* sounds easy, but actually it isn't. Rephrasing the main ideas of a reading in a short paragraph is a time-consuming task—not to be undertaken in the last hour before class. However, if you practice writing summaries conscientiously, you will improve as a reader and will be able to write concise, clear, smooth paragraphs. These skills will then carry over into your reading and writing for other courses.

A Sample Reading

Read the following excerpt from the book *Bollywood Crafts—20 Projects Inspired by Popular Indian Cinema*. It will be followed by a sample summary.

BOLLYWOOD FILM FACTS

Bollywood is the biggest film industry in the world. Approximately one thousand films are made in India under the "Bollywood" umbrella each year (that is double the amount of Hollywood films) and over 12 million Indians watch a Bollywood film every day. The films are also popular throughout the Middle East, Russia and Africa, and, increasingly, Western audiences are surrendering to the charms of Indian cinema.

Bollywood is also referred to as Hindi cinema—there are 22 official languages spoken in India; however, the major movies are made in Hindi as it is the country's dominant language, though films in other languages, such as Tamil and Urdu, are also made. Although the main hub of production companies are based in Mumbai (Bombay), films are shot in locations all over the country and recent films have even been set abroad [in England, Europe, Australia, and America].

Like mainstream Hollywood movies, Bollywood films also fall into specific genres, such as action or romance, but most are multi-genre, family movies. In India, going to the movies is a family event, and often several generations watch a film together. This means the content has to appeal to all. It also means filmmakers have to be creative in their approach to telling narratives. How they express emotions is a key element. Emotions are represented not just through acting, but also through the use of spectacle—songs and dance.

The key to a successful [Bollywood] movie is to have a popular soundtrack, and for the choreography that accompanies it to be equally impressive. Song sequences usually start in the middle of a dialogue and are a break from the reality of the storyline. Characters are transported to different locations and their costumes become very significant; a leading lady can go through several costume changes per dance scene, which makes for compelling viewing! When you're watching a song from a film, it's best to ignore the subtitles and instead let yourself be entertained by the visuals. The choreography is a mixture of Indian dancing styles with global influences such as MTV. Extras play a key role in bringing the dances to life, and as a viewer, I often want to get up and join in!

Some Bollywood films are inspired by Hollywood tales, but most are original ideas, often based on moral or family dilemmas. Like Hollywood, the star system is an important part of Bollywood and the biggest actors and actresses are celebrities in their own right. Unlike Hollywood, however, Indian actors often work on several films at one time, even switching between movie sets in the same day. And while Hollywood left behind its musicals in the 1950s, Bollywood films always contain a performance element. Actors have to demonstrate impeccable dancing skills as well as acting ability.

If you have yet to watch a Bollywood movie, don't worry! They are far more accessible than you may think, with cinemas and rental stores responding to audience demands by showing and stocking new movies. Don't be alarmed by the length; Bollywood movies are longer than other films to allow for the songs, but there is always an interval [intermission].

Bollywood films are an exciting and original contribution to the filmmaking world and, as the popularity of Bollywood continues to spread around the globe, Indian filmmakers are getting more progressive with their plots, special effects and visuals. This means that films will develop stylistically even further and continue to get better—something I'm really looking forward to!

Source: Momtaz Begum–Hossain is a freelance crafts maker and runs a customized clothing service, www.momtazbh.co.uk

A good summary begins with a statement of the reading's "biggest" idea, written in your own words. An effective summary does not just translate or re-order the words of the original. Some single words from the original—"India," "Hollywood," and "Bollywood," in this case—may be used in a summary when they lack a substitute. However, as the writer of an effective summary, you must find new ways to phrase the original reading's ideas, present them in a condensed form, and reveal your understanding of the original in the process.

A Sample Summary

In "Bollywood Film Facts," Momtaz Begum-Hossain explains that India has its own version of Hollywood—called Bollywood—that produces movies that are growing in popularity worldwide. Bollywood releases twice as many movies a year as Hollywood does. Unlike Hollywood movies, Bollywood movies can include different languages besides India's main language, Hindi. These films also include more music and dancing than Hollywood movies do. Elaborate, well-performed songs are essential and unique to Bollywood films. Therefore, movie stars in India have to act well and dance well, too. Indian movies are longer than Hollywood movies and might require subtitles, but they continue to attract new audiences because of their high entertainment value and universal appeal.

Writing Exercise 13

WRITE A SHORT SUMMARY: ASK YOURSELF, "WHAT'S THE BIG IDEA?"

Return to Patricia Lara's biography of Rachel Carson on page 224, and read it carefully. Then follow the instructions below to write a practice summary:

A good way to begin the summary of a reading is to identify the most general idea that the author (in this case, Patricia Lara) wants to get across to the reader. Write your own sentence expressing the main idea of "The Green Pioneer" now.

You may have written a sentence like this:

Rachel Carson challenged ideas about female scientists and began the fight to save our environment.

Next, it's important to add the author's name and the reading's title to identify what you are summarizing:

> In "The Green Pioneer," Patricia Fara explains that Rachel Carson challenged ideas about female scientists and began the fight to save our environment.

Now that you have your first sentence, summarize the rest of the reading by rephrasing only its "big ideas." Be sure to use your *own* words. It's not difficult if you remember to put the reading aside and write as if you're telling a friend the essay's main ideas in your own way. The first draft of your summary may be too long. Cut it down by including only the essential points and by omitting any of Lara's details or examples. Stay within a limit of 100–120 words.

When you have written the best summary you can, then compare it with the sample summary on the last page of the Answers section. If you look at the sample sooner, you'll cheat yourself of the opportunity to learn the valuable skill of writing summaries. If you read the sample summary before writing your own, it will be impossible not to be influenced by it. So do your own thinking and writing, and then compare.

SUMMARY CHECKLIST

Even though your summary is different from the sample, it may be just as good. If you're not sure how yours compares, consider these questions:

1. Have you included the writer's main ideas *without* adding your own reactions or opinions?
2. Have you written the summary in your own words *without* using any quotations?
3. Have you left out all of the writer's examples and supporting details?
4. Does your summary read smoothly?
5. Would someone who had not read the article get a clear overview of it from your summary?

X. REVISING, PROOFREADING, AND PRESENTING YOUR WORK

Great writers don't just sit down and write a final draft. They write and revise. You may have heard the expression, "Easy writing makes hard reading." True, it is *easier* to turn in a piece of writing as soon as you finish the first draft. But your reader (and eventually you) will probably be disappointed by the results. Try to think of revision as an opportunity instead of a chore, as a necessity instead of a choice.

Whenever possible, you should write a paper several days before it is due. Let it sit for a while. When you reread it, you'll see many ways to improve the organization, add more details, and clarify phrasing. After revising the paper, put it away for another day, and try again to improve it. Save all of your drafts along the way to see the progress you've made or possibly to find text deleted in an early draft that fits in again after revision.

Don't call any paper finished until you have worked through it several times. Revising is one of the best ways to improve your writing.

A Sample Rough Draft

Take a look at an early draft of the student essay you read on page 224 about learning to draw a self-portrait. Notice that the student has revised her rough draft by crossing out weak parts, correcting word forms, and adding new phrasing or reminders for later improvement.

Drawing a Blank

~~If at First You Don't Succeed . . . Try, Try Again~~

On the day ~~that~~ my drawing class started to learn about self-portraits last year, each of us had to bring a mirror to class. *In backpacks and purses* ~~There~~ were make-up mirrors, dressing table mirrors—large and small mirrors of every shape and kind. I was nervous about drawing a self-portrait, so I brought *only* a tiny plastic pocket mirror. That way if I didn't do a good job, it would be my mirror's fault. *Add a thesis*

I had never done well on human figure drawing. ~~Anyway~~, *First* *, Ms. Newman, demonstrated* our teacher ~~showed us how to do~~ the proportion of a human figure; *she explained that* ~~something like~~ a human body measures about seven times a human head. She used a tiny piece of chalk to draw on the board while she was talking. Then she ~~also~~ showed how to sketch ~~out~~ the face, from eyebrows to eyes, nose, mouth, and ears. After ~~all that~~ *her lecture*, she ~~led~~ *told* us to ~~start~~ *begin* ~~our~~ drawing *our self-portraits.*

we all ~~Everyone in the class~~ set up ~~their~~ *our* mirrors; ~~and~~ *T*he ceiling danced with ~~all of~~ the reflections they made. *as we got to work.* ~~Then we started to draw.~~ I looked down at my little square *of* scratched-up *plastic* ~~mirror~~ and started to draw gingerly on my ~~drawing~~ paper. I ~~looked at my face, eyebrows, eyes,~~ ~~nose, mouth, and ears~~. I tried to put ~~what~~ *the eyes, nose, and mouth* I had seen on

the paper. ~~Then~~ *When* I finished, I ~~was like~~ *wondered,* "Who the heck is

this?" The drawing *didn't look anything* ~~was totally bad. Nothing looked~~ like

me. I was ~~so~~ frustrated and sank down in my chair. After

a minute, I told myself, "Try again*,"* ~~the next one will be~~

~~better.~~ I drew another one, and it was a little better.

~~It looked a little like me. Nevertheless,~~ *But* I could not

really ~~say that~~ *call* it ~~was~~ a self-portrait because it did not

look exactly like me.

   I asked ~~my teacher to come over and help me out.~~ *Ms. Newman for help.* She

~~saw~~ *glanced at* my previous ~~drawings~~ *attempts* and said, "A good self-portrait

doesn't just look like you, it also shows your personal-

ity and ~~characteristics.~~ *your feelings."* ~~From my drawing~~ *s*he did not see

any of these. *in my other drawings.* So I tried again*.* I borrowed my friend's

big glass mirror and stared into it; I was not only looking

at my face, but also deep inside my face. This time,

I freely sketched ~~out~~ *the shape of* my face *.* ~~shape first.~~ Then *I* roughly

placed my eyebrows, eyes, nose, mouth, and ears. ~~And I~~

looked *into* ~~at~~ the mirror *again and* ~~, seeing my reflection closely. I~~

drew ~~what I felt to be like in the mirror.~~ *the expression I saw there.*

   When my ~~drawing~~ *Portrait* was finished, I wondered at ~~what an~~ *the*

amazing work I had done. Even though it did not perfectly

look like me, it really showed my *personality and emotions* ~~characteristics~~ through

the *contrast of* light and dark. When ~~my teacher~~ *Ms. Newman* saw it, she applauded*.*

~~my drawing and she really liked it.~~ Not only did I get an

A ~~in~~ *on* this project; it also became one of the strongest

pieces in my portfolio. I ~~recognized~~ *realized* that ~~nothing could~~ *few things can*

be done successfully the first time. If I ~~gave~~ *had given* up after

my first try, I would never have ~~known I could have done~~ *captured the real me.*

~~such a great job. Now I know I will succeed no matter how~~

~~many times I must try.~~

242 Part 4 Writing

Can you see why each change was made? Analyzing the reasons for the changes will help you improve your own revision skills.

Writing Exercise 14

IS THE GLASS HALF EMPTY OR HALF FULL?

The old test of optimism and pessimism is to look at a glass filled to the midpoint. An optimist, or positive thinker, would see it as "half *full.*" But a pessimist, or negative thinker, would consider it "half *empty.*" Is it better to be an optimist or a pessimist? What are the consequences of focusing on the bright side or on the dark side? Think about these questions, do some free writing or clustering about them, come up with a thesis statement, and organize your results into the structure of a brief essay.

Write a rough draft of the paper and set it aside. A day or two later, reread your paper to see what improvements you can make to your rough draft. Use the following checklist to help guide you through this or any other revision.

REVISION CHECKLIST

Here's a checklist of revision questions. If the answer to any of these questions is no, revise that part of your paper until you're satisfied that the answer is yes.

1. Does the introductory paragraph introduce the topic clearly and include a thesis statement that the paper will explain or defend?
2. Do all of the body paragraphs support the thesis statement?
3. Does each body paragraph begin with a clear topic sentence and focus on only one supporting point?
4. Do the body paragraphs contain relevant details, and are transitional expressions well used?
5. Do the final thoughts expressed in the concluding paragraph bring the paper to a smooth close?
6. Does your (the writer's) voice come through?
7. Do the sentences read smoothly and appear to be correct?
8. Are words well chosen and are spelling and punctuation consistent and correct?

Exchanging Papers (Peer Evaluations)

The preceding checklist can also be used if you exchange papers with another student. Since you both have written a response to the same assignment, you will understand what the other writer has been going through and learn from the differences between the two papers.

Proofreading Aloud

Finally, you should read your finished paper *aloud*. If you read it silently, your eyes will see what you *think* is there, but you are sure to miss some errors. Read your paper aloud slowly, pointing to—and listening carefully to—each word as you read it. When you *hear* your sentences, you will notice missing words and find errors in spelling and punctuation. Reading a paper to yourself this way may take fifteen minutes to half an hour, but it will be time well spent. You can also ask a friend or relative to read your paper to you. This method can be fun as well as helpful. If you don't like the way something sounds, don't be afraid to change it! Make it a rule to read each of your papers *aloud* before handing it in.

PRESENTING YOUR WORK

Part of the success of a paper could depend on how it looks. The same paper written sloppily or typed neatly might even receive a completely different grade. It is human nature to respond positively to an object created and presented with care. Here are some general guidelines to follow.

Paper Formats

Following instructions and standard formats is essential. Your paper should be typed, double-spaced, or written neatly in ink on 8 1⁄2-by-11-inch paper. A 1-inch margin should be left around the text on all sides for your instructor's comments. The beginning of each paragraph should be indented.

Most instructors specify a particular format for presenting your name and the course material on your papers. Always follow such instructions and other formats carefully in preparation for following more complicated formats in the future.

Titles

You should spend some time thinking of a good title for any paper long enough to deserve one. Just as you're more likely to read a magazine article with an interesting title, so your readers will be more eager to read your paper if you give it a good title. Which of these titles from student papers would make you want to read further?

An Embarrassing Experience	Super Salad?
American Beauty: Diversity	Paper on Immigration in America
Argument Essay	Got Elk?

Learn these three rules about titles, and you'll always write them correctly:

1. Capitalize only the first, the last, and the important words within a title. Don't capitalize articles (*a, an,* or *the*), prepositions (*to, at, in, around* . . .), or the connecting words (*and, or, but* . . .) in the middle of a title. (See page 193.)

    A Night on Eagle Rock   To the Limit of Endurance and Beyond

2. Don't use quotation marks unless your title includes a quotation or the title of an article, a poem, a song, or other short work. (See page 187.)

   Mozart's "Divine" Talent   The Call of "The Raven"

3. Don't underline or use italics in your title unless it includes the title of a book, movie, magazine, or other long work. (See page 187.)

   Promises in <u>The Pact</u>   *Avatar* Sinks *Titanic*

Remember that "Haste is the assassin of elegance." Instead of rushing to finish a paper and turn it in, take the time to give your writing the polish that it deserves.

Answers

GUIDELINES FOR DOUBLING A FINAL LETTER (PP. 6–7)

EXERCISE 1

1. tapping
2. clasping
3. defending
4. cleaning
5. referring
6. filling
7. smashing
8. playing
9. padding
10. deploying

EXERCISE 2

1. sewing
2. reviewing
3. dealing
4. clogging
5. clicking
6. unhooking
7. quizzing
8. pushing
9. aiming
10. delivering

EXERCISE 3

1. snipping
2. buzzing
3. mixing
4. rowing
5. tampering
6. performing
7. conferring
8. gleaming
9. clipping
10. permitting

EXERCISE 4

1. patting
2. sawing
3. feeding
4. playing
5. occurring
6. brushing
7. gathering
8. knotting
9. offering
10. boxing

EXERCISE 5

1. helping
2. flexing
3. assisting
4. needing
5. selecting

6. wishing
7. towing
8. constructing
9. polishing
10. leading

WORDS OFTEN CONFUSED, SET 1 (PP. 13–17)

EXERCISE 1

1. know
2. are, no
3. A, affect
4. a
5. an

6. new
7. an, an, effect
8. a, an, due
9. It's, accept
10. do

EXERCISE 2

1. an, advice
2. a, choose
3. effect
4. already, affect
5. knew

6. its
7. clothes
8. effect
9. accept
10. No

EXERCISE 3

1. are, our
2. course
3. an, a, dessert
4. its
5. due, an

6. knew
7. new
8. fill
9. complement
10. have

EXERCISE 4

1. already, do
2. clothes, choose
3. have, its
4. course, dessert
5. Due

6. feel, conscious
7. advice
8. have, complimented
9. course, do
10. except

EXERCISE 5

1. an, choose
2. course, it's
3. advice, an
4. effect
5. its, due

6. cloths, no, coarse
7. break
8. all ready, feel, it's
9. compliments
10. clothes

PROOFREADING EXERCISE

~~Its~~ *It's* hard to ~~except~~ *accept* criticism from friends. The other day, my friend Jane told me that my voice is always too loud when I talk on the phone. She said that the way I talk hurts her ears and makes her hold the phone away from her head. I ~~no~~ *know* that she didn't mean to hurt my feelings, but that was the ~~affect~~ *effect* of what she said. I should ~~of~~ *have* told her that she snores whenever we go camping in the ~~dessert~~ *desert*. Next time, I will record her snoring so that she can ~~here~~ *hear* herself. I don't really want Jane's criticism to ~~brake~~ *break* up ~~are~~ *our* friendship, so I'll probably just talk to her and tell her how I ~~fill~~ *feel*.

WORDS OFTEN CONFUSED, SET 2 (PP. 22–26)

EXERCISE 1

1. whose
2. quite
3. than, personnel
4. whether
5. their, principle

6. led, to
7. were
8. to
9. passed
10. than

EXERCISE 2

1. past
2. principal
3. quiet
4. piece
5. led, right

6. lose, their
7. passed
8. were
9. too
10. passed

EXERCISE 3

1. through
2. You're
3. whose, too, to
4. past, there
5. peace, quiet, their

6. through, they're
7. there, lose, their, right, personal
8. where
9. Then, to, than
10. Whether, you're, quite

EXERCISE 4

1. were
2. weather
3. led
4. past, whether
5. passed

6. past, there
7. quiet
8. lose, two, right
9. through, past
10. piece, weather

EXERCISE 5

1. whether, write
2. who's, You're, your
3. right, through, quite
4. led, too, write, personal
5. past

6. Personnel
7. They're, past, than
8. woman, principal
9. where
10. lose, than, lose

PROOFREADING EXERCISE

In the ~~passed~~ *past,* if you wanted ~~too~~ *to* hear a ~~peace~~ *piece* of music, you turned on ~~you're~~ *your* stereo. Later, you could even listen ~~too~~ *to* tunes on your computer. Now, with the ~~write~~ *right* equipment, you can play music ~~threw~~ *through* a vase of flowers. The sound doesn't come from the vase, but from the flowers themselves. Let's Corp., a company in Japan, has created a gadget called Ka-on, which means "flower sound" in Japanese. With the Ka-on device, sound is ~~past~~ *passed* up the stems of the flowers, into the delicate blossoms, and out into the room. If you touch the petals, you can feel ~~there~~ *their* vibrations. The Ka-on sound is supposed to be softer ~~then~~ *than* music played through ordinary speakers.

THE EIGHT PARTS OF SPEECH (PP. 30–32)

EXERCISE 1

```
        n    prep adj   n    v    adj   adj      n
1. The mall near my house has a new movie theater.

   pro  v     adj      conj    adj       n
2. It shows American and international films.

        n   prep adj    n     v prep adj     n     conj v    adj       n
3. The films from other countries are in foreign languages but have English subtitles.

     pro prep    adj    n   v   prep  n
4. Many of the foreign films come from India.

   pro  v   v   adj   adj   v   adv    adv  conj  v    v   pro  adv   adv
5. I have seen three Indian films there already and have liked them very much.

    adj      adj       n    v  adv conj pro v      v
6. These Bollywood movies are not what I had expected.

   pro v    v    prep adj   adj    n   conj adj   n    adj prep  n
7. I had heard about their bright colors and their songs full of dancing.

     adv    pro v    adv      v       n    conj    n   prep adj    n
8. However, I have particularly enjoyed the stories and characters in these films.

         n    v   adv  v    adj      conj  v   adv    v   pro prep n
9. The acting has also been impressive and has often moved me to tears.

    pro  v   conj pro v   v    pro     n  prep    n        adv
10. I guess that I can call myself a fan of Bollywood now.
```
    [Note that the word *Bollywood* was used as both an adjective and a noun in this exercise.]

EXERCISE 2

```
    conj    n    v    pro      pro  adv  v
1. When babies want something, they often cry.

    adv  adj    n    v   adj    n   prep adj    n
2. Now some parents teach sign language to their babies.

   adj    n   prep    n     v   adj    n   prep adj  n  prep     n
3. One professor of psychology tried sign language with her baby in the 1980s.

    adv pro    v       n     prep adj    n
4. Then she repeated the experiment with other children.

        n    v   conj prep adj     n    prep n  adj    n    v  adj
5. The results showed that at twelve months of age, most babies are ready.

    pro   v    v   adj   n   adv  adv
6. They can control their hands fairly well.
```

conj   n   v   n prep adj   n   n   v   v   pro
7. If a parent repeats signs for a few months, a child can learn them.

n   v   n   prep   n   pro   v   adj   n
8. Studies report benefits for babies who learn sign language.

adv   adj   adj   adj   n   v   adj
9. Later, their verbal test scores are high.

adv   pro   v   adv adv prep adj   n
10. Also, they score very well on IQ tests.

EXERCISE 3

prep   n   prep n   adj   n   v   adj   n
1. In the summer of 2005, London Zoo opened a temporary exhibit.

n   prep   n   v   adj   n
2. The title of the exhibit was "The Human Zoo."

adj   n   v   adj   adj   n
3. Zoo officials selected eight human volunteers.

adv pro v   n   prep   n   prep adj   n
4. Then they put the humans on display for several days.

n   prep n   v   v   adv   prep   n
5. Dozens of people had applied online for the project.

n   v   adj   n   conj adj   n
6. The exhibit showcased three males and five females.

pro   v   prep adj adj   n   pro   v   adj   n   conj adj   n
7. They dressed in fake fig leaves that covered their shorts and bikini tops.

prep adj adj   n   conj adj   n   n   v   adv
8. With its rocky ledges and cave-like structures, the enclosure had previously

v   n
housed bears.

adj   n   v   v   n   conj   v   n prep   n
9. The eight humans talked, played games, and received a lot of attention.

prep   n   n   v   n   prep   adj   n   n   conj   n
10. Outside the exhibit, the zoo posted signs about human diet, habitat, and behavior.

EXERCISE 4

n   v   n   conj   n
1. Plants need water and sunlight.

adv   n   v   adv
2. Sometimes houseplants wither unexpectedly.

      n   adv   v   pro adv   adj   n conj adv   adj   n

3. People often give them too much water or not enough water.

  pro v   n   prep   adj   n   adv

4. I saw an experiment on a television show once.

  pro   v   adj   n

5. It involved two plants.

        adj   n   v   adj   n   prep   n   conj   n

6. The same woman raised both plants with water and sunlight.

        n   v prep adj   adj   n

7. The plants grew in two different rooms.

  pro   v prep adj   n   conj   v   adj   n   prep   pro

8. She yelled at one plant but said sweet things to the other.

       adv   adj   n   v   adv   conj   adj pro   v

9. The verbally praised plant grew beautifully, but the other one died.

     n   v   n   adv

10. Plants have feelings, too.

EXERCISE 5

      n   v   n   pro v   adv   adj

1. Rabies is a disease that is usually fatal.

  adv adj   n   prep adj   n   v   adv   v

2. Only five people with rabies symptoms have ever survived.

  adj   n   pro   v   v   v   adj   n   conj   adj   n   v

3. Most people who are bitten get rabies shots before any symptoms begin.

  adj   n   v   v   adj   n   prep   n

4. These patients can avoid the deadly results of the disease.

      n   prep   n   v   adj

5. Jeanna Giese from Wisconsin is unique.

   pro   v   n   prep   n   conj   n   v pro prep adj   n

6. She survived a case of rabies after a bat bit her at her church.
   (Note that *her* plays two different parts of speech in Sentence 6.)

   pro   adv   v   n   prep n   conj pro v prep   n

7. She already showed symptoms of rabies when she went to the hospital.

    n   v adv   v   n   adj   n

8. Doctors did not give Giese the rabies vaccine.

   pro   v   n   prep   n   adv

9. They put the teenager into a coma instead.

    adj   n   v   conj pro   v   n prep adj   n prep   n

10. Their treatment worked, and it promised hope for rabies patients in the future.

PARAGRAPH EXERCISE

adj   n   v   adv adj n adv   pro v   adv conj pro   v

Your eyelids blink regularly all day long. They stop only when you sleep.

n   v   adj   adj   n prep   n   conj   pro   v   prep

Blinking protects your delicate eyes from injury. When something flies toward

pro   adv   adj   n   v   adv   conj   v   adj   n

you, usually your lids shut quickly and protect your eyes.

n   adv   v   n prep adj   n   pro v   adj   n   adv conj

Blinking also does a kind of washing job. It keeps your eyelids moist. If

n prep n   v   prep adj   n   adj   adj   n   v pro adv   adj   n

a speck of dirt gets past your lids, your moist eyeball traps it. Then your eyes

v prep   n   adj   n   v   conj   n   v   adv prep adj   n

fill with water, your lids blink, and the speck washes out of your eye.

ADJECTIVES AND ADVERBS (PP. 36–39)

EXERCISE 1

1. adjective adding to the noun *buildings*

2. adverb adding to the adjective *impressive*

3. adjective adding to the noun *columns*

4. adverb adding to the adjective *smooth*

5. adjective adding to the noun *quad*

6. adjective adding to the noun *walkways*

7. adjective adding to the noun *students*

8. adjective adding to the noun *patterns*

9. adjective adding to the noun *studying,* which is a *verbal.* (To learn more, see "Recognizing Verbal Phrases" on p. 123.)

10. adverb adding to the verb *allows*

EXERCISE 2

1. adjective adding to the noun *coupon*

2. adverb adding to the adjective *one*

3. adjective adding to the pronoun *I*

4. adverb adding to the verb *sells*

5. adjective adding to the noun *software*

6. adjective adding to the noun *hardware*

7. adjective adding to the noun *Spanish*

8. adjective adding to the noun *students*

9. adjective adding to the noun *child*

10. adjective adding to the pronoun *she*

EXERCISE 3

1. close	**6.** badly
2. closely	**7.** very happily
3. close	**8.** very happy
4. badly	**9.** good
5. bad	**10.** well

EXERCISE 4

1. the smallest	**6.** newer
2. a small	**7.** better
3. smaller	**8.** the best
4. the newest	**9.** better
5. newer	**10.** more important

EXERCISE 5

　　　　　　　　　adv　　adj　　adj
1. I took a very unusual art class over the summer.

　　　　　　adj　　　　　　　　　　　　　adj
2. The intriguing title of the class was "Frame-Loom Tapestry."

　　　　　　　　　adj　　adj　　　　　　　adj
3. We created small colorful tapestries on a wooden frame.

　　　　　　　adj　　adj　　　adj　　　　adj　adj　　　adj　adj
4. We started with four wooden stretcher bars, two long ones and two short ones.

　　adv　　　adv　　　　　　　　　　　　　　　　adj
5. Then we carefully joined them at the corners to make a rectangular frame.

　　adv　　　　　　adj　adj　　　　　　　　　　adv
6. Next, we wound white cotton string around the frame lengthwise.

        adv   adj

7. We finally had the basis for our tapestries.

            adv   adj   adj

8. We took brightly colored yarns and fabric strips and wove them between the strings.

         adv   adj

9. I was very happy with the results.

    adj adj   adj

10. My first tapestry looked like a beautiful sunset.

PROOFREADING EXERCISE

    I didn't do very ~~good~~ *well* in my last year of high school. I feel ~~badly~~ *bad* whenever I think of it. I skipped my classes and turned in messy work. My teachers warned me about my negative attitude, but I was ~~real~~ *really* stubborn. Now that I am a college student, I am even ~~stubborner~~ *more stubborn*. I go to every class and do my best. Now, success is ~~only~~ my *only* goal.

CONTRACTIONS (PP. 41–45)

EXERCISE 1

1. There's, that's, doesn't

2. It's, doesn't

3. aren't

4. you'd

5. they're

6. it's

7. can't

8. no contractions

9. don't, it's

10. you're

EXERCISE 2

1. There's

2. it's

3. someone's

4. person's

5. no contractions

6. there's, we'll, we're

7. We'll

8. there's

9. they're

10. That's

EXERCISE 3

1. we'd
2. didn't, I'd
3. couldn't, hadn't
4. wasn't
5. didn't

6. weren't, they're
7. isn't, didn't, I'd
8. no contractions
9. we'd
10. we're, couldn't

EXERCISE 4

1. who's
2. I'm
3. You're
4. that's
5. It's

6. wouldn't, we'd
7. They're
8. wasn't
9. that's
10. hasn't (*Its* is used twice as a posessive.)

EXERCISE 5

1. there's, I'm
2. I've
3. We've, haven't
4. We'll, can't
5. she's, we've

6. it's
7. aren't
8. we're, we'll
9. That's, I'll, it's
10. there's

PROOFREADING EXERCISE

~~Ive~~ *I've* heard about a new Web site created to allow people to share ~~there~~ *their* books with complete strangers. ~~Its~~ *It's* called BookCrossing.com, and when ~~your~~ *you're* finished reading a book, it can be ~~past~~ *passed* on to a ~~knew~~ *new* reader just by leaving it on a park bench, at a cafe, or wherever you like. Before you pass it on, you just register the book on the Web site, get its ID number, and tell ~~wear~~ *where* you're going to leave it. Then you place a note or a sticker in the book with ~~a~~ *an* identification number and the Web address telling the person ~~whose~~ *who's* going to find it what to do next. This way, people can keep track of the books they decide to "release into the wild," which is how the Web site phrases it. The best part about "bookcrossing" is that it's anonymous, and ~~its~~ *it's* free!

POSSESSIVES (PP. 47–51)

EXERCISE 4

1. child's
2. baby's
3. building's (Note: No apostrophe is needed for the possessive pronoun *its*.)
4. nanny's
5. baby's

6. stroller's
7. bystanders'
8. parents'
9. no possessive nouns (Note: No apostrophe is needed for the possessive pronoun *Its*.)
10. model's

EXERCISE 5

1. Claude Monet's
2. London's
3. fog's
4. weather's
5. no possessive nouns
6. no possessive nouns

7. People's (Note: No apostrophe is needed for the possessive pronoun *its*.)
8. no possessive nouns
9. artist's
10. "Monet's London."

PROOFREADING EXERCISE

I'm not satisfied with my ~~cars~~ *car's* ride; it's too rough. For instance, when a ~~roads~~ *road's* surface has grooves in it, the wheels get pulled in every direction. My ~~tires~~ *tires'* treads seem too deep for ordinary city driving. Bumps and potholes usually send my ~~passenger's~~ *passengers'* heads straight into the roof. When I bought my car, I asked about ~~it's~~ *its* stiff suspension and heavy-duty tires. The salesperson told me that the suspension's elements would eventually soften for a smoother ride, but they haven't. I should have known not to trust ~~anyones~~ *anyone's* words more than my own instincts.

REVIEW OF CONTRACTIONS AND POSSESSIVES (PP. 52–53)

1. There's, Valentine's
2. I'm, You're
3. America's, that's
4. Necco's, they've
5. heart's (or hearts'), it's

6. company's, cookie's
7. candy's
8. country's
9. New Year's, year's, Valentine's
10. they'll

BOWLING FOR VALUES

[Note: We have added the necessary apostrophes to show contractions and posses-sives in this exercise. Check carefully to see if your apostrophes match up.]

Growing up as a child, I didn't have a set of values to live by. Neither my mother nor my father gave me any specific rules, guidelines, or beliefs to lead me through the complicated journey of childhood. My parents' approach was to set me free, to allow me to experience life's difficulties and develop my own set of values.

They were like parents taking their young child bowling for the first time. They hung their values on the pins at the end of the lane. Then they put up the gutter guards and hoped that I'd hit at least a few of the values they'd lived by themselves.

If I had children today, I'd be more involved in developing a set of standards for them to follow. I'd adopt my mom and dad's philosophy of letting them discover on their own what they're interested in and how they feel about life. But I'd let them bowl in other lanes or even in other bowling alleys. And, from the start, they'd know my thoughts on religion, politics, drugs, sex, and all the ethical questions that go along with such subjects.

Now that I'm older, I wish my parents would've shared their values with me. Being free wasn't as comfortable as it might've been if I'd had some basic values to use as a foundation when I had tough choices to make. My children's lives will be better, I hope. At least they'll have a base to build on or to remodel—whichever they choose.

PROGRESS TEST (P. 54)

1. B. We should *have* taken separate classes to stay focused.
2. A. If *you're* looking for a new place to eat lunch, try food trucks.
3. B. Some *people's* sunglasses don't enhance their style.
4. A. Big summer movies often have *too* many special effects.
5. A. Learning to drive was easier *than* I thought it would be.
6. A. I received several *compliments* on my presentation.

7. B. A student *led* the rehearsal, and we never sounded better.

8. A. I took my doctor's *advice* and signed up for a yoga class.

9. A. Music *affects* people in different ways.

10. A. My computer has a problem with *its* DVD player.

SENTENCE STRUCTURE

FINDING SUBJECTS AND VERBS (PP. 59–62)

EXERCISE 1

1. Harold Lloyd became a star of comic films during the silent era of Hollywood.

2. In a fun twist, his character's name in many of his films was also Harold.

3. Harold worked in Hollywood at the same time as Charlie Chaplin and Buster Keaton.

4. One accessory distinguished Harold from the others: a pair of round eyeglasses.

5. The glasses had no lenses but fit his face and suited his character perfectly.

6. A suit and a straw hat completed Harold's simple yet effective costume.

7. Unlike Chaplin and Keaton's clownish characters, Harold looked like an ordinary young man but was physically ready for anything—from great fun to a good fight.

8. Harold performed incredible stunts in spite of a hand injury from an explosion early in his career.

9. In his most famous film, *Safety Last!*, Harold climbed a building and dangled dangerously from its clock.

10. Luckily, Harold Lloyd's movies are now available on DVD for the enjoyment of future generations.

EXERCISE 2

1. Travelers often carry food and other products from one country to another.

2. They ride trains or take planes to their new destinations.

3. Customs officials check passengers for illegal foods or other contraband.

   4. Sometimes, customs <u>officers</u> <u>catch</u> smugglers of very unusual items.

   5. One <u>woman</u> from Australia <u>made</u> the news recently.

   6. There <u>were</u> two odd <u>things</u> about her skirt.

   7. It <u>looked</u> very puffy and <u>made</u> a sloshing noise.

   8. Customs <u>officers</u> <u>found</u> fifty-one live tropical fish in an apron under her skirt.

   9. The <u>apron</u> <u>had</u> special pockets and <u>held</u> fifteen plastic bags.

  10. <u>Officials</u> <u>arrested</u> the woman and <u>confiscated</u> her cargo.

EXERCISE 3

   1. Chris <u>Lindland</u> <u>had</u> a simple idea.

   2. <u>He</u> <u>used</u> an ordinary fabric in an extraordinary way.

   3. <u>Lindland</u> <u>invented</u> "Cordarounds."

   4. <u>Cordarounds</u> <u>are</u> corduroy pants with a twist.

   5. The corduroy <u>ridges</u> <u>go</u> across instead of down the pant legs.

   6. These new <u>pants</u> <u>have</u> their own Web site.

   7. The <u>Web site</u> <u>is</u>, predictably, cordarounds.com.

   8. There <u>are</u> different <u>colors</u> and <u>styles</u> of Cordarounds.

   9. <u>They</u> <u>cost</u> a little more than regular corduroy pants.

  10. <u>Lindland</u> <u>sells</u> other new styles of clothes on his Web site.

EXERCISE 4

   1. <u>Cats</u> <u>are</u> extremely loyal and determined pets.

   2. <u>They</u> <u>form</u> strong attachments to their families.

   3. One cat recently <u>showed</u> her love for the Sampson family very clearly.

   4. The <u>Sampsons</u> <u>made</u> a temporary move and <u>took</u> Skittles, the cat, with them.

   5. The <u>Sampsons</u> and <u>Skittles</u> <u>spent</u> several months 350 miles away from home.

   6. Before the end of their stay, <u>Skittles</u> <u>disappeared</u>.

   7. The <u>family</u> <u>returned</u> home without their beloved cat and <u>considered</u> her lost.

   8. Seven months later, there <u>was</u> a <u>surprise</u> on their doorstep.

   9. <u>Skittles</u> somehow <u>navigated</u> her way home but barely <u>survived</u> the 350-mile trip.

  10. This incredible <u>story</u> <u>proves</u> the loyalty and determination of cats.

1. There <u>are</u> a <u>number</u> of world-famous trees in California.

2. <u>One</u> of them <u>is</u> the oldest tree on the planet.

3. This <u>tree</u> <u>lives</u> somewhere in Inyo National Forest.

4. The <u>type</u> of tree <u>is</u> a bristlecone pine.

5. <u>Scientists</u> <u>call</u> it the Methuselah Tree.

6. <u>They</u> <u>place</u> its age at five thousand years.

7. The <u>soil</u> and <u>temperatures</u> around it <u>seem</u> too poor for a tree's health.

8. But the <u>Methuselah Tree</u> and its <u>neighbors</u> obviously <u>thrive</u> in such conditions.

9. Due to its importance, the Methuselah Tree's exact <u>location</u> <u>is</u> a secret.

10. Such important natural <u>specimens</u> <u>need</u> protection.

The 1960s and 1970s: Renewal through Independence

The golden <u>age</u> of cinema <u>was</u> over. A new <u>generation</u> of filmmakers . . . <u>emerged</u> on the scene during this period of crisis.

Worldwide Awakening

Everywhere there <u>was</u> a <u>renewal</u> of film and cinema. In Latin America, the Brazilian <u>Glauber Rocha</u> <u>provided</u> the impetus for *Cinema Novo* with his cinema as political allegories. In the U.S., a <u>group</u> of young directors, actresses, and actors <u>responded</u> to the creative standstill of the large studios—the <u>first</u> [were] Dennis Hopper and Peter Fonda with their naively pessimistic interpretation of the American Dream in "Easy Rider" (1969). <u>George Lucas</u> ("THX 1138," 1970) and <u>Steven Spielberg</u> ("Duel," 1971) <u>made</u> their debut. <u>Martin Scorsese</u> ("Mean Streets," 1973; "Taxi Driver," 1976; "Raging Bull," 1980) and <u>Francis Ford Coppola</u> ("The Conversation," 1974; "The Godfather," 1972; "Apocalypse Now," 1979) <u>directed</u> their best films. The <u>decade</u> of "New Hollywood" <u>was</u> a stroke of luck for cinema and the film industry.

LOCATING PREPOSITIONAL PHRASES (PP. 65–68)

EXERCISE 1

1. Roald Dahl is the author (of *Charlie and the Chocolate Factory*).

2. (In his youth), Dahl had two memorable experiences (with sweets).

3. One (of them) involved the owner (of a candy store).

4. Dahl and his young friends had a bad relationship (with this particular woman).

5. (On one visit) (to her store), Dahl put a dead mouse (into one) (of the candy jars) (behind her back).

6. The woman later went (to his school) and demanded his punishment.

7. He and his friends received several lashes (from a cane) (in her presence).

8. (During his later childhood years), Dahl became a taste-tester (for the Cadbury chocolate company).

9. Cadbury sent him and other schoolchildren boxes (of sweets) to evaluate. [*To evaluate* is a verbal, not a prepositional phrase. See p. 123 for more.]

10. Dahl tried each candy and made a list (of his reactions and recommendations).

EXERCISE 2

1. A killer whale (at MarineLand) (in Canada) actually invented his own stunt.

2. (After feeding time), gulls often ate the leftover fish (on the surface) (of the water).

3. One orca found a way to benefit (from the gulls' habit). [*To benefit* is a verbal, not a prepositional phrase. See p. 123 for more.]

4. He filled his mouth (with fish chunks) and squirted them (on top) (of the water).

5. Then he sank (beneath the surface) and waited (for a gull).

6. The whale caught the gull and had it (for dessert).

7. This whale then taught his new trick (to some) (of the other whales).

8. One main aspect (of the whales' behavior) fascinated scientists.

9. These whales taught the trick (to themselves) and (to each other) (without human guidance).

10. Luckily, cameras captured all (of the learning) (on film) (for study) (in the future).

1. My <u>family</u> and <u>I</u> <u>live</u> (in a house) (at the top) (of a hilly neighborhood) (in Los Angeles).

2. (On weekday mornings), nearly <u>everyone</u> <u>drives</u> (down the steep winding roads) (to their jobs) or (to school).

3. (In the evenings), <u>they</u> all <u>come</u> back (up the hill) to be (with their families).

4. (For the rest) (of the day), <u>we</u> <u>see</u> only an occasional delivery van or compact school bus.

5. But (on Saturdays and Sundays), there <u>is</u> a different <u>set</u> (of drivers) (on our roads).

6. (On those two days), <u>tourists</u> (in minivans) and prospective home <u>buyers</u> (in convertibles) <u>cram</u> our narrow streets.

7. (For this reason), <u>most</u> (of the neighborhood residents) <u>stay</u> (at home) (on weekends).

8. Frequently, <u>drivers</u> unfamiliar (with the twists and turns) (of the roads) (in this area) <u>cause</u> accidents.

9. The <u>expression</u> "Sunday driver" really <u>means</u> something (to those) (of us) (on the hill).

10. (In fact), even "<u>Saturday drivers</u>" <u>are</u> a nuisance (for us).

1. <u>Most</u> (of us) <u>remember</u> playing (with Frisbees) (in our front yards) (in the early evenings) and (at parks or beaches) (on weekend afternoons).

2. Fred <u>Morrison</u> <u>invented</u> the original flat Frisbee (for the Wham-O toy company) (in the 1950s).

3. Ed <u>Headrick</u>, designer (of the professional Frisbee), <u>passed</u> away (at his home) (in California) (in August) (of 2002).

4. Working (at Wham-O) (in the 1960s), <u>Headrick</u> <u>improved</u> the performance (of the existing Frisbee) (with the addition) (of ridges) (in the surface) (of the disc).

5. Headrick's <u>improvements</u> <u>led</u> (to increased sales) (of his "professional model" Frisbee) and (to the popularity) (of Frisbee tournaments).

6. (After Headrick's redesign), <u>Wham-O</u> <u>sold</u> 100 million (of the flying discs).

7. <u>Headrick</u> also <u>invented</u> the game (of disc golf).

8. (Like regular golf) but (with discs), the <u>game</u> <u>takes</u> place (on special disc golf courses) (like the first one) (at Oak Grove Park) (in California).

9. (Before his death), <u>Headrick</u> <u>asked</u> (for his ashes) to be formed (into memorial flying discs) (for select family and friends). [*To be formed* is a verbal. See p. 123.]

10. <u>Donations</u> (from sales) (of the remaining memorial discs) <u>went</u> (toward the establishment) (of a museum) (on the history) (of the Frisbee and disc golf).

Exercise 5

1. An engraved <u>likeness</u> (of Pocahontas), the famous Powhatan princess, <u>is</u> the oldest portrait (on display) (at the National Portrait Gallery).

2. (In 1607), <u>Pocahontas</u>—still (in her early teens)—single-handedly <u>helped</u> the British colonists (in Virginia) to survive. [*To survive* is a verbal. See p. 123.]

3. Later, (in 1616), <u>Pocahontas</u> <u>traveled</u> (to England) (after her marriage) (to John Rolfe) and (after the birth) (of their son).

4. <u>She</u> <u>visited</u> the court (of King James I) and <u>impressed</u> the British (with her knowledge) (of English) and (with her conversion) (to Christianity).

5. (For her new first name), <u>Pocahontas</u> <u>chose</u> Rebecca.

6. (During her seven-month stay) (in England), <u>she</u> <u>became</u> extremely ill.

7. (At some point) (before or during her illness), <u>Simon Van de Passe</u> <u>engraved</u> her portrait (on copper).

8. The <u>portrait</u> <u>shows</u> Pocahontas (in a ruffled collar and fancy English clothes) but (with very strong Native American features).

9. Successful <u>sales</u> (of prints) (from the portrait) <u>illustrate</u> her fame abroad.

10. <u>Pocahontas</u> <u>died</u> (on that trip) (to England) (at the age) (of twenty-two).

Paragraph Exercise

Even the Liberty Bell came (to the fair) (during that summer)—after seventy-five thousand St. Louis school children had signed a petition requesting its visit. (On June 8), the cracked bell arrived (on a flat wagon) pulled (by a team) (of horses) and surrounded (by policemen) (from Philadelphia). Crowds lined the edges (of the Plaza) (of St. Louis), hoping to get a glimpse (of this famous artifact). Mayor Rolla Wells pronounced the occasion Liberty Bell Day and called off school (in the city) so that children could come (to the fair).

[Note: *After* begins a dependent clause, not a prepositional phrase, in the first sentence of the previous paragraph. *To get* begins a verbal phrase, not a prepositional phrase, in the third sentence. *Off* adds to the verb *called* in the final sentence. Together, *called off* means "canceled."]

UNDERSTANDING DEPENDENT CLAUSES (PP. 71–75)

EXERCISE 1

1. When people visit Google's homepage on one evening in March each year, they are often surprised.

2. They notice immediately that the whole page is black instead of white.

3. After they look into it further, they discover the reason for the temporary color change.

4. The black page signifies that Google is a participant in Earth Hour.

5. In 2008, Google joined countless cities, companies, and individuals who turn their lights off for one hour in an international effort to encourage energy conservation.

6. People around the globe cut their electricity and live in the dark as soon as the clock strikes 8 pm in their locations.

7. When the hour is up at 9 pm, they turn the electricity back on.

8. Earth Hour is an idea that began in Australia.

9. In 2007, the first Earth Hour that the Australians celebrated occurred between 7:30 and 8:30 pm on March 31.

10. Even though some people dismiss Earth Hour as a minor event, others believe in its power as a symbol of environmental awareness.

EXERCISE 2

1. The world is a miserable place when you have an upset stomach.

2. Whether you get carsick, airsick, or seasick, you probably welcome any advice.

3. Motion sickness is most common when people are between the ages of seven and twelve.

4. Motion sickness happens to some people whenever the brain receives mixed messages.

5. If the inner ear feels movement but the eyes report no movement, the brain gets confused.

6. This confusion results in dizziness and the feeling that all is not well.

7. Experts suggest that you sleep well and eat lightly to avoid motion sickness.

8. When you travel by car, you should sit in the middle of the back seat and look straight out the windshield.

9. On an airplane or a boat, the best seat is one that allows a view of the clouds or horizon.

10. Whenever the queasy feeling comes, you should sip small amounts of water.

EXERCISE 3

1. The Breathalyzer is a machine that measures a person's blood alcohol level.

2. Police officers use the device when they suspect a drunk driver.

3. Robert F. Borkenstein was the man who invented the Breathalyzer.

4. Before Borkenstein created the portable measuring device, officers took suspects' breath samples in balloons back to a laboratory for a series of tests.

5. Borkenstein's Breathalyzer was an improvement because all testing occurred at the scene.

6. The Breathalyzer was so reliable and became so feared that one man went to extremes to avoid its results.

7. While this man waited in the back of the police car, he removed his cotton underwear and ate them.

8. He hoped that the cotton cloth would soak up all the alcohol in his system.

9. When the desperate man's case went to court, the judge acquitted him.

10. The judge's decision came after spectators in the court laughed so hard that they could not stop.

EXERCISE 4

1. On June 8, 1924, George Mallory and Andrew Irvine disappeared as they climbed to the top of Mount Everest.

2. Earlier, when a reporter asked Mallory why he climbed Everest, his response became legendary.

3. "Because it is there," Mallory replied.

4. No living person knows whether the two British men reached the summit of Everest before they died.

5. Nine years after Mallory and Irvine disappeared, English climbers found Irvine's ice ax.

6. In 1975, a Chinese climber spotted a body that was frozen in deep snow on the side of the mountain.

7. He kept the news secret for several years but finally told a fellow climber on the day before he died himself in an avalanche on Everest.

8. In May 1999, a team of mountaineers searched the area that the Chinese man described and found George Mallory's frozen body still intact after seventy-five years.

9. After they took DNA samples for identification, the mountaineers buried the famous climber on the mountainside where he fell.

10. The question remains whether Mallory was on his way up or down when he met his fate.

EXERCISE 5

1. I read an article that described the history of all the presidents' dogs.

2. George Washington cared so much about dogs that he interrupted a battle to return a dog that belonged to a British general.

3. Abraham Lincoln, whose dog's name was actually Fido, left his loyal pet in Illinois after the Lincolns moved to the White House.

4. Teddy Roosevelt met and adopted Skip, the dog that he loved best, after the little terrier held a bear at bay in the Grand Canyon.

5. Franklin Delano Roosevelt also adored his dog Fala, another stout terrier who was so famous that a separate statue of him sits next to FDR at the Franklin Delano Roosevelt Memorial in Washington, D.C.

6. Nikita Khrushchev traveled from Russia with Pushinka, a dog that he gave to John F. Kennedy's daughter Caroline.

7. At a gas station in Texas, Lyndon Johnson's daughter Luci found a little white dog, Yuki, whom President Johnson loved to have howling contests with in the Oval Office.

8. Of course, Nixon had his famous Checkers, and George Bush Sr. had Millie, the spaniel who wrote her own best-selling book with the help of Barbara Bush.

9. And just when it seemed that all presidents prefer dogs, Bill Clinton arrived with Socks, a black-and-white cat.

10. In 2009, Barack Obama's <u>family</u> <u>chose</u> Bo, a Portuguese Water Dog, as the
White House pet because one <u>daughter</u> <u>is</u> allergic to other dog breeds.

PARAGRAPH EXERCISE

New England <u>is</u> a tightrope where the <u>weather</u> usually <u>balances</u> between
warm maritime air and the periodic flows of cold continental air from the
northwest. So if ever there <u>was</u> a <u>place</u> where amateur folklore weather <u>prophets</u>
<u>do</u> their best work, <u>I</u> <u>might</u> <u>suggest</u> New England. The <u>tightrope</u> between the two
air masses often <u>waves</u> and <u>writhes</u>, causing sunny weather in one spot while <u>rain</u>
<u>is</u> only a mile or two away. <u>You</u> <u>can't</u> <u>show</u> that sort of thing on a weather map. A
New England weather <u>prophet</u> just <u>has</u> to know his sky and wind and <u>remember</u>
by past experience <u>what</u> <u>follows</u> which sky phenomena. [The verb forms *causing*
and *to know* are not real verbs in this paragraph; they are verbals. See page 123
for more.]

CORRECTING FRAGMENTS (PP. 78–82)

EXERCISE 1
Possible revisions to make the fragments into sentences are *italicized.*

1. Correct

2. *They don't think* about the consequences.

3. Correct

4. Correct

5. About half of the people *change their minds*, to be exact.

6. Correct

7. *It involves* lasers to remove the pigment in the skin.

8. Correct

9. *They are* used on different colors and in different combinations.

10. Correct

Changes used to make the fragments into sentences are *italicized.*

1. Correct

2. Correct

3. *Jerry had to wear the shirt* on TV.

4. *He did it* to help Kramer's friend, a fashion designer.

5. Correct

6. Dorothy's ruby slippers from *The Wizard of Oz are also on display there.*

7. *The museum holds* other famous objects, like the original Kermit the Frog from *Sesame Street.*

8. Correct

9. Correct

10. *It's* because the shirt had the combination of a funny design and a funny name.

1. It's almost impossible to find a parking space on or near campus without getting up really early.

2. Hoping for the best, I always pay my sixty dollars a year for a parking permit.

3. My car's old engine, stalling or backfiring every few minutes, can't tolerate long periods of waiting.

4. In order to get a space close to my first class, I follow anyone who is walking towards a parked car.

5. Rarely offering signs of encouragement, students usually keep walking through the parking lots, down the street, and toward the bus stop.

6. Due to their own struggles with parking, visitors who return to their cars sometimes offer help.

7. There is one foolproof way to ensure a perfect parking place: getting to campus before 6:30 am.

8. Every morning, I see the early birds in their cars with their seats back, sleeping there for hours before class.

9. Because of my late-night study habits, I can barely make it to school by 8:00 am.

10. Due to increases in enrollment, the parking problem is here to stay.

Answers may vary, but here are some possible revisions.

1. We were writing our in-class essays when suddenly the emergency bell rang.

2. Everyone in the class looked at each other first and then at the teacher. He told us to gather up our things and follow him outside.

3. The series of short rings continued as we left the room and noisily walked out into the parking lot beside the main building.

4. The sunlight was very warm and bright compared to the classroom's fluorescent lights, which always make everything look more clinical than natural.

5. As we stood in a large group with students and teachers from other classes, we wondered about the reason for the alarm.

6. I have never heard an emergency alarm that was anything but a planned drill.

7. Without the danger of injury, a party atmosphere quickly developed since we all got a break from our responsibilities.

8. I've noticed that the teachers seem the most at ease because they don't have to be in control during these situations.

9. After we students and the teachers chatted for ten minutes or so, the final bell rang to signal the end of the drill.

10. When we sat down at our desks again, the teacher asked us to continue writing our essays until the end of the hour.

Answers may vary, but here are some possible revisions. (Changes are in *italics*.)

1. *I am surprised* whenever I see a seagull up close.

2. After lunch on Tuesdays, our club *meets* in the gym.

3. After we turned in our research assignments, *the librarians celebrated*.

4. Traveling overseas without a lot of planning *is risky*.

5. The pizza *arrived* within thirty minutes of our call.

6. It *was* the hardest question on the test.

7. *I have discovered* that people often stretch the truth.

8. *Discuss* the topic with the person next to you.

9. Even though "wet paint" signs were still on the walls, *people leaned against them.*

10. *The book explains* how a series of paragraphs becomes an essay.

Italics identify a suggested correction for each of the six fragments. Your revisions may differ. Note that italics also punctuate the two book titles in this paragraph.

We are all familiar with photos that have been digitally altered to enhance some part of the *image, whether* it's a celebrity's waistline or a country's coastline. Questioning the reliability of photographs is not a new practice. One example from the early 1900s *involves* the infamous pictures of the Cottingley Fairies. The story of these photos began in 1918 when two girls from the small English town of Cottingley took pictures of themselves surrounded by tiny dancing figures. *Then the girls insisted* that the creatures in the photos were real live *fairies caught* on film in their natural habitat for the first time. Scientific tests, the girls' assurances, and people's desire to believe led many to accept that the Cottingley fairies actually existed. Even Sir Arthur Conan Doyle, creator of Sherlock Holmes, wrote a book called *The Coming of the Fairies, which* he published to stress the importance of the photographs in 1920. Eventually, the girls revealed that the figures in the photographs were only drawings of *fairies and* that they had destroyed the drawings and buried them after taking the pictures. *Fairy Tale: A True Story* (1997) is a popular film that is based on these events.

CORRECTING RUN-ON SENTENCES (PP. 85–89)

Your answers may differ depending on how you chose to separate the two clauses.

1. Mary Mallon is a famous name in American history, but she is not famous for something good.

2. Most people know Mary Mallon by another name, and that is "Typhoid Mary."

3. The sentence is correct.

4. The sentence is correct.

5. Mary Mallon was the first famous case of a healthy carrier of disease, but she never believed the accusations against her.

6. Mallon, an Irish immigrant, was a cook; she was also an infectious carrier of typhoid.

7. By the time the authorities discovered Mallon's problem, she had made many people ill. A few of her "victims" actually died from the disease.

8. A health specialist approached Mallon and asked her for a blood sample; she was outraged and attacked him with a long cooking fork.

9. Eventually, the authorities dragged Mallon into a hospital for testing, but she fought them hysterically the entire time.

10. The lab tests proved Mallon's infectious status, and health officials forced Mary Mallon to live on an island by herself for twenty-six years.

EXERCISE 2

Your answers may differ depending on how you chose to separate the two clauses.

1. Frank Epperson invented something delicious and refreshing, and it comes on a stick.

2. In 1905, Epperson was an eleven-year-old boy. He lived in San Francisco.

3. The sentence is correct.

4. The sentence is correct.

5. There was a record-breaking cold snap that evening, and the drink froze.

6. In the morning, Frank Epperson ate his frozen juice creation; it made a big impression.

7. Epperson grew up and kept making his frozen "Epsicles"; they came in seven varieties.

8. The sentence is correct.

9. Epperson's kids loved their dad's treat, and they always called them "pop's sicles."

10. So Popsicles were born, and people have loved them ever since.

EXERCISE 3

Your answers may differ since various words can be used to begin dependent clauses.

1. *When* I went to the orthodontist last month, she told me that I needed braces.

2. I was happy *because* I always wanted them.

3. The sentence is correct.

4. The sentence is correct.

5. *After* my dentist told me about many types of braces, I wanted the invisible kind.

6. *Once* the dentist said that the invisible ones were perfect for my case, she began the process.

7. The sentence is correct.

8. The company made a series of sets of clear braces, *which* I will wear for several weeks each.

9. *Because* the first set fits my teeth perfectly, they are almost totally invisible.

10. I am glad that orthodontists offer this new type of braces *that* are just right for me.

EXERCISE 4

Your answers may differ since various words can be used to begin dependent clauses.

1. Since I've been reading about sleep in my psychology class, I know a lot more about it.

2. Sleep has five stages, which we usually go through many times during the night.

3. The first stage of sleep begins as our muscles relax and mental activity slows down.

4. The sentence is correct.

5. Stage two takes us deeper than stage one so that we are no longer aware of our surroundings.

6. The sentence is correct.

7. Next is stage three, in which we become more and more relaxed and are very hard to awaken.

8. Stage four is so deep that we don't even hear loud noises.

9. The fifth stage of sleep is called REM (rapid eye movement) sleep because our eyes move back and forth quickly behind our eyelids.

10. Although REM sleep is only about as deep as stage two, we do all our dreaming during the REM stage.

Your answers may differ depending on how you chose to connect the clauses.

1. Boston Red Sox fans have a tradition, *which* they celebrate at every home game without question.

2. Very few people know how the tradition began, but most people don't care to know.

3. It happens in the eighth inning, and everyone looks forward to it.

4. *When* the loud speakers at Fenway Park play the song "Sweet Caroline," all of the fans sing along.

5. There is problem with the tradition; the original song has no link to Boston or baseball.

6. Neil Diamond sings the thirty-year-old song, but his last name is only a baseball coincidence.

7. In the past, other teams played the song at stadiums, but in 2002, Boston started playing it at every game.

8. The sentence is correct.

9. The Red Sox won the 2004 World Series even though no one really expected that they would.

10. Players and teams in sports are often superstitious. Singing "Sweet Caroline" is a lucky charm that the fans, the players, and the management love.

REVIEW OF FRAGMENTS AND RUN-ON SENTENCES (P. 89)

Your revisions may differ depending on how you chose to correct the errors.

With the focus on cleanliness lately in advertising for soaps and household cleaning products, people are surprised to hear that we may be too clean for our own good. This phenomenon is called the "hygiene hypothesis," and recent studies support its validity. For instance, one study shows the benefit of living with two or more pets. Babies may grow up with healthier immune systems and be less allergic if they live with a dog and a cat or two dogs or two cats. The old thinking was that young children would become more allergic living with many pets, but they don't. Somehow the exposure to pets and all their "dirty" habits gives youngsters much-needed defenses. There may be as much as a seventy-five percent lower allergy risk, according to this study.

IDENTIFYING VERB PHRASES (PP. 92–96)

Exercise 1

1. People from all over the world entered a dog-cloning contest in June 2008.
2. The "Golden Clone Giveaway" was sponsored by BioArts and Best Friends Again, a dog-cloning company in California.
3. BioArts had succeeded in cloning the company owner's dog, Missy, in 2007.
4. The company's Web site showed pictures of Missy and three of her clones: Mira, Chingu, and Sarang.
5. To enter the "Golden Clone Giveaway" contest, applicants submitted an application and wrote a short essay describing why their dog would be perfect to clone.
6. James Symington was chosen from all the applicants as the winner of the first "Golden Clone Giveaway."
7. Symington had written his essay about Trakr, a rescue dog who had worked at Ground Zero on 9/11 and had even found the last person alive in the debris.
8. For those who could afford to pay for the service, BioArts and Best Friends Again also conducted auctions for their dog-cloning procedures.
9. The auctions occurred in July 2008; each auction opened with a $100,000 starting bid.
10. After the company had successfully cloned the five dogs that were purchased in the auctions, it stopped all operations and issued a press release "Six Reasons Why We're No Longer Cloning Dogs."

[Note: The word forms "dog-cloning," "describing," "to clone," "starting," and "to pay" are not acting as real verbs here, but as *verbals*. To learn more, see page 123.]

Exercise 2

1. Scientists successfully cloned a dog for the first time in 2005.
2. Cloning experts had been attempting to clone a dog for many years.
3. They had had success with horses, cats, and even rats before they could clone a dog.

4. The scientists who eventually <u>succeeded</u> <u>were</u> from Seoul National University in South Korea.

5. They <u>named</u> the cloned dog Snuppy as a tribute to the university where the accomplishment <u>was made</u>, and they <u>pronounced</u> the name "Snoopy."

6. Of course, Snuppy <u>could thank</u> his "parent" dog, a three-year-old Afghan hound, for all of his great physical features.

7. Both dogs <u>had</u> long glossy black fur that <u>was accentuated</u> by identical brown markings on their paws, tails, chests, and eyebrows.

8. Unfortunately, the cloning procedure <u>does</u> not <u>guarantee</u> that the clone of a dog <u>will share</u> the unique features of the original dog's personality.

9. Nevertheless, now that dog cloning <u>has been achieved</u>, many people <u>have shown</u> an interest in cloning their own dogs.

10. Although some people <u>may</u> not <u>be</u> happy with just a physical copy of a beloved pet, for others, a copy <u>is</u> better than nothing.

[Again the word forms "cloning," "to clone," and "cloned" in "the *cloned* dog," are not acting as real verbs, but as *verbals*. To learn more, see page 123.]

EXERCISE 3

1. I <u>have</u> always <u>wondered</u> how an Etch A Sketch <u>works</u>.

2. This flat TV-shaped toy <u>has been</u> popular since it first <u>arrived</u> in the 1960s.

3. Now I <u>have learned</u> the secrets inside this popular toy.

4. An Etch A Sketch is <u>filled</u> with a combination of metal powder and tiny plastic particles.

5. This mixture <u>clings</u> to the inside of the Etch A Sketch screen.

6. When the pointer that <u>is connected</u> to the two knobs <u>moves</u>, the tip of it "<u>draws</u>" lines in the powder on the back of the screen.

7. The powder at the bottom of the Etch A Sketch <u>does</u> not <u>fill in</u> these lines because it is too far away.

8. But if the Etch A Sketch is <u>turned</u> upside down, the powder <u>clings</u> to the whole underside surface of the screen and "erases" the image again.

9. Although the basic Etch A Sketch <u>has</u> not <u>changed</u> since I <u>was</u> a kid, it now <u>comes</u> in several different sizes.

10. Best of all, these great drawing devices <u>have</u> never <u>needed</u> batteries, and I <u>hope</u> that they never <u>will</u> [need batteries].

EXERCISE 4

1. During my last semester of high school, our English teacher assigned a special paper.

2. He said that he was becoming depressed by all the bad news out there, so each of us was asked to find a piece of good news and write a short research paper about it.

3. I must admit that I had no idea how hard that assignment would be.

4. Finally, I found an article while I was reading my favorite magazine.

5. The title of the article was a pun; it was called "Grin Reaper."

6. I knew instantly that it must be just the kind of news my teacher wanted.

7. The article explained that one woman, Pam Johnson, had started a club that she named The Secret Society of Happy People.

8. She had even chosen August 8 as "Admit You're Happy Day" and had already convinced more than fifteen state governors to recognize the holiday.

9. The club and the holiday were created to support people who are happy so that the unhappy, negative people around will not bring the happy people down.

10. As I was writing my essay, I visited the Society of Happy People Web site, *www. sohp.com*, and signed my teacher up for their newsletter.

EXERCISE 5

1. Donald Redelmeier was sitting in front of his television a few years ago, and he was not alone.

2. He was enjoying the Academy Awards along with millions of other TV viewers.

3. Redelmeier focused on the nominees as they were waiting for the announcement of the winners' names.

4. Suddenly, he was struck by the good health and lively mannerisms of them all.

5. Redelmeier's experiences as a doctor of ordinary people did not match w^ was seeing on TV.   ᴐn on

6. He devised a study that would explore the effects of success and re^ health.   ᴐf subjects

7. He would use the winners and losers of Academy Awards as ^ for his data.

8. He <u>wondered</u> if Oscar winners <u>would live</u> longer than losers and those who <u>had</u>
never <u>been nominated</u>.

9. The results of his study <u>showed</u> that the winners <u>do live</u> an average of four years
longer than the losers.

10. Luckily, nominees who <u>lose</u> also <u>live</u> a few months longer than those who <u>are</u> not
<u>nominated</u>, so they <u>do get</u> some benefits.

REVIEW EXERCISE

The Physics—Our Homemade Cloaking Device

If <u>we</u> <u>were</u> to make ourselves invisible, an <u>observer</u> <u>would</u> not <u>see</u> us,
but <u>would</u> <u>see</u> <u>whatever</u> <u>is</u> (on the other side) (of us). (In order) to do this, <u>we</u>
<u>would have</u> to prevent light (from reflecting) off (of us), and also somehow <u>bend</u>
the light (from objects) (behind us) (into the prying eyes of inquisitive observers).
<u>We</u> <u>would need</u> to create a mirage.

(For our purposes) <u>we</u> <u>will play</u> around (with a couple) (of optical concepts).
<u>We</u> <u>will redirect</u> light (in order) to create a crude "cloaking device"/mirage. Maybe
<u>we</u> <u>won't be</u> invisible, but at least <u>we</u> <u>might confuse</u> and <u>irritate</u> our adversary (for
a second). [First <u>we</u> <u>will make</u>] our imaginary spaceship completely black so that
no <u>light</u> <u>will be reflected</u> off (of its surface). Then <u>we</u> <u>will try</u> to create the mirage
ᶠ the background stars and planets) where an <u>observer</u> <u>would be looking</u> (at the

᠆᠆We <u>will consider</u> applying the following methods to make our homemade
opʟ

ᶜeption: (1) <u>surround</u> the ship (with fiber optics cables), and (2) <u>find</u> a
way tᶜ

light (around the ship).

The fiber optics idea is pretty simple. All [that] we need to do is [to] use total internal reflection (inside the cables) to bend light (around the ship). . . .

Will this work? Well it depends what we mean (by "work.") We can divert light such that we create a mirage (in front) (of the ship), but we are going to have problems (with reflections) off (of the exterior) (of the cables), and not all (of the light) will necessarily be totally internally reflected because it depends (on the angle) (of the rays) relative (to the cables). This means [that] *we will be able to see the cables*. (In addition), light rays can diffuse as they pass (through the cables) so that the image/mirage won't be as sharp (as the original). Will we be invisible? Not really. Will it be a pretty cool effect? I think so!

USING STANDARD ENGLISH VERBS (PP. 99–102)

EXERCISE 1
1. packs, packed
2. are, were
3. walk, walked
4. has, had
5. need, needed
6. does, did
7. is, was
8. like, liked
9. have, had
10. am, was

EXERCISE 2
1. do, did
2. are, were
3. has, had
4. type, typed
5. counts, counted
6. have, had
7. opens, opened
8. does, did
9. plan, planned
10. am, was

EXERCISE 3

1. do, don't
2. had, decided
3. was, played
4. talked
5. asked, was
6. was
7. were, were
8. enjoyed, liked
9. started, stopped
10. am, plan

EXERCISE 4

1. changed, want
2. had
3. signed, turned
4. was, were
5. did, were, did
6. observed, had
7. watched, helped
8. had
9. imagined, had
10. needs, are, am

EXERCISE 5

1. assigned
2. had
3. asked
4. liked
5. did
6. was, was
7. wanted
8. was, was
9. based, had
10. seemed, had

PROOFREADING PARAGRAPH

Most people believe that they ~~has~~ *have* the best pets. I think that we have the cutest pet hamster in the world. Her name is Toots. The name ~~come~~ *comes* from the little dog that ~~die~~ *dies* in the movie *Lassie Come Home.* Our Toots ~~don't~~ *doesn't* look like that dog, but she ~~have~~ *has* something about her that reminds us of it. The dog in the movie ~~protect~~ *protects* her owner from some really mean men. When the men try to beat the man who ~~own~~ *owns* her, Toots is so brave. She ~~jump~~ *jumps* in front of her owner and saves him. Our hamster is small but fearless too, so her name is Toots.

USING REGULAR AND IRREGULAR VERBS (PP. 107–111)

EXERCISE 1
1. eat
2. eat
3. eating
4. eaten
5. ate

6. eats
7. eat
8. eaten
9. ate
10. eat

EXERCISE 2
1. buy, bought
2. know, knew
3. is, are
4. agree, agree
5. told, telling

6. sit, sat
7. having, have
8. got, getting
9. need, need
10. am, are

EXERCISE 3
1. took, supposed
2. did, earned
3. called, told, feel
4. thought, was
5. leaving, drove, saw

6. felt, knew, tell
7. tried, went
8. been, undo
9. wishes, take
10. used, called, does

EXERCISE 4
1. use, puts
2. does, do
3. transfers, spend
4. is, like, choose
5. does, wants

6. trusts, is
7. imagine, made
8. talking, asked, worries
9. looked, said, lived, understand
10. wonder, is

EXERCISE 5
1. lying, fell
2. was, done
3. wearing, shielded
4. lain, woke, realized, happened
5. felt, started

6. passed, turned, began
7. describe, experienced
8. was, felt, saw
9. looked, taped, was, protected, wearing
10. had, felt

PROGRESS TEST (P. 112)

1. B. (incorrect verb form) As soon as I *finished* the test, the bell rang.

2. A. (fragment) Textbooks *are* available online.

3. A. (run-on) Our class took a field trip to the museum, and I loved it.

4. B. (incorrect word form) I should *have* gone to the library sooner.

5. A. (incorrect word form) We were *supposed* to lock the door after class.

6. B. (incorrect word form) *They're* going away for spring break, and I'm staying at home.

7. B. (incorrect word form) We were *surprised* that it was delivered on time.

8. A. (incorrect verb form) In my math class, we've already *taken* three quizzes.

9. B. (run-on) Nothing worked, so we all got off the bus and waited for another one.

10. A. (fragment) I don't like the taste of grapefruits or lemons.

MAINTAINING SUBJECT-VERB AGREEMENT (PP. 116–119)

EXERCISE 1

1. wrinkles
2. is
3. absorbs
4. absorb
5. soak, have

6. swells, expands
7. result
8. doesn't
9. block
10. take, get

EXERCISE 2

1. are, involve
2. suffer
3. are
4. come, lead
5. start, works, plays

6. starts
7. are
8. cause
9. is
10. warn

EXERCISE 3

1. is
2. has
3. starts
4. puts, wants
5. likes

6. have, looks
7. let, wants
8. have
9. helps, turn
10. am, is

EXERCISE 4

1. think, picture
2. are, live
3. is
4. encounter
5. goes, looks

6. have, defend
7. tease, taunt, gives, leaves
8. run, make
9. is, flicks, kicks
10. work, swoop, pounce

EXERCISE 5

1. is, call
2. is, are, has
3. is, are, is
4. have, is
5. are, are

6. experiences, has
7. are, functions
8. determine
9. seems
10. affect, tend

PROOFREADING EXERCISE

    I exercise in a large park near my house several times a week. The fresh air and pretty scenery ~~refreshes~~ *refresh* me and make me happy. There ~~is~~ *are* several paths I can follow each day. One of my favorite walks ~~go~~ *goes* up a steep hill and down through a grove of ferns. The droplets of water on the ferns ~~splashes~~ *splash* on me as I brush past them. Then the path ~~open~~ *opens* into a grassy area that ~~take~~ *takes* my breath away sometimes. The late afternoon sunlight ~~shine~~ *shines* through the branches of a few large trees, and it ~~create~~ *creates* beautiful shadows on top of the grass. Another of the paths goes straight between a row of tall, narrow trees. The trunks of the trees ~~is~~ *are* smooth, but their leafy tops ~~sways~~ *sway* in the wind because they are so high. I love my afternoon walks in the park.

AVOIDING SHIFTS IN TIME (PP. 121–122)

1. Plastic surgery helps many people look better and feel better about themselves. Of course, there *are* stories of unnecessary surgeries and even heartbreaking mistakes. People *can* make their own decisions about whether plastic surgery *is* right for them. Dogs, however, can't communicate what they want. Nevertheless, some people *take* their dogs in for cosmetic surgeries, such as tummy tucks and face-lifts. Just like humans, dogs sometimes *need* surgery to correct painful or unhealthy conditions. A dog with a low-hanging tummy *can* get an infection from scratches that *are* caused by rocks on the ground. And another dog may need a face-lift to help it stay clean when it eats. Animal lovers *are* worried that some canine plastic surgeries *are* done without good reasons.

2. The paragraph is correct.

3. I really enjoyed my winter break this year. It was too short, of course, but I *made* the most of the time I had. My extended family had a reunion at my aunt's house in St. Louis. I didn't pack enough coats and sweaters, but the loving atmosphere *kept* me warm. Once I *was* back in the same house with my cousins, we goofed off just the way we used to when we were kids. One night my four closest cousins and I *stayed* up after everyone else *was* in bed. We played board games and ate buttery popcorn and got the game pieces all greasy just like the old days. Overall, my trip to St. Louis with its late-night game marathon *was* the highlight of my winter vacation.

RECOGNIZING VERBAL PHRASES (PP. 124–128)

EXERCISE 1

1. Mark Twain lived [to become one of the most [admired] Americans of his time].

2. [Traveling across the U.S. and to countries around the world], Twain formed [unwavering] opinions, both favorable and unfavorable, of the people and places he visited.

3. Twain began [to write his autobiography] in the last years before he died in 1910.

4. [Hoping to be honest and thorough], he decided [to dictate his thoughts as they struck him].

5. However, he knew that it might be impossible [to be as honest] as he wanted [to be].

6. [Being truthful] meant [including statements that could hurt or upset the people that he knew], and he knew almost everyone.

7. Twain <u>thought</u> of a way [to avoid [causing that potential pain or embarrassment]].

8. He <u>decided</u> not [to publish his autobiography until 100 years after his death].

9. In that way, Twain <u>did</u> not <u>need</u> [to hold back any of his strong opinions].

10. In 2010, the first volume of *The Autobiography of Mark Twain* <u>was</u> finally <u>released</u>, [making it one of the most [anticipated] books of all time].

EXERCISE 2

1. The idea of [home-schooling children] <u>has become</u> more popular recently.

2. Many parents <u>have decided</u> [to teach kids themselves] instead of [sending them to public or private school].

3. There <u>are</u> many different reasons [to choose [home-schooling]].

4. In Hollywood, for instance, child actors often <u>must use</u> [home-schooling] due to their schedules.

5. The [home-schooling] option <u>allows</u> for one of their parents, or a special teacher, [to continue] [to instruct them on the set].

6. Other parents simply <u>want</u> [to be directly involved in their child's [learning]].

7. Many school districts <u>have</u> special independent study "schools," [offering parents the structure and materials] that they <u>need</u> [to provide an appropriate curriculum on their own].

8. Children <u>do</u> all of their [reading] and [writing] at home, with their parents [guiding them along the way].

9. The family <u>meets</u> with the independent study school's teacher regularly [to go over the child's work] and [to clarify any points of confusion].

10. Many parents <u>would like</u> [to have the time] [to home-school their children].

EXERCISE 3

1. [Finding the exact origin of the game of poker] <u>is</u> probably impossible.

2. Some <u>think</u> that it <u>started</u> as a game [played in China around a thousand years ago].

3. Others <u>have</u> a theory [placing its origins in an ancient Persian game] that <u>involves</u> [using twenty-five cards with five suits].

4. Poker also <u>has</u> similarities to the game "poque," [played by the French when they <u>colonized</u> New Orleans in the 1700s].

5. [Betting] and [bluffing] <u>were</u> both aspects of poque.

6. So <u>was</u> a deck of cards [containing the four suits] [used in modern poker]: diamonds, hearts, spades, and clubs.

7. In the 1800s, Jonathan H. Green <u>wrote</u> about a pastime [called the "[cheating] game."]

8. He <u>observed</u> that people [traveling down the Mississippi river] <u>enjoyed</u> this card game.

9. Green <u>used</u> the name "poker" for the first time [to identify it].

10. Since human [beings] <u>have</u> always <u>loved</u> games, [tracing the history of one game] <u>can be</u> difficult.

EXERCISE 4

1. Some travelers <u>want</u> [to know how [to behave in other countries]].

2. *Behave Yourself!* <u>is</u> a book [written [to help such people]].

3. It <u>outlines</u> what [to do] and what not [to do] in countries around the world.

4. In Austria, for example, [cutting your food with a fork] <u>is</u> more polite than [cutting it with a knife].

5. In Egypt, [nodding the head upward]—not [shaking the head from side to side]—<u>means</u> "no."

6. In the Netherlands, [complimenting people about their clothes] <u>is</u> not a good idea.

7. An Italian diner <u>will fold</u> lettuce into a bite-size piece with the fork and knife instead of [cutting it].

8. A common mistake that people <u>make</u> in many countries <u>is</u> [to stand with their hands on their hips].

9. This posture and [pointing at anything with the fingers] <u>are thought</u> [to be very rude] and even [threatening].

10. Travelers <u>should study</u> any country before [visiting it] in order [to avoid [confusing] or [offending] anyone].

EXERCISE 5

1. John Steinbeck, author of *The Grapes of Wrath,* was the first native of California [to receive the Nobel Prize for literature].

2. [Calling his hometown of Salinas "Lettuceberg,"] Steinbeck's [writing] made the area famous.

3. At the time, not everyone liked the attention [brought by his portrayals of life in *Cannery Row* and other works].

4. Steinbeck's father was the treasurer of Monterey County for ten years, [working also for the Spreckels company].

5. John Steinbeck tried [to find satisfaction in his birthplace], [enrolling in and quitting his studies at Stanford University many times].

6. Finally, Steinbeck moved to New York, [distancing himself from his California roots].

7. Steinbeck won the Nobel Prize in 1962, [revealing the literary world's esteem for his work].

8. Not [writing anything of the caliber of the Salinas stories] while [living in New York], Steinbeck did return to California before he died in 1968.

9. In 1972, the Salinas library changed its name, [to be known thereafter as the John Steinbeck Library].

10. And the house Steinbeck was born in became a restaurant and then a full-[fledged] museum [chronicling the life of Salinas' most [celebrated] citizen].

PARAGRAPH EXERCISE

Somewhere amid the narrow lanes, the [congested] wharves, the stables, workshops, forges, and fairs of the medieval city of Strasbourg, Frau Troffea stepped outside and began [to dance]. So far as we can tell no music was playing and she showed no signs of joy as her skirts flew up around her rapidly [moving] legs. To the consternation of her husband, she went on [dancing throughout the day]. And as the shadows lenghtened and the sun set behind the city's half-[timbered] houses, it became clear that Frau Troffea simply could not stop. Only after many hours of [crazed] motion did she collapse from exhaustion. [Bathed in sweat] and [twitching], she finally <u>sank</u> into a brief restorative sleep. Then, a few hours later, she <u>resumed</u> her solitary jig. Through much of the [following] day she <u>went</u> on, fatigue [rendering her movements increasingly violent and erratic]. Once again, exhaustion <u>prevailed</u> and a weary sleep <u>took</u> hold.

SENTENCE WRITING

Your sentences may vary, but make sure that your verbals are not actually the main verbs of your clauses. You should be able to double underline your real verbs, as we have done here.

[Shopping for holiday food] <u>is</u> fun.

[Earning enough money for a vacation] <u>can take</u> a long time.

I <u>like</u> [giving my dog a bath].

My dog <u>hates</u> [wearing a leash].

We <u>tried</u> [to drive all the way up the coast in one day].

Neither of them <u>knows</u> how [to sew].

They <u>need</u> [to talk about their problems].

[Given a chance], I <u>could climb</u> that rope.

The [baked] apples <u>tasted</u> delicious.

Projects [built by Habitat for Humanity] <u>are supported</u> by the community.

CORRECTING MISPLACED OR DANGLING MODIFIERS (PP. 130–132)

Answers may vary. Corrections are in *italics.*

EXERCISE 1

1. *As I was walking up the stairs,* I found a cell phone.

2. *Because that play was full of surprises, we loved it* and want to see it again.

3. *The tires on his car* need to be replaced.

4. *Because I scribbled it quickly,* I could not read the phone number.

5. The sentence is correct.

6. With outdated functions and styling, *my cell phone needs to be upgraded.*

7. *After I took several photographs,* the shadows on the trees disappeared.

8. The sentence is correct.

9. The sentence is correct.

10. *After he talked to the doctor,* his ear started to feel better.

EXERCISE 2

1. The sentence is correct.

2. The sentence is correct.

3. *In the store,* she kicked her mother by accident.

4. *Searching outside the house,* the inspector found a few termites.

5. The sentence is correct.

6. *Waiting in line at the new restaurant, I couldn't wait to taste the food.*

7. The sentence is correct.

8. *The State of California offers a test for students who are sixteen to get out of high school early.*

9. The sentence is correct.

10. The sentence is correct.

EXERCISE 3

1. They finally found their lost credit card; *it had been lying under the table for a week.*

2. *Walking down the hall, she located the door to the auditorium.*

3. The sentence is correct.

4. *My doctor told me to drink extra water after taking an aspirin.*

5. The sentence is correct.

6. Our mail carrier *tripped on a crack in the sidewalk and fell.*

7. *Since we argued nonstop,* the road trip was not as much fun as we hoped it would be.

8. The sentence is correct.

9. The sentence is correct.

10. The students immediately liked their substitute teacher, *who smiled nicely at everyone.*

1. *After I got a headache from the fumes,* the ferry finally made it across the river.

2. *That carnival sold cotton candy full of empty calories, but it was the best I'd ever tasted.*

3. *Two months after we moved out,* our old apartment is still empty.

4. *In her e-mail message,* she promised to return the library books.

5. *Sitting in small groups,* the students took the notes.

6. *Before we said goodnight,* the porch light burned out.

7. Our hostess showed us her favorite room; *it was decorated beautifully.*

8. *I saw a tiny gray mouse* scampering along the baseboards of the cabin.

9. The sentence is correct.

10. All along the highway, volunteers *wearing special T-shirts* planted trees.

EXERCISE 5

1. Feeling the excitement of the first day of school, *I left my backpack behind.*

2. We saw the new movie that everyone is talking about; *it was full of explosions.*

3. My cousins and I, *wearing our pajamas,* always wrapped our gifts on the night before the holiday.

4. *Now that he practices for an hour a day,* his tennis has improved.

5. *Rising and falling several times a year,* the price of gasoline fluctuates.

6. The sentence is correct.

7. *Hiking in the nearby mountains,* they discovered a new trail.

8. She felt pressure *from her parents* to get good grades.

9. The sentence is correct.

10. The sentence is correct.

PROOFREADING EXERCISE

Corrections are *italicized.* Yours may differ slightly.

Hoping to become famous and wealthy, a man in Edinburgh, Scotland, has invented a device. *Located just above the trunk and visible from behind,* the device is a variation on the center-mounted brake light used in the design of many new cars. Instead of just a solid red brake light, however, this invention displays to other drivers *words* written in bold, red-lighted letters.

With simplicity in mind, *the inventor limited the machine's vocabulary* to three words: "Sorry," "Thanks," and "Help." After making an aggressive lane change, *we could use the machine* to apologize. Or after being allowed to go ahead of someone, we could thank the considerate person responsible. Of course, *with the use* of the "Help" display, we could summon fellow citizens for assistance.

And there is no need to worry about operating the device while driving. With three easy-to-reach buttons, *we could activate the messages* without taking our eyes off the road.

FOLLOWING SENTENCE PATTERNS (PP. 135–139)

EXERCISE 1

```
       S   LV            Desc
```
1. Sleep is an important part (of life).

```
       S              S    AV    Obj
```
2. Animals and humans use sleep (as a vacation) (for their brains and bodies).

```
          S                      AV        Obj
```
3. Some facts (about sleep) might surprise people.

```
          S      AV      Obj          S     AV
```
4. Large animals require less sleep than small animals do.

```
        S        AV
```
5. A typical cat will sleep (for twelve hours) (in a day).

```
                 S        AV
```
6. An ordinary elephant will sleep (for only three hours).

```
          S    AV      Obj          Obj
```
7. Smaller animals use their brains and bodies (at higher rates).

```
            S    AV      Obj
```
8. Therefore, they need many hours (of sleep).

```
          S     LV Desc
```
9. The reverse is true (for large animals).

```
         S      AV
```
10. Humans fall (between cats and elephants) (for their sleep requirements).

EXERCISE 2

```
         S    AV            Obj
```
1. Many people get migraine headaches.

```
          S        LV            Desc
```
2. These headaches can be extremely painful.

        S   AV

3. People (with migraines) <u>may</u> also <u>suffer</u> (from nausea and dizziness).

                   S   AV   Obj   Obj

4. Migraine <u>sufferers</u> <u>avoid</u> bright lights and loud sounds.

                  S   AV   Obj

5. These <u>sensations</u> <u>cause</u> a different kind (of discomfort).

               S   AV   Obj

6. Some <u>medicines</u> <u>reduce</u> the pain (of migraine headaches).

               S   AV

7. Other <u>drugs</u> <u>help</u> (with the additional symptoms).

               S   LV   Desc

8. No migraine <u>treatment</u> <u>is</u> perfect (for everyone).

          S   AV   Obj

9. <u>Scientists</u> <u>have been studying</u> migraine headaches (for years).

          S   LV   Desc

10. A <u>cure</u> (for migraines) <u>is</u> long overdue.

          S   LV   Desc

1. Horatio <u>Greenough</u> <u>was</u> a sculptor (in the 1800s).

          S   AV   Obj

2. <u>Greenough</u> <u>created</u> a controversial statue (of George Washington).

          S   AV   Obj   S   LV   Desc

3. The <u>statue</u> <u>weighed</u> twelve tons, but its <u>weight</u> <u>was</u> not the reason (for the controversy).

                  S   AV   Obj

4. The controversial <u>aspect</u> (of the statue) <u>involved</u> Washington's clothes.

         S   AV   Obj

5. The <u>statue</u> <u>portrayed</u> Washington (in a toga-like garment).

            S   S   S   LV   Desc   Desc

6. His <u>stomach</u>, <u>chest</u>, and <u>arms</u> <u>were</u> bare and very muscular.

        S   AV

7. One part (of the toga) draped (over the statue's raised right arm).

                 S   AV

8. The bare-chested statue (of Washington) stood (in the rotunda) (of the Capitol) (for only three years).

        S   AV   Obj

9. Officials moved the statue many times.

                  S AV

10. (In 1962), it arrived (in its final home) (at the American History Museum).

EXERCISE 4

      S   LV   Desc   Desc

1. Cakes can be plain or fancy.

                      S   S   AV Obj

2. Most grocery stores and almost all bakeries sell cakes.

      S   AV

3. They range (in price) depending (on size, occasion, and amount of decoration).

    [*Depending* begins a verbal phrase.]

       S   AV

4. A cake (with a "Happy Birthday" inscription) will usually cost thirty (to fifty)

   Obj
   dollars.

                 S   LV   Desc

5. Wedding cakes, however, are often very expensive.

                         S   AV   Obj

6. An elaborate wedding cake may cost several hundred or even a thousand dollars.

                                 S   LV

7. The multilayered traditional white wedding cake still seems the most popular

   Desc
   kind.

                     S   AV   Obj

8. These delicate structures need special care (during transportation).

         S   AV   Obj

9. Some couples order two or more smaller cakes (for the occasion).

        S   AV   Obj   Obj

10. People sometimes save a slice or section (of their wedding cake) (as a memento).

                                                      S   AV   Obj

1. (In 1998), Sotheby's auction house sold a piece (of sixty-year-old wedding cake) (for an amazing price).

   S   AV

2. It had belonged (to the Duke and Duchess) (of Windsor).

                                  S   AV

3. (On June 3, 1937), the famous couple married (in France).

                                    S   AV   Obj

4. (On the day) (of their wedding), they put a piece (of cake) (in a pink box) and

   AV   Obj

tied a pink bow (around it).

   S   AV   Obj   S   AV

5. They identified its contents as "a piece of our wedding cake"; they initialed and

   AV   Obj   S AV Obj

dated the box, and they kept it (as a memento) (for the rest) (of their lives).

                         S   S   AV   LV Desc

6. This couple's relationship, which began (in the 1930s), was one (of the most famous love affairs) (in history).

          S   AV   Obj

7. The Duke (of Windsor) gave up the throne (of England) to be (with Wallis

                                 S   AV

Simpson), the woman that he loved. [*To be* begins a verbal phrase.]

                         S   LV   Desc

8. Unfortunately, she was a divorced American woman and could not, therefore,

   AV   Obj   S   AV

marry the king (of England), so he abdicated.

                                     S

9. The pre-auction estimate (for the box) containing the piece (of their wedding

         LV   Desc

cake) was five hundred (to a thousand) dollars. [*Containing* begins a verbal phrase.]

                        S   AV   S   LV

10. When the gavel came down, the high bid (by a couple) (from San Francisco) was

   Desc

$29,900.

PARAGRAPH EXERCISE

    [S] Armstrong [AV] released [Obj] his grip (on the handrail) (of the ladder) and [AV] stepped fully (off the foot pad). [S] Walter Cronkite proudly [AV] told [Obj] his CBS audience that a 38-year-old [S] American [AV] was now standing (on the surface) (of the Moon). When [S] Armstrong [AV] scraped [Obj] his foot (across the surface), [S] he [AV] noticed [Obj (dep. clause)] that the dark powdery [S] material [AV] coated his overshoe. "The [S] surface [LV] is [Desc] fine and powdery. [S] I [AV] can kick [Obj] it up loosely (with my toe). [S] It [AV] adheres (in fine layers) (like powdery charcoal) (to the sole and sides) (of my boots)." Although his [S] boots only slightly [AV] impressed the [Obj] surface, the [S] material [AV] preserved [Obj] the imprint (of his boots) very well. "[S] I only [AV adv] go in a small fraction (of an inch)—maybe one-eighth (of an inch)—but [S] I [AV] can see the [Obj] prints (of my boots) and the [Obj] treads (in the fine, sandy particles)."

AVOIDING CLICHÉS, AWKWARD PHRASING, AND WORDINESS (PP. 140–144)

Your revisions may differ.

    1. My favorite class in high school was the cooking class I took in tenth grade. The class was an independent study, so I got to choose my own meals to cook and eat. The assignments were all the same: research a meal from a particular country or culture, buy the ingredients for the meal, and learn to cook it. To get a grade, I brought my teacher a sample of the food along with my report about making it. Then I received my grade.

    2. *While You Were Sleeping* is one of my favorite holiday movies. I love the scenes in the snow and at holiday parties. In the story, Sandra Bullock's character saves a man's life after he is injured at the train station where she works. He goes into a coma, and she pretends to be his fiancée. While he is unconscious, she gets close to his whole family, especially his brother. Suddenly, the man in the coma wakes up. Eventually, everyone realizes that Bullock's character and the man's brother belong together, and the story ends happily.

3. Ancient civilizations mummified the remains of adults, children, and animals. Mummification was a way to help these beings enter the next world and to show them respect. One mummy of an Eskimo baby found in Greenland dated back to the 1400s. It was wrapped in beautiful fur to protect it from the cold. In Egypt, archeologists discovered the mummies of cats, crocodiles, cows, baboons, and birds. In Alaska, experts found a huge, perfectly preserved bison mummy that was over 35,000 years old. A big lion's tooth in its neck revealed how it probably died.

CORRECTING FOR PARALLEL STRUCTURE (PP. 145–150)

Your answers may differ from these possible revisions.

EXERCISE 1

1. Preparing for emergencies involves two steps: planning for anything and gathering certain supplies.

2. The sentence is correct.

3. The sentence is correct.

4. Where would you go, and how would you get there?

5. Have you made a list of phone contacts inside and outside the area?

6. Do the adults, teenagers, and children in the family carry those phone numbers with them?

7. Are the most important supplies ready at hand, including water, food, flashlight, radio, and batteries?

8. Have you assembled your own first-aid kit or bought a ready-made one?

9. Do you stay prepared by reading, understanding, and updating your important insurance policies?

10. By planning for anything and stocking up on the right supplies, you can prepare yourself and your family for emergencies.

EXERCISE 2

1. I have read about many foods that can help people stay healthy and live longer.

2. Eating whole wheat bread benefits the brain and increases energy.

3. Apples contain ingredients to aid memory, keep lungs healthy, and prevent cancer.

4. Kidney beans can reduce cholesterol, increase energy, and stabilize moods.

5. Oranges fight inflammation and loss of eyesight.

6. Substances found in fish can prevent heart problems, depression, and high cholesterol.

7. Milk boosts the nervous system and postpones aging.

8. Antioxidants in red grapes benefit the heart, protect the brain, and prevent cancer.

9. The sentence is correct.

10. By eating these foods, people can live longer, stay stronger, and be happier.

EXERCISE 3

1. I like coffee and tea.

2. I've heard that coffee is bad for you, but tea is good for you.

3. It must not be the caffeine that's bad because both coffee and tea have caffeine.

4. The sentence is correct.

5. All teas are supposed to be healthy, but green tea is supposed to be the healthiest.

6. The sentence is correct.

7. I love orange pekoe tea with tons of milk and sugar.

8. The sentence is correct.

9. I know that all coffee comes from coffee beans, but I didn't know that all tea comes from *Camellia sinensis* leaves.

10. The sentence is correct.

EXERCISE 4

1. I was washing my car two weeks ago and noticed a few bees buzzing around the roof of my garage.

2. I didn't worry about it at the time, but I should have.

3. The sentence is correct.

4. The sentence is correct.

5. They flew in a pattern as if they were riding on a roller coaster or over waves.

6. The sentence is correct.

7. There was nothing I could do but wait in my car until they went away.

8. Finally, the bees flew straight up into the air and disappeared.

9. Once inside my house, I opened the phone book and called a bee expert.

10. The sentence is correct.

EXERCISE 5
Your revisions may differ.

1. The sentence is correct.

2. First, avoid getting frustrated if you have to wait a long time in the reception area or the exam room.

3. Always answer the doctor's questions first; then ask your own questions.

4. Inquire about a referral to a specialist if you think you need one.

5. Find out about other treatments besides the one the doctor first recommends.

6. Ask about any tests that the doctor orders and determine how to get in touch with the doctor about the results.

7. Take the time to ask about prescription drugs' side effects and optional medicines.

8. Try to be calm in your discussions with the doctor.

9. Finally, be prepared to wait in a long line at the pharmacy.

10. If you follow these suggestions when visiting a doctor, you will be more informed and feel more involved in your own treatment.

PROOFREADING EXERCISE
Your revisions may differ.

The world knows relatively little about the life of William Shakespeare. Stanley Wells' book *Is It True What They Say about Shakespeare?* addresses the questions that people continue to have about the famous poet and playwright. Because of Shakespeare's talent and reputation, everyone wants to know when he was born, which schools he went to, where he traveled, who his friends or lovers were, what he looked like, as well as how and when he wrote each of his poems and plays. Wells starts with the basic question "Is it true that . . .?" Throughout the book, he identifies commonly held beliefs about Shakespeare, discusses the historical evidence, and judges each belief to be "true," "untrue," or something in between. Wells even examines the numerous theories that someone else wrote the works of Shakespeare but finds no evidence strong enough to convince him of their validity.

USING PRONOUNS (PP. 151–157)

EXERCISE 1

1. I

2. I

3. she and I

4. she

5. she and I

6. I

7. she

8. her and me

9. her

10. me

EXERCISE 2

Your revisions may differ.

1. its

2. its

3. its

4. their

5. One day last week, the passengers had to gather their belongings . . . .

6. their

7. their

8. The passengers did their best to hide their annoyance . . . .

9. As the passengers stepped off the bus at the end of the line, the driver thanked them for their patience and understanding.

10. it

EXERCISE 3

Your revisions may differ slightly.

1. me

2. he (. . . taller than *he was.*)

3. She and he (or *They* are working . . . .)

4. The dentists received gift bags full of toothbrushes and dental floss. (To avoid wordiness, we deleted the *his or her* pronouns, as well as *Each of* in the beginning.)

5. their

6. I (*I* was the person responsible . . . .)

7. The audience expressed its opinion of the performances with its applause. (To avoid wordiness, we changed the subject to *audience* and used the pronoun *its*.)

8. its

9. I (. . . better than *I do*.)

10. she

EXERCISE 4

1. I (. . . as *I am*.)

2. she (. . . than *she does*.)

3. she

4. their

5. its

6. Everyone must use *a* password to enter the network.

7. me (. . . or *by me*.)

8. she (*She* and Justin were the winners. . . .)

9. their

10. us (. . . judge sent *us* a message.)

EXERCISE 5

1. me

2. Students will buy *their* own materials for the jewelry class.

3. their

4. I

5. Due to the holiday, everyone was allowed to turn *the* essay in late.

6. she

7. he (. . . than *he is*.)

8. I

9. me

10. her

Corrections are *italicized.*

My daughter and *I* drove up the coast to visit a little zoo I had heard about. *The zoo was a hundred miles away, and the drive took* about two hours. Once *she* and I arrived, we saw the petting zoo area and wanted to pet the baby animals, but *the zoo employees* wouldn't let us. They said that it was the baby animals' resting time, so we couldn't pet them. Then we got to the farm animals. There was a prize-winning hog. *When the huge pig was lying down, it was as big as a couch.* My daughter liked the hog best of all, and as she and I drove home in the car, *that big pig* was all she could talk about.

AVOIDING SHIFTS IN PERSON (PP. 158–160)

1. Americans have always had more than they actually need. Americans have gotten used to having as much food, water, and clothes as they want. Restaurants throw away plates and plates of food every day. If people don't want something, they throw it in the trash. But a lot of people have started to think differently. Recycling doesn't just involve aluminum cans and plastic bottles. Americans can recycle food, water, and clothes if they think more creatively and responsibly than they've been doing in the past. People can change the society's view of recycling by just doing it.

2. The paragraph is correct.

3. If I had a choice to live in the city or the country, I would choose the city. I would choose the city because I am surrounded by other people there, and it feels friendly. The country is too quiet. There is dirt everywhere, flies flying around in the sky, bugs—which I hate—crawling on the floor inside and out. The city is a place where the lights are always on. Yes, I deal with pollution, smog, and crowds, but it just feels like home to me. A city house can be any size, shape, and color. All the houses in the country look the same to me. No matter who the country people are, they have a white house and a big red barn. I have to admit that I have only been to the country a couple of times to visit my relatives, but the city would have to be the place for me.

REVIEW OF SENTENCE STRUCTURE ERRORS (PP. 161–163)

Your corrections may differ.

1. B. not parallel (We *saw* two shows by Cirque du Soleil, *made* several trips to the buffet, and *won* some money at the roulette table.)
2. A. subject-verb agreement error (A huge stack of textbooks *was* blocking the main aisle. . . .)

3. A.   shift in time (As the teacher entered the classroom on the first day, she *took* out an instant camera.)

4. B.   incorrect pronoun (They've taught my classmates and *me* how to proofread. . . .)

5. A.   fragment (If students apply for financial aid in the middle of a school year, they might not receive money in time to pay their registration and tuition fees.)

6. A.   incorrect pronoun (All of my friends are better gamblers than *I am*).

7. B.   run-on sentence (The fans were confused, and so were the players.)

8. A.   shift in time (I *was* interested in business; it was my original choice of major.)

9. B.   awkward phrasing (She told me that *I needed to learn perspective.*)

10. A.   misplaced modifier (*We could see dangerous-looking electrical wires hanging from the clock in the classroom.*)

11. A.   wordy (*I hate to buy a used book* full of someone else's notes and markings.)

12. B.   cliché (It seems as though I am *constantly* working.)

13. B.   misplaced modifier (Mom, Dad, aunts, uncles, cousins, and brothers—we all surprised her by jumping out of closets and from behind furniture.)

14. B.   pronoun agreement error (*We were all holding our hands over our ears.*)

15. A.   dangling modifier (At the age of seven, *Jake* moved to my neighborhood.)

PROOFREADING EXERCISE

MOTHER TELLS ALL

I have learned the most memorable lessons about myself from my children. A mother is always on display; she has nowhere to hide. And children are like parrots; they repeat whatever they hear. If I change my mind about something, they will remind me of every word I said.

For example, last summer I told my kids that I planned to take an exercise class and lose about forty pounds. I did lose some weight, and I attended an exercise class. But I started to feel like a balloon losing air. I decided that I did not want to lose any more weight or exercise anymore. I expected my children to accept my decision.

When I stopped, one of my sons said, "Mom, you need to go back to exercise class." Then they all started telling me what to eat, and I felt horrible. I had given up these things because I wanted to, but my words were still being repeated like a nonstop alarm clock. Finally, my kids got bored with the idea of my losing weight.

Sometimes, when one of them makes a joke about my "attempt" to lose weight, it hurts me that they don't understand.

From this experience, I have learned not to tell my children about a plan unless I am going to finish it. Otherwise, they will never let me forget.

PUNCTUATION AND CAPITAL LETTERS

PERIOD, QUESTION MARK, EXCLAMATION POINT, SEMICOLON, COLON, DASH (PP. 167–171)

Your answers may vary slightly, especially in the use of optional pieces of punctuation (the exclamation point and the dash).

EXERCISE 1

1. Have you noticed that light bulbs don't last as long as they used to?

2. Some seem to burn out after only a month or two.

3. Would you believe that one light bulb has lasted for 110 years?

4. Well, it's true—believe it or not! (or.)

5. At a fire station in Livermore, California, the same bulb has been burning since 1901.

6. The now famous light bulb is treated like a celebrity by the firefighters.

7. They are proud of its history, and who wouldn't be?

8. The famous bulb doesn't get cleaned or covered by any type of shade; no one wants to risk damaging it or making it burn out after so many years.

9. The Livermore Light Bulb, as it's called, has even made it into the *Guinness Book of World Records* as the longest running light bulb.

10. Anyone who wants to see this famous bulb in action can visit its 24-hour webcam online.

EXERCISE 2
1. Have you heard of the phenomenon known as a "milky sea"?

2. Sailors throughout history have described this eerie condition.

3. A milky sea occurs when ocean water turns almost completely white.

4. What accounts for this milky color?

5. It is due to huge amounts of bacteria that glow with white light.

6. Until recently, no one had photographs or other visual proof of this condition.

7. In 1995, however, people took the first pictures of a milky sea off the coast of Somalia.

8. Scientists later reviewed satellite images from the same period and discovered their own startling documentation that milky seas exist.

9. The satellite photos clearly showed a long glowing white stretch of ocean water.

10. It was the size of the state of Connecticut. (or !)

EXERCISE 3

1. People can learn foreign languages in several new ways these days: by practicing with a partner, by studying on long plane flights, and by listening to foreign news on the radio or watching movies in other languages.

2. The Internet allows people—especially those who want to learn a language—to correspond easily with people from other countries.

3. The exchange goes something like this: one person wants to know French; he contacts a person in France who wants to learn English.

4. The two exchange e-mails; then, as they correct each other's phrasing, they learn more about the other's language.

5. Certain audio programs and books have been designed for one purpose: to offer airline passengers a quick course in a foreign language.

6. Portable music devices usually hold book-length works; therefore, these in-flight language programs are easy to use.

7. The sentence is correct.

8. It's easy to find foreign news sites on the Internet; these radio programs feature reporters who speak clearly and use many common phrases.

9. There is a variation that anyone with a DVD player can use: most DVD menus include the option of listening to the movie dubbed in another language.

10. In this way, movies can be even more entertaining; they can also be more educational.

EXERCISE 4

1. Nancy Cartwright is a well-known actress on television; however, we never see her when she is acting.

2. Cartwright is famous for playing one part: the voice of Bart Simpson.

3. Besides her career as the most mischievous Simpson, Cartwright is married and has children of her own—a son and a daughter.

4. The sentence is correct.

5. The sentence is correct.

6. The sentence is correct.

7. Bart is a boy; Cartwright is obviously a woman.

8. Bart is perpetually ten years old; Cartwright is in her fifties.

9. The sentence is correct.

10. When they yell for her to "Do Bart! Do Bart!" she declines by saying, "No way, man!"

EXERCISE 5

1. What do math and origami—Japanese paper folding—have to do with each other?

2. Erik Demaine and other origami mathematicians would answer, "Everything." (or "Everything!")

3. If you have never heard of the field of origami mathematics, you're not alone.

4. Origami math is a relatively new field; back in 2003, Demaine won a "genius" award partly due to his work with origami and its applications in many fields.

5. The MacArthur Foundation awarded Demaine more than just the title "genius"; it awarded him half a million dollars. (or !)

6. At twenty, Demaine was hired as a professor by the Massachusetts Institute of Technology; he became the youngest professor MIT has ever had.

7. Erik Demaine has his father to thank for much of his education: (or ;) Martin Demaine home-schooled Erik as the two of them traveled around North America.

8. Erik was always intensely interested in academic subjects; during his travels, he and his father would consult university professors whenever Erik had questions that no one else could answer.

9. Erik Demaine continues to investigate one area in particular: the single-cut problem.

10. This problem involves folding a piece of paper—then making one cut; the result can be anything from a swan to a star, a unicorn, or any letter of the alphabet.

PROOFREADING EXERCISE

The ingredients you will need for a lemon meringue pie are lemon juice, eggs, sugar, cornstarch, flour, butter, water, and salt. First, you combine flour, salt, butter, and water for the crust and bake until lightly brown; then you mix and cook the lemon juice, egg yolks, sugar, cornstarch, butter, and water for the filling. Once the filling is poured into the cooked crust, you whip the meringue. Meringue is made of egg whites and sugar. Pile the meringue on top of the lemon filling; place the pie in the hot oven for a few minutes, and you'll have the best lemon meringue pie you've ever tasted!

COMMA RULES 1, 2, AND 3 (PP. 173–178)

EXERCISE 1

1. An unusual 400-year-old mechanical clock went up for auction in 2007, and someone paid $135,000 for it.

2. The clock is made of brass covered in gold, but that's not what makes it valuable.

3. The clock's value lies in its unique design, for it's shaped like a skull resting on top of two crossed bones.

4. To view the time, a person must lift the skullcap, but the clock might scare the person away in the process.

5. The sentence is correct.

6. The sentence is correct.

7. The sentence is correct.

8. The sentence is correct.

9. This golden skull clock is definitely not for everyone, yet it is intriguing.

10. It may have been created four centuries ago, but it looks like a prop from a modern horror movie or graphic novel.

1. I graduated from high school on June 25, 2006, in San Antonio, Texas.

2. I was lucky to have an English teacher in high school who was young, enthusiastic, and highly motivated.

3. We read essays, stories, poems, and research articles in her class.

4. One time we read a short play, chose parts to memorize, and gave a performance of it in front of the whole school.

5. The sentence is correct.

6. She was trying to teach us how to follow directions, how to explain something clearly, and how to think about what she called our "tone of voice" when we wrote.

7. We had to write a real letter of complaint about a product, a service, or an experience that was unsatisfactory to us.

8. Then we sent a copy of our letter to the company's business address, to our home address, and to Ms. Kern's school address.

9. Ms. Kern assured us that we would receive a response from the company if we explained our complaint well, asked for a reasonable solution, and used an appropriate tone.

10. In the big envelope from my company was a letter of apology, a bumper sticker, and an impressive discount coupon to use at any of the company's stores.

1. Most people don't know how coffee is decaffeinated, do you?

2. Although there are three methods used to decaffeinate coffee, one of them is the most popular.

3. The most popular method is called water processing, drawing the caffeine from the coffee beans into a water solution and removing most of it.

4. After going through the natural water processing method, the coffee may be a little less flavorful.

5. To decaffeinate coffee another way, manufacturers add a chemical solution to the beans and then steam them to remove the leftover chemicals.

6. Compared to the water processing method, the chemical method is more "scientific" and removes more of the caffeine.

7. Finally, there is the method that infuses coffee beans with carbon dioxide gas to get rid of the caffeine.

8. Since carbon dioxide is plentiful and nontoxic, this process is also popular.

9. Even though the carbon dioxide method is the most expensive of the three ways to decaffeinate coffee, it also removes the most caffeine.

10. Whenever I drink a cup of decaf in the future, I'll wonder which method was used to remove the caffeine.

EXERCISE 4

1. When the government issued the Susan B. Anthony dollar coin on July 2, 1979, it met with some disapproval.

2. People didn't dislike the person on the coin, but they did dislike the size and color of the coin.

3. It was nearly the same size as a quarter, had a rough edge like a quarter's, and was the same color as a quarter.

4. It differed from a quarter in that it was faceted around the face, was lighter in weight, and was worth four times as much.

5. Due to these problems, the Susan B. Anthony dollar was discontinued, and in January 2000, the government issued a new golden dollar.

6. Like the Anthony dollar, the new coin portrayed the image of a famous American woman.

7. She was the young Native American guide and interpreter for the Lewis and Clark expedition, and her name was Sacagawea.

8. Although the Sacagawea dollar was roughly the same size as the Anthony dollar, it had a smooth wide edge, and its gold color made it easy to distinguish from a quarter.

9. Sacagawea's journey included hardship, suffering, and illness, but it also revealed her incredible knowledge, courage, and strength.

10. However, because the Sacagawea dollar coins were not popular either, the government decided to issue dollar coins with U.S. presidents on them.

EXERCISE 5

1. In the past, people believed that emeralds held magical powers.

2. They were supposed to cure disease, lengthen life, and protect innocence.

3. Part of their appeal was their rarity, for emeralds are even rarer than diamonds.

4. Geologists have been mystified by emeralds because they are produced through a unique process, the blending of chromium, vanadium, and beryllium.

5. These substances almost never occur together, except in emeralds.

6. In South Africa, Pakistan, and Brazil, emeralds were created by intrusions of granite millions of years ago.

7. These areas are known for their beautiful gems, but emeralds from Colombia are the largest, greenest, and most sparkling of all.

8. In Colombia, the makeup of the sedimentary rock accounts for the difference.

9. Instead of the granite found in other emerald-rich countries, the predominant substance in Colombia is black shale.

10. Even though emeralds can be synthesized, a real one always contains a trapped bit of fluid, and jewelers call this tiny imperfection a "garden."

PROOFREADING EXERCISE

I couldn't believe it, but there I was in the pilot's seat of an airplane. I had casually signed up for a course in flying at the aviation school and hadn't expected to start flying right away. The instructor told me what to do, and I did it. When I turned the stick to the right, the plane turned right. When I turned it to the left, the plane went left. Actually, it was very similar to driving a car. Most of my practice involved landing, bringing the plane in softly and safely. After many hours of supervised flying, my time to solo came, and I was really excited. I covered the checklist on the ground, took off without any problems, and landed like a professional. On May 8, 2010, I became a licensed pilot, so now I can pursue my dream of being a private pilot for a rock star.

SENTENCE WRITING

Here are some possible combinations. Yours may differ.

I like to watch golf and baseball, but I love to play hockey and soccer.

Tutors will not correct a student's paper, but they will explain how to clarify ideas, add stronger details, and improve organization.

When Meg and Charlie bought their first car, they bought a big one and got a good price, but they should have thought more about gas mileage because now they spend over two hundred dollars a month on gas.

COMMA RULES 4, 5, AND 6 (PP. 181–185)

EXERCISE 1

1. The sentence is correct, or commas could be used around "Ms. Gonzalez."

2. The sentence is correct.

3. My daughter's friend Harry doesn't get along with her best friend, Jenny.

4. My daughter's best friend, Jenny, doesn't get along with one of her other friends, Harry.

5. The tiger, which is a beautiful and powerful animal, symbolizes freedom.

6. The sentence is correct.

7. The sentence is correct.

8. Kim and Teresa, who helped set up the chairs, were allowed to sit in the front row.

9. My car, which had a tracking device, was easy to find when it was stolen.

10. The sentence is correct.

EXERCISE 2

1. We trust, of course, that people who get their driver's licenses know how to drive.

2. The sentence is correct.

3. The sentence is correct.

4. Mr. Kraft, who tests drivers for their licenses, makes the streets safer for all of us.

5. The sentence is correct.

6. The sentence is correct.

7. The driver's seat, we know, is a place of tremendous responsibility.

8. The sentence is correct.

9. The sentence is correct.

10. No one, we believe, should take that responsibility lightly.

EXERCISE 3

1. This year's Feast of Lanterns in Pacific Grove, I think, was better than last year's.

2. The sentence is correct.

3. The sentence is correct.

4. The sentence is correct.

5. The sentence is correct.

6. Laurie and Jane, who decorated their houses with lanterns, were among the unsung heroes of the weeklong festival.

7. The sentence is correct.

8. Adrienne and Andrea, two volunteers at the Pet Parade, were also dancers in the ballet.

9. The salads at the Feast of Salads, I have to say, were better last year.

10. The sentence is correct.

EXERCISE 4

1. Arthur S. Heineman, a California architect, designed and built the world's first motel in the mid-1920s.

2. He chose the perfect location, the city of San Luis Obispo, which was midway between Los Angeles and San Francisco.

3. Heineman, an insightful man of business, understood the need for inexpensive drive-in accommodations on long motor vehicle trips.

4. Hotels, which required reservations and offered only high-priced rooms within one large structure, just didn't fulfill the needs of motorists.

5. Heineman envisioned his "Motor Hotel," or Mo-Tel, as a place where the parking spaces for the cars were right next to separate bungalow-style apartments for the passengers.

6. Heineman's idea was so new that, when he put up his "Motel" sign, several residents of the area told him to fire the sign's painter, who couldn't even spell the word *hotel.*

7. The sentence is correct.

8. Heineman's Milestone Mo-Tel, the world's first motel, opened in San Luis Obispo in 1925.

9. Before Heineman's company, the Milestone Interstate Corporation, could successfully trademark the name "Mo-Tel," other builders adopted the style and made *motel* a generic term.

10. Some of the original Milestone Mo-Tel building, now called the Motel Inn, still stands on the road between L.A. and San Francisco.

1. I bought a book, *The Story of the "Titanic,"* because I am interested in famous events in history.

2. This book, written by Frank O. Braynard, is a collection of postcards about the ill-fated ocean liner.

3. The book's postcards, four on each page, can be pulled apart and mailed like regular ones.

4. The sentence is correct.

5. The blank sides, where messages and addresses go, include brief captions of the images on the front of the cards. (Note: This sentence could be left without commas.)

6. The book's actual content, the part written by Braynard, offers a brief history of each image relating to the *Titanic*.

7. One of my favorite cards shows the ship's captain, Edward Smith, and its builder, Lord Pirrie, standing on the deck of the *Titanic* before it set sail.

8. Another card is a photograph of *Titanic* passengers on board the *Carpathia,* the ship that rescued many survivors.

9. There is also a picture of two small children, survivors themselves, who lost their father in the disaster but were later reunited with their mother.

10. The most interesting card, a photo of the ship's gymnasium, shows that one of the pieces of exercise equipment for the passengers was a rowing machine.

PROOFREADING EXERCISE

Do you know, Ryan, that there is a one-unit library class that begins next week? It's called Library 1, Introduction to the Library, and we have to sign up for it before Friday. The librarians who teach it will give us an orientation and a series of assignment sheets. Then, as we finish the assignments at our own pace, we will turn them in to the librarians for credit. Ms. Kim, the librarian that I spoke with, said that we will learn really valuable library skills. These skills, such as finding books or articles in our library and using the Internet to access other databases, are the ones universities will expect us to know. I, therefore, plan to take this class, and you, I hope, will take it with me.

SENTENCE WRITING
Here are some possible combinations. Yours may differ.

Samantha Jones, a great boss, recognizes hard work and rewards dedicated employees.

Samantha Jones is a great boss who recognizes hard work and rewards dedicated employees.

We should, I believe, start a savings account to help us prepare for financial emergencies.

I believe that we should start a savings account to help us prepare for financial emergencies.

Leslie, my roommate, got a job in the bookstore to get good discounts on books.

My roommate Leslie got a job in the bookstore to get good discounts on books.

COMMA REVIEW EXERCISE (P. 186)

I'm writing you this note, Monica, to ask you to do me a favor. [4] Before you leave for work today, would you take the pizza dough out of the freezer? [3] I plan to get started on the salads, soups, and desserts as soon as soon as I wake up. [2] I will be so busy, however, that I might forget to thaw out the dough. [5] It's the first time I've cooked all the food for pizza night by myself, and I want everything to be perfect. [1] The big round pizza pan, the one in the cupboard above the refrigerator, should be the best place to keep the dough as it thaws. [6]

Thanks for your help.

QUOTATION MARKS AND UNDERLINING/*ITALICS* (PP. 188–192)

EXERCISE 1

1. "Marks" is the title of a poem by Linda Pastan.

2. I'll never understand what "No news is good news" means.

3. The student asked the librarian, "Can you help me find an article on spontaneous human combustion?"

4. Whatever happened to The Book of Lists?

5. <u>My Antonia</u> is the title of one of Willa Cather's most famous novels.

6. "Let's begin," the relaxation expert said, "by closing our eyes and imagining ourselves in an empty theater."

7. Television series like <u>Frontier House</u> and <u>Colonial House</u> have made PBS a real competitor for reality-TV-hungry audiences.

8. "I can't keep this a secret anymore," my neighbor told me. "Your son has a tattoo that he hasn't shown you yet."

9. <u>Phil Gordon's Little Green Book</u> is the whole title of his book, and the subtitle is <u>Lessons and Teachings in No Limit Texas Hold'em</u>.

10. I was shocked when my high school English teacher told us, "Most of Shakespeare's stories came from other sources; he just dramatized them better than anyone else did."

EXERCISE 2

1. Emilie Buchwald once noted, "Children are made readers on the laps of their parents."

2. Have you read Mark Twain's book <u>The Adventures of Tom Sawyer?</u>

3. I took a deep breath when my counselor asked, "How many math classes have you had?"

4. "Let's start that again!" shouted the dance teacher.

5. Last night we watched the Beatles' movie <u>Help!</u> on DVD.

6. "Books," wrote Jonathan Swift, "are the children of the brain."

7. Voltaire stated in <u>A Philosophical Dictionary</u> that "Tears are the silent language of grief."

8. Why do dentists ask questions like "How are you?" as soon as they start working on your teeth?

9. "Time is the only incorruptible judge" is just one translation of Creon's line from the Greek play <u>Oedipus Rex</u>.

10. My favorite essay that we have read this semester has to be "The Pie" by Gary Soto.

EXERCISE 3

1. "Do you need any help with your homework?" my father asked.

2. In William Zinsser's book <u>On Writing Well</u>, he explains that "Readers want the person who is talking to them to sound genuine."

3. Sigmund Freud had this to say about the intensity of a particular dream: "The dream is far shorter than the thoughts which it replaces."

4. Cat People and The Curse of the Cat People are two movies about people who turn into panther-like cats.

5. "All for love, and nothing for reward" is a famous quotation by Edmund Spenser.

6. Forrest Gump made many sayings famous, but "Life is like a box of chocolates" is the most memorable.

7. My teacher wrote "Well done!" at the top of my essay.

8. Poker expert Phil Gordon admits that "Everyone makes mistakes." "A bad poker player," he adds, "will make the same mistake over and over again."

9. Donna asked, "What time is the meeting?"

10. My family subscribes to The New Yorker, and we all enjoy reading it.

EXERCISE 4

1. Alfred Tonnelle defined art this way: "The artist does not see things as they are, but as he is."

2. I found a vintage children's book called Baby Island at the thrift store; it was a fascinating story.

3. A Russian proverb says, "When money speaks, the truth is silent."

4. When someone suggested that Walt Disney run for mayor of Los Angeles following the success of Disneyland, Disney declined, saying, "I'm already king."

5. About trying new foods, Swift said, "It was a bold man who first ate an oyster."

6. Mark Twain noted about California, "It's a great place to live, but I wouldn't want to visit there."

7. There is a French expression *L'amour est aveugle; l'amitié ferme les yeux,* which translates as follows: "Love is blind; friendship closes its eyes."

8. "Let's keep our voices down," the librarian said as we left the study room.

9. One of Emily Dickinson's shortest poems begins, "A word is dead/When it is said/Some say."

10. Dickinson's poem ends like this: "I say it just/Begins to live/That day."

EXERCISE 5

1. In Booker T. Washington's autobiography <u>Up from Slavery</u>, he describes his early dream of going to school.

2. "I had no schooling whatever while I was a slave," he explains.

3. He continues, "I remember on several occasions I went as far as the schoolhouse door with one of my young mistresses to carry her books."

4. Washington then describes what he saw from the doorway: "several dozen boys and girls engaged in study."

5. "The picture," he adds, "made a deep impression upon me."

6. Washington cherished this glimpse of "boys and girls engaged in study."

7. It contrasted directly with his own situation: "My life had its beginning in the midst of the most miserable, desolate, and discouraging surroundings."

8. "I was born," he says, "in a typical log cabin, about fourteen by sixteen feet square."

9. He explains, "In this cabin I lived with my mother and a brother and sister till after the Civil War, when we were all declared free."

10. As a slave at the door of his young mistress's schoolhouse, Booker T. Washington remembers, "I had the feeling that to get into a schoolhouse and study in this way would be about the same as getting into paradise."

PARAGRAPH EXERCISE

Yesterday, I was looking through a book of quotations in the library. When I got to the section with quotes about books and reading, I noticed that the people who have been most affected by books are writers themselves. For instance, one long quotation by the popular author Amy Bloom begins, "When I was little, maybe eight or nine, the books that made an enormous impression on me, and didn't fade, were <u>The Scarlet Pimpernel</u>, <u>A Tale of Two Cities</u>, and all of the Superman comic books." Then Bloom points out what these classic readings have in common: "They all involve the same idea, which is someone who is ineffective and foppish on the surface but powerful and effective and mysterious and unstoppable in secret." Bloom concludes by saying, "They encouraged me to develop the notion that you might appear one way but really be another." Bloom's quotation about stories with unlikely heroes makes me want to read—or write—a new one right now!

CAPITAL LETTERS (PP. 194–197)

EXERCISE 1

1. I recently saw the movie *V for Vendetta,* and I wanted to learn more about it.

2. I found out that it's based on an extensive series of comic books.

3. They were written by Alan Moore and illustrated by David Lloyd.

4. The original episodes of *V for Vendetta* were published in black and white within a British comic series called *Warrior.*

5. Once the series caught on in the United States, DC Comics began to publish it.

6. At that time, the creators added color to the drawings.

7. The letter V in the title *V for Vendetta* stands for the main character, a mysterious costumed figure who calls himself V.

8. However, many other connections between the letter V and the Roman numeral 5, which is written as a V, come up throughout the story.

9. V wears a mask that people in the United Kingdom refer to as a Guy Fawkes mask.

10. Guy Fawkes was an English historical figure famous for his involvement in the Gunpowder Plot, which failed on the fifth of November in 1605.

EXERCISE 2

1. J.K. Rowling is a very famous British writer.

2. Her Harry Potter novels are among the most popular books ever written.

3. The series begins with the book *Harry Potter and the Sorcerer's Stone.*

4. In England, the first book is called *Harry Potter and the Philosopher's Stone.*

5. Next comes *Harry Potter and the Chamber of Secrets,* which introduces the character of Tom Riddle.

6. In *Harry Potter and the Prisoner of Azkaban,* everyone is trying to catch the supposed criminal named Sirius Black.

7. The fourth book in the series is *Harry Potter and the Goblet of Fire.*

8. Harry's friends Ron and Hermione aggravate him in *Harry Potter and the Order of the Phoenix.*

9. Readers learn more about Harry's nemesis, Voldemort, in *Harry Potter and the Half-Blood Prince*.

10. Rowling's seventh and final book finishes off the story and is called *Harry Potter and the Deathly Hallows*.

EXERCISE 3

1. When my art teacher asked the class to do research on Frida Kahlo, I knew that the name sounded familiar.

2. Then I remembered that the actress Salma Hayek starred in the movie *Frida,* which was about this Mexican-born artist's life.

3. Frida Kahlo's paintings are all very colorful and seem extremely personal.

4. She painted mostly self-portraits, and each one makes a unique statement.

5. One of these portraits is called *My Grandparents, My Parents, and I.*

6. Kahlo gave another one the title *The Two Fridas*.

7. But my favorite of Kahlo's works is *Self-Portrait on the Borderline between Mexico and the United States*.

8. In an article I read in *Smithsonian* magazine, Kahlo's mother explains that after Frida was severely injured in a bus accident, she started painting.

9. Kahlo's mother set up a mirror near her daughter's bed so that Frida could use herself as a model.

10. In the *Smithsonian* article from the November 2002 issue, Kahlo is quoted as saying, "I never painted dreams. I painted my own reality."

EXERCISE 4

1. Hidden beneath the church of St. Martin-in-the-Fields in London is a great little place to have lunch.

2. It's called The Café in the Crypt, and you enter it down a small staircase just off Trafalgar Square.

3. The café is literally in a crypt, the church's resting place for the departed.

4. The food is served cafeteria-style: soups, stews, sandwiches, and salads.

5. You grab a tray at the end of the counter and load it up with food as you slide it toward the cash register.

6. Although the café is dark, the vaulted ceilings make it comfortable, and you can just make out the messages carved into the flat tombstones that cover the floor beneath your table.

7. One of London's newspapers ranked The Café in the Crypt high on its list of the "50 Best Places to Meet in London."

8. The Café in the Crypt can even be reserved for private parties.

9. The café has its own gallery, called—what else?—The Gallery in the Crypt.

10. So if you're ever in London visiting historic Trafalgar Square, don't forget to look for that little stairway and grab a bite at The Café in the Crypt.

EXERCISE 5

1. My mom and dad love old movie musicals.

2. That makes it easy to shop for them at Christmas and other gift-giving occasions.

3. For Mom's birthday last year, I gave her the video of Gilbert and Sullivan's comic opera *The Pirates of Penzance.*

4. It isn't even that old; it has Kevin Kline in it as the character called the Pirate King.

5. I watched the movie with her, and I enjoyed the story of a band of pirates who are too nice for their own good.

6. Actually, it is funnier than I thought it would be, and Kevin Kline sings and dances really well!

7. Dad likes musicals, too, and I bought him tickets to see the revival of *Chicago* on stage a few years ago.

8. He loves all those big production numbers and the synchronized choreography.

9. Thanks to Baz Luhrmann and others, movie musicals made a comeback.

10. *Moulin Rouge* and the film version of *Chicago* are just two examples.

REVIEW OF PUNCTUATION AND CAPITAL LETTERS (P. 198)

1. The Alamo is the most popular historical site in Texas.

2. Have you ever seen the first episode of The Simpsons?

3. The Thompsons remodeled their garage, and now their daughter uses it as an apartment.

4. "How much will the midterm affect our grades?" the nervous student asked.

5. We have refunded your money, Ms. Jones, and will be sending you a confirmation letter.

6. One of the teachers who visited the library left a textbook on the checkout counter.

7. The United Parcel Service, better known as UPS, was hiring on campus yesterday.

8. Even though I am enjoying my Latin class, I wish I had taken Chinese instead.

9. You always remember the date of my birthday, March 20, but you forget your own.

10. Pink is a calming color—but not if it's hot pink. (or !)

11. Pam, Martha, Justin, and Luke left class early to practice their presentation in the hallway.

12. Finding a good deal for a new car online takes time, patience, and luck.

13. My friend is reading a Shakespeare play in her women's studies class.

14. I wonder how much my History of Textiles book will cost.

15. In 2008, Bill Gates stepped down as the CEO of Microsoft; now he focuses on his charity, The Bill & Melinda Gates Foundation.

COMPREHENSIVE TEST (PP. 199–200)

1. ro (The twins spent their summer vacation at a computer camp, and they loved it.)

2. s-v agr (Either the employees or the company *has* to take a cut in earnings.)

3. sp (My counselor's *advice* has helped me so much.)

4. s-v agr (A bus full of high school students always *passes* me on my way to school.)

5. ro (Amanda has the highest grade in the class; I have the second highest.)

6. wordy (*I have a question or two* about your return policy.)

7. ww/sp (I love spring and summer; *they're* my favorite seasons.)

8. pro (The officer gave my sister and *me* a ticket for jaywalking.)

9. cs (Camping can be fun, *but* it can also be a nightmare.)

10. adj (The students felt *bad* about mistreating the substitute.)

11. cs (She is very creative; however, she is not a professional artist.)

12. mm (I found a wrench *left under the hood of my car by a careless mechanic.*)

13. p (Have you read the essay called "Superman and Me," by Sherman Alexie?)

14. pro agr (Everyone on the committee needed to cast *a* separate vote.)

15. c (As we stepped outside, the bright sunlight hurt our eyes.)

16. ww/sp (Some people take *compliments* well; others don't like to hear praise.)

17. ww/sp (Your research paper uses more sources *than* mine, but mine has a better thesis.)

18. ww/apos (*It's* a perfect time of year to visit the rose garden.)

19. wordy (We don't know *whether our application was approved or not.*)

20. awk/mm (The students held a debate *about* the proposed parking structure.)

WRITING

ORGANIZING IDEAS (P. 219)

EXERCISE 1 TOPIC, FACT, OR THESIS?

1. FACT	**6.** FACT
2. TOPIC	**7.** FACT
3. THESIS	**8.** TOPIC
4. TOPIC	**9.** TOPIC
5. THESIS	**10.** THESIS

WRITING EXERCISE 8: ADDING TRANSITIONAL EXPRESSIONS (P. 222)

Whenever I plan a trip that involves driving long distances, I go through the following routine. *First,* I make sure that I have a recent map of the highways so that if I get lost along the way, I won't panic. *Next,* even if I do have a map to the city of my destination, I go online to get specific driving directions to the hotel from the highway. *Another* way that I prepare is to check my car's tires and get its engine serviced, if necessary. I know how important cell phones are on long drives; *therefore,* I never forget to bring mine. *Finally,* before I leave my house on the day of the trip, I call the Highway Patrol hotline to see if there are any highway closures. This routine has always worked for me. *However,* I would give it up for a car with its own navigation system.

WRITING EXERCISE 13: WRITE A SHORT SUMMARY (P. 238)

In "The Green Pioneer," Patricia Fara explains that Rachel Carson challenged ideas about female scientists and began the fight to save our environment. Some people believe that the influence of women in science is limited. Rachel Carson's early works didn't challenge those views. She succeeded in two areas: observing positive truths about nature and recording her unique observations in her writing. After WWII, however, Carson could not continue to write supportively about the future of nature. The use of chemicals at nature's expense had changed everything. She wrote *Silent Spring* as a warning to her fellow scientists and human beings. With that book, Carson started the fierce environmental debate that continues today.

Index